D A N T E

DANTE

LAYMAN
PROPHET
MYSTIC

REV. JAMES J. COLLINS

ALBA · HOUSE　　NEW · YORK

SOCIETY OF ST. PAUL, 2187 VICTORY BLVD., STATEN ISLAND, NEW YORK 10314

Library of Congress Cataloging-in-Publication Data

Collins. James J . 1938-
    Dante - - layman. prophet. mystic / James J. Collins
        p   cm
    Includes bibliographical references (p   )
    ISBN 0-8189-0564-6
    1. Dante Alighieri. 1265-1321 — Biography   2. Dante Alighieri.
  1265-1321 — Religion 3. Authors. Italian — To 1500 — Biography
  I. Title
  PQ4335 C65 1989
  851' 1 — dc20   89-38909
  [B]   CIP

Designed. printed and bound in the United States of
America by the Fathers and Brothers of the
Society of St. Paul. 2187 Victory Boulevard,
Staten Island. New York 10314. as part of their
communications apostolate

Printing Information:

Current Printing - first digit 1 2 3 4 5 6 7 8 9 10 11 12

Year of Current Printing - first year shown
  1989   1990   1991   1992   1993   1994   1995   1996

DEDICATION

In loving memory of my parents
John and Marie,
and of Lisa Marie Stanton,
called already to that
"fellowship of those chosen to feast
at the great supper of the Lamb of God
Who feeds you, satisfying all your needs."
(Par. XXIV, 1)

ACKNOWLEDGMENTS

I should like to express my gratitude to the many Dante scholars whose works I have consulted and quoted in this book. Particular recognition should be given to Mark Musa for his eloquent English translation of Dante's *Commedia* and *Vita Nuova* as well as for his masterly commentaries on those works. His encouragement and friendship during my sojourn in Florence in 1987 was a source of inspiration. Thanks should also be given to the *Soctieà Dantesca Italiana*, whose excellent library in Florence I used for much of my research.

Another Dante scholar, the late Bishop Giovanni Fallani, deserves special mention since he was my first teacher of Dante. His enthusiastic lecture and books were and remain invaluable.

Special thanks should be extended to Raphael Brown, scholar and writer on Franciscan spirituality, who gave me so much advice and support during the preparation and completion of this work. His expertise in medieval spirituality and his interest in making that wealth available to today's Christians have greatly helped me.

My gratitude should also be expressed to Nancy Johnston, whose generous support helped to make this work possible, and to Jacqueline De Leo, whose expert typing provided such a fine manuscript.

I should also thank two close friends, Angelo Randazzo and Anna Maria Stango, for their support through the arduous task of composition.

Particular recognition and gratitude should be given to the many publishers who granted permission to print excerpts from their publication of Dante studies. Special mention should be made of:

Indiana University Press for *Dante's Vita Nuova: A Translation and an Essay* by Mark Musa (copyright 1973) and *The Divine Comedy*, also translated in three volumes by Mark Musa (copyright 1984, 1985, and 1986).

Penguin Books for *Confessions* by St. Augustine, translated by R.S. Pine-Coffin (copyright 1961).

Simon & Schuster, Inc. for *The Closing of the American Mind* by Allan Bloom (copyright 1987).

CONTENTS

CHRONOLOGY

Dante's life and works	Historical events

1265 Dante born, probably May 25

1267   Guelph rule in Florence under protection of Charles of Anjou

1274   Death of Thomas Aquinas

1282   Growing influence of guilds in Florence

1283 Dante begins his association with the poet Guido Cavalcanti

1289 Dante at Battle of Campaldino   Florence defeats Arezzo and Ghibelline factions at Campaldino and extends her supremacy in Tuscany

1290 Death of Bice (Beatrice) Portinari

1292 Dante begins the *Vita Nuova* (vernacular lyric poems with prose narrative and commentary)

1294   Election and abdication of Pope Celestine V; election of Pope Boniface VIII

1295 Dante probably completes *Vita Nuova*; enrolls in a guild; begins five years of active participation in the political life of the Florentine Commune

1300 Dante elected to the office of Prior

1301		Entry of Charles of Valois into Florence; defeat of the White Guelphs
1302	Dante in his absence sentenced to death by the ruling Black faction; exile begins	
1303	Dante seeks refuge for the first time in Verona;	Death of Pope Boniface VIII
1304	Probably begins the *Convivio* (vernacular prose interpretation of three philosophical lyrics) and *De Vulgari Eloquentia* (Latin treatise on vernacular language and poetry)	
1305		Pope Clement V detained in Avignon
1307	Possible date for beginning of *The Divine Comedy*	
1308		Henry of Luxemburg elected Emperor
1310	Dante's Epistle to Henry;	Henry enters Italy
1312	Possible date for the beginning of *De Monarchia* (Latin work on political philosophy)	Henry crowned Emperor in Rome
1313		Emperor Henry VII dies; Boccaccio born
1314	Dante returns to Verona under protection of Can Grande della Scala	
1316		Election of Pope John XXII
1318	Dante at Ravenna: close contacts with Guido Novello da Polenta	
1321	Dies at Ravenna, Sept. 14	

INTRODUCTION

The Church in the late twentieth century has often been described as a Church in crisis: dissent and confusion seem to reign; the question of authority seems to be the source of much unrest and turmoil; unity and harmony seem to have disappeared. Anger and resentment have been expressed publicly on a variety of issues: moral issues as well as issues of Church discipline and practices. Traditional teachings are challenged and the very teaching authority of the Church itself is held in contempt, or simply ignored. Church attendance and fidelity to traditional practices, such as confession, have significantly waned. Indifference to the Church and her teachings is rampant.

And yet on the brighter side we can point to a marvelous renewal and an almost unbelievable enthusiasm which has regenerated the spiritual lives of so many members of the Church — laity, religious and clergy. The reforms initiated by the Second Vatican Council and the proliferation of so many "movements" within the Church have truly renewed the faith and lives of many. The abiding activity of the Spirit has been manifested in so many unexpected ways in the post-Vatican II era. Pope John XXIII's words about "a new Pentecost" were truly prophetic. Angelo Roncalli, elected much to the surprise of many, surprised the Church by calling an ecumenical council. Such surprises continue in the Church's life. We keep seeing the surprises of God's activity: the Spirit blows when and where He wills. The present participation and collaboration of the laity in the mission and ministries of the Church were unheard of twenty-five years ago. The rediscovery of the Scriptures, the renewed liturgy and the interest in genuine spirituality have revolutionized the Church's life in countless ways.

The Church's prophetic role in the world has also been rediscovered. Her role as a servant to the world in its quest for justice and peace is being exercised with bold words and actions. Church leaders are finally taking the side of the poor and oppressed and giving them a voice. Popes, bishops, religious and laity have witnessed — many with their own blood — to God's compassion for His people. Liberation theology has spoken a prophetic word which echoes the Hebrew prophets and Christ's love for the hungry and dispossessed of the world.

To this Church and to this world of the late twentieth century can a voice from the very distant world of the late thirteenth and early fourteenth century have anything relevant to say? Can Dante speak to us today? If we consider Dante as a layman, prophet and mystic, we can, I believe, hear and see a very relevant message for us. These three aspects of Dante seem to be of particular relevance to our age and to us. He gives us a vision that can illuminate us, give direction and enliven our own faith, hope and love as we live out our little lives in a troubled Church and an even more troubled world.

This book does not intend to be a thorough biography of Dante Alighieri nor a complete spiritual or psychological portrait of him. Since Dante has not left us a "journal of his soul," a full spiritual biography of him is impossible to compose. There is just not enough evidence in his works. True, his letters (the few that have survived) and works such as his *Vita Nuova* and his *Commedia* do provide much autobiographical material. I have investigated this material and hope to present a work, which though not entirely scholarly in the technical sense — it does not pretend to break new ground in Dante studies — does intend to present a spiritual portrait of Dante based on scholarly research. I do hope this work has avoided being too scholarly. I often digress into some complex historical and theological considerations for the sake of clarifying Dante's position on the issue in question. But many more scholarly works are available. There is a steady flow of scholarly Dante studies which only the initiated can understand and appreciate. I have tried to address the general reader who is educated and interested in the implications of Christian faith and theology.

But what is the exact nature and purpose of this book? For whom is it written specifically? In general it is an invitation to all readers to know a great man who is so unknown today. Some would call him, in the words of John Ruskin, "the central man of all the world" because of his sublime poetic, moral and intellectual gifts. He was truly one of the greatest poets of all times. He was also a great scholar and statesman. But he was an outstanding Christian — the main focus of this book. So this work is addressed first of all to believers who share Dante's Christian faith. Even more specifically (but not exclusively), Catholic Christians — laity, religious and clergy — could find this book a source of inspiration and hope by discovering in Dante a model for their lives. Since Dante was a layman, his life as a layman in the Church should interest in a special way laypersons of this late twentieth century confronted with a changing world, a changing Church, alarming injustices and threats in the world as well as disturbing currents in a Church where abuses of authority as well as deviations from authoritative teaching by both clergy and laity are lamentable realities. But the signs of our times are not only crisis and dissent. There are abundant signs of healthy growth and deep spirituality. The pains of growth and development in the aftermath of Vatican II can be seen in the distant mirror of the medieval Church which, after the great Reform Councils and spiritual revolutions such as the Franciscan movement, was in a state of tension characterized by inquisitions, spiritual enthusiasm, intellectual explosions and so many factors which made of that time an extremely exciting period of history.

In Dante's time there was scandalous abuse of ecclesiastical authority, profound upheavals in society, revolutions in the intellectual world of the universities, an emerging laity, intense spiritual renewal and enthusiasm generated by the Franciscan, Dominican and many lay movements. Dante's life and writings reflect this complex and turbulent period of history. So in this respect his life as a layman in the Church, as a prophet to both Church and secular world, and as a deeply spiritual man whose faith matured through rejection and suffering into an experience which can be called "mystical," could be a very relevant model for Catholic laypersons today as well as for all Christians in general.

This book will investigate Dante's public and private life to the extent that his writings and other contemporary documents shed light on his life and personality. But more than any aspect of his life I shall pursue Dante's role as a prophet whose "mystical" experience is the prophetic message he felt compelled — and divinely called — to communicate to a Church and world in chaos. His message will have the ring of righteous indignation, so typical of prophets whose passion for God's justice erupts in wild tirades and invectives. But beneath the harsh words is an experience of God's loving providence for His Church and world. Dante's passion is, like Jeremiah's, an expression of God's passionate love — a lover's jealousy — which calls His children back to justice, responsibility and authentic love when He sees them going astray, blinded by greed, power and lust.

Dante's own soul, we shall see, was affected by serious deviations from the "right path." His own need for conversion is expressed in his works, particularly in the *Comedy,* which is really the story of his conversion and encounter with Christ who condemns his sin, but forgives him, heals him and gives him a vision of His powerful love and glorious triumph over evil. Christ will be the central focus of Dante's spirituality — the spirituality of every Christian graced with faith, hope and love. Dante lived these gifts; and throughout the terrible crises of his life grew in his faith, hope and love even to the point of reaching an overwhelming vision of that lasting city where God's love filled him with peace and joy.

Even though Dante perceived himself as a pilgrim and exile in this earthly "city" — the community of mankind united by natural bonds and a common civilization — he expressed the deepest concern and even passionate love for this world. But the realization that God's perfect justice and peace is an eschatological event projected his soul into a consideration — a contemplative vision — of that lasting and perfect City in Paradise, where God's peace fulfills all human desires.

Dante's life and works illustrate, I believe, what a Christian pilgrim can and should be: an indefatigable "activist" for peace and justice in this world in spite of opposition, indifference and failures; a prophet who fearlessly speaks out from an authentic faith experience; a lover of his fellow pilgrims and a lover of the God Who loves him and all passionately.

This, then, is the main purpose of this book: to provide a picture of a man who lived out his Christian faith even, and especially, in the depths of near despair. Through his dark experiences — comparable to a Jeremiah, Job or John of the Cross — he reached a heightened awareness and a more profound experience of God's mysterious love which brought His Son out of defeat into glory. Dante's story follows the pattern of Christ's — God's — design of defeat, death and resurrection for all His Son's followers. Dante's life will remain for us a powerful story which not only speaks to us today but connects us once again with our one Source and our one End — our Alpha and Omega — who remains with us pilgrims through His Church, Word and Sacraments. Dante, the loyal and faithful son of that Church, experienced Christ's presence in His Spouse; and this felt presence gave him the unwavering faith, the persistent hope and the passionate love which he expressed in his life — a life which is a most meaningful and eloquent model for all of us today.

Dante's perennial significance for the Church is expressed so well by Raphael in his monumental fresco called "The Disputation on the Sacrament" in the *Stanza della Segnatura* of the Vatican. Dante is portrayed there among the great theologians and doctors of the Church — the only layman in this group which surrounds the Sacrament of the Eucharist enthroned on the altar. The painting is actually a kind of pictorial *Summa Theologiae,* since it depicts the Trinity: the Father above all with the Son below Him surrounded by the saints of the Old and New Testaments; below Christ is the Spirit descending as a Dove surrounded with angels bearing the Gospels. Directly below them is the Sacrament surrounded by the theologians, among whom is Dante in the company of Augustine, Thomas Aquinas, Bonaventure and others.

The scene shows the Church triumphant with Christ in glory and the Church on earth which focuses on Christ's presence in the Eucharist. Dante's presence there reveals Raphael's — and the Renaissance's — esteem for Dante as a theologian. Although we may not consider Dante a theologian in the technical sense of the term today, we see in this painting Dante's union with the Church, turned in loving contemplation toward the supreme manifestations of the Father's love for the world: His Son, His gift of the Spirit, His Word and Sacrament — all still present on earth for us, celebrated in poetry by Dante, always the model pilgrim for us and with us.

DANTE

Chapter One

THE FLORENTINE

A visitor to Florence today cannot help being impressed by the charm and sophistication of that unique city, even in spite of the rude encroachments of late twentieth-century "civilization": the air pollution, the horrendous automobile traffic, the hordes of tourists crowding into its beautiful churches and museums, and the endless frustrations of a small city bursting its seams with so much business and not enough space in which to conduct it. And yet with all these blights, it is still a lovely city, full of delights and cultural treasures at every step. It is not a sterile, dead monument to a glorious past; it lives and thrives through its continuing artistic and economic creativity. It bustles with the same energy and enterprise as in Dante's time, and its fine products in leather, fashionable clothes and art objects are still much in demand throughout the world today.

Dante's time, one of political turmoil, economic boom, intellectual and spiritual vitality, cultural revolutions and population explosion, was truly an exciting and invigorating, albeit chaotic, time in the history of Western civilization. In many ways the late thirteenth century was not unlike our late twentieth century. Such an observation risks falling into the cliché of "history repeats itself," but a closer look at the cultural and social conditions of Dante's epoch will reveal some striking resemblances which confirm the oft-repeated adage.

By observing some similarities between Dante's age and ours I hope to bridge the gap which separates us from that remote world. I cannot offer a detailed analysis of how Dante's world is similar to ours, but some of the innate constants of human nature and human society surface in the comparison. Many institutions — the Church primarily, but also other institutions such as political and economic systems, labor guilds, schools, etc. — survive today, although their structures in most cases have changed considerably. Nonetheless, human nature and institutions display today the same limitations and blatant flaws as well as the same prodigious potentials and amazing accomplishments. Pascal so well identified these poles as *la misere* and *la grandeur* of the human being. Dante, too, was a most keen observer of *la grandezza* and *la miseria* of the human condition.

To describe the Florence of Dante's time would be a formidable task, but some acquaintance with it is necessary and will enable the modern reader to appreciate better the world in which Dante lived and even some of his personality traits which reflect characteristics common to the Florentines. They were a proud people, deeply aware of their roots, which they traced back to an elite of noble Roman families chosen by Julius Caesar to settle there. According to a legend the name of the city was derived from the heroic Roman consul Fiorinus, who died in battle there. According to another source the name of Florence came from *fiore* (flower), since many flowers, especially white lilies, grew in that beautiful valley along the river Arno.

The lily became, and still is, the emblem of the city and abundant flowers still adorn the gardens and public places of the city today. The emblem was engraved on its famous gold piece, the florin, which in Dante's time was the most respected monetary unit on the international trade market. A few years ago we could have compared it to the American dollar; perhaps the Japanese *yen* would be a more exact comparison today.

The Roman connection formed a link with a glorious past and provided the Florentines with a profound civic pride which partly explains Dante's perception of himself as a citizen not only of Florence but also of the Roman Empire, which he considered the divinely chosen institution for attaining peace and happiness in this world. The Roman memory was also traced to a Florentine martyr, St. Miniato, who was decapitated by order of the Roman Emperor Decius in 250. According to the account of the chronicler Giovanni Villani, a friend of Dante, St. Miniato, by a miracle of Christ, carried his severed head to the high hill on the other side of the Arno where there was an oratory dedicated to

St. Peter, in which many martyrs were buried. On that site today is the beautiful church of St. Miniato, built in the eleventh century. Dante mentioned the church and the steep climb to it in his *Comedy (Purg.* XII, 101) and the visitor today can admire its magnificent mosaics and geometrical designs in colored marbles. It is a gem of the Tuscan Romanesque style and the view of Florence from the church is unforgettable.

These links with Rome and the early Christian martyrs were so engraved in Dante's memory and imagination that the symbols of the Empire and Christ's Church — the eagle and the cross — became the two fundamental images which permeate his major work, the *Comedy.* Rome in Dante's mind was the "holy city chosen by God," where God's two "suns" — the Pope, the successor of St. Peter, and the Emperor, the successor of Caesar — should guide humanity towards her two goals: eternal and temporal happiness. Dante would even describe the heavenly Paradise as "that Rome where Christ is a Roman."

A famous Roman of the fifth century, Boethius, a distinguished consul, philosopher, poet and theologian, most likely served as a role model for Dante. One could say that he was one of Dante's patron saints, given the many allusions Dante makes to his works and the place that Dante gives him among the great doctors in the heavenly sphere of the sun. He has St. Thomas Aquinas describe him in these words:

> Wrapped in the vision of all good, rejoices
> the sainted soul who makes most manifest
> the world's deceit to one who reads him well.
> The body that was torn from him below
> Cieldauro now possesses; to this peace
> he came from exile and from martyrdom.
> (*Par.* X, 124-129)

That Boethius was regarded as a saint and martyr in the Middle Ages is attested by the chronicler Villani who reported that Theodoric, the Arian Christian king of the Ostrogoths and the master of Italy, had Boethius exiled, imprisoned and horribly murdered. Apparently Boethius' enemies, out of envy, convinced the king that Boethius was plotting against him. Without a trial Boethius was banished, his property confiscated, and he was sentenced to death. Boethius' fate reminds us so much of Dante's personal history: the trumped-up charges and the unjust sentences of confiscation, exile and death.

The similarities, however, go far beyond these: Boethius composed his most famous work, *The Consolation of Philosophy,* while an exile in prison. That work, one of the most widely read books in the Middle Ages, exercised a profound influence on Dante, especially after the death of Beatrice. It probably also influenced Dante during his long exile when he composed his most famous work, the *Comedy.* Both men overcame cruel fate, injustices and despair by creating masterpieces that are enduring testimonies to their faith and hope. Both their works remain as lasting triumphs of the spirit.

Because of certain prejudices of historians and critics the theological works of Boethius have been little known and appreciated. Today scholars accept them as authentic. Among them are the treatises *On the Trinity* and *On the Catholic Faith.* They both reveal Boethius as a competent, if not brilliant, Catholic theologian and even as a forerunner of St. Thomas Aquinas. In those works he makes clear distinctions between reason and faith which anticipate the precision of the thirteenth century Scholastics. He was an important link between the great Fathers of the Church and the medieval doctors.

Boethius' work also served as a bridge between the classical world of Greco-Roman culture and the Middle Ages. He translated and commented on Plato and Aristotle and bequeathed to Europe's Middle Ages knowledge and interest in the great Latin orators and poets. He wrote splendid Latin verses, whose style and content inspired some of Dante's works. Boethius' combination of poetry and prose in his *Consolation of Philosophy* probably provided the model for Dante's *Vita Nuova.*

Just as Boethius summarized and transmitted the wisdom of the Greeks and Romans to the Middle Ages, so Dante encapsulated the vast achievement of medieval intellectual culture — its splendid integration of Greek philosophy and Christian faith — and passed it on to the Renaissance. Both men were traditionalists as well as original thinkers and poets; both were capable statesmen and intrepid teachers of philosophical and theological truth; both eventually died as victims and martyrs.

Another significant similarity between the two is that they were both laymen, married and fathers of children. It seems that Dante saw in Boethius a man who incarnated his ideal of the Catholic layman who fulfills his responsibilities to this world as well as his commitments to the Church and to God. This extraordinary integration of the active and contemplative lives was an accomplishment of both Boethius and Dante, and can well serve as a model for laypersons today.

Laypersons in the Middle Ages were not excluded from the religious culture of their time, although their participation in the life of the Church was greatly limited, if compared with today's practices in the post-Vatican II age. The Middle Ages, often eulogized by Catholic historians as "the age of faith" are sometimes described by other historians as "the age of acquiescence," when the laity was held captive in a state of fear of hell-fire by a hierarchy driven by the twin lusts of power and greed. Some historians with an anti-clerical bias take great delight in exposing the tyrannical control that the clergy exercised over the entire lives and consciences of the faithful. Many blatant examples of scandalous abuse of spiritual powers and offices are historically true, particularly in Dante's time. The term "bad popes," applied to some of the medieval popes, corresponds to the reality of the lives and policies of most of the popes during Dante's lifetime — popes guilty of simony, fraud, unjustified warfare, greed and authoritarianism.

One of Dante's vivid childhood memories was no doubt a period of four years when Florence was under an interdict imposed by Pope Gregory X in 1272, when Dante was only seven. During those years all sacramental and liturgical rites were forbidden except the administration of the "viaticum" to the dying. One can imagine the somber pall cast over a city which used to enjoy its festive celebrations of baptisms, marriages and processions honoring the Blessed Sacrament and the saints. To deprive people of the precious "Bread of Life" was the ultimate weapon wielded by these unscrupulous popes determined to force people to obey their political and economic policies. Such overtly malicious abuse of sacred power aroused the animosity and outrage of many laypersons in Dante's time: he was not the only critic of these abominations, but he was one of the most outspoken ones.

And yet Dante the layman always had the deepest respect for the Petrine office itself. In a moving passage on Mount Purgatory he encounters a former pope, Adrian V, who had held the office for only three months in 1276. Dante kneels in his presence and exclaims: "Your dignity commands. My conscience would not let me stand up straight." (*Purg.* XIX, 132) Adrian was there purging himself of the sin of greed. Divine Justice bound him and the other avaricious souls face down to the ground because their love of worldly goods had kept them earth-bound. The former pope addresses Dante as "my brother" and tells him not to kneel: "I am a servant too with you and all the others of One Power." He explains that his temporary office as pope — that "great mantle" which weighed him down on earth — has been dissolved and they are brothers now.

Greed was the sin which Dante targeted the most in his writings. A Florentine in his time would readily observe this vice, since Florence was then the economic capital of Europe. Her bankers operated a powerful system of loans with interest which controlled the whole economic life of Italy and Europe. It also had far-reaching effects in the Middle East because of the prosperous trade opened up by the Crusades. Medieval popes, who found themselves leaders of a Church thoroughly enmeshed in the social and economic fabric of their time, were dependent on the Florentine bankers, who collected taxes for them from all parts of Europe. This international tax-collecting machinery served the popes in their operation of the complex Roman Curia, the highest court of appeal for all Christendom then. It also supported the governance of vast territories which the pope ruled.

This papal incursion into temporal affairs had a long, complicated history, too lengthy to describe here. Many factors contributed to this lamentable situation: the disintegration of the Roman Empire after the barbarian invasions during the Dark Ages, the failure of local civil governments to organize and control social and economic changes, and many other factors. Temporal affairs often fell to the responsibility of Church leaders, whose authority was the only one recognized throughout centuries of political chaos in the Dark Ages. In Dante's time this secular involvement of the popes was justified by the legend of Constantine's donation to the bishop of Rome of temporal dominion over the entire Western part of the Empire. Although Dante did not question the authenticity, or the good will, of this forged document, he denied the very right of Constantine to hand over land ownership and temporal rule to the pope; he also condemned the papal acceptance of an office not intended for him by Christ. Dante's criterion was the Gospel, which he felt clearly prohibited the apostles from owning any property at all and from exercising any temporal rule.

In Dante's time there was also the odious double standard from which the Church operated: on the one hand she condemned usury as a serious sin and on the other she actually licensed and encouraged the Florentine bankers in this practice. Clerics, too, were permitted to borrow money to pay papal fees on their benefices. All this worldly business of usury and, worse still, of simony were often the targets of Dante's outrage, expressed so often in his works. When Dante described the glorious triumph of Christ and His Church in Paradise he has St. Peter burst into a searing condemnation of Pope Boniface VIII, the pontiff reigning when Dante wrote the passage:

> He who on earth usurps that place of mine,
> that place of mine, that place of mine which now
> stands vacant in the eyes of Christ, God's Son,
> has turned my sepulchre into a sewer
> of blood and filth, at which the Evil One
> who fell from here takes great delight down there.
>
> .   .   .
>
> The bride of Christ was not nourished on blood
> that came from me, from Linus and from Cletus,
> only that she be wooed for love of gold;
>
> .   .   .
>
> From here we see down there in all your fields
> rapacious wolves who dress in shepherd's clothes.
> O power of God, why do You still hold back?
> (*Par.* XXVII, 22-57)

Such blistering attacks on Pope Boniface VIII were matched and surpassed by Jacopone da Todi, a saintly Franciscan mystical poet and contemporary of Dante, who went so far as to call Boniface "a new Lucifer on the papal throne."[1] In Dante's *Inferno* Boniface's place in Hell among the simoniacs is announced by a predecessor, Nicholas III.

When Nicholas, confined upside down in one of the pouches of the simoniacs, hears Dante's voice he mistakes it for Boniface's:

> Is that you, here, already, upright?
> Is that you here already upright, Boniface?
> By many years the book has lied to me!
> Are you fed up so soon with all that wealth
> for which you did not fear to take by guile
> the Lovely Lady, then tear her asunder?
> (*Inf.* XIX, 52-57)

Dante responds to Nicholas in these words:

> Well, tell me now: what was the sum of money
> that holy Peter had to pay our Lord
> before He gave the keys into his keeping?
> Certainly He asked no more than 'Follow me.'
>
> .   .   .
>
> And were it not for the reverence I have
> for those highest of all keys that you once held
> in the happy life — if this did not restrain me,
> I would use even harsher words than these,
> for your avarice brings grief upon the world,
> crushing the good, exalting the depraved.
>
> .   .   .
>
> You have built yourselves a God of gold and silver!
> How do you differ from the idolator,
> except he worships one, you worship hundreds?
> O Constantine, what evil did you sire,
> not by your conversion, but by the dower
> that the first wealthy Father got from you!
> (*Inf.* XIX, 90-117)

Although Dante respected the sacred office of the papacy, and even reprimanded the French authorities for their abuse of Boniface, "the vicar of Christ," he was uncompromising in his invectives against the individual popes who disgraced their office. Boniface VIII represented for Dante the very betrayal of that sacred office. Boniface's glaring sins of avarice and simony were matched by his arrogant assertion of universal power over the entire earth. His notorious bull *Unam Sanctam* claimed supreme authority in all matters, both spiritual and temporal.

This papal bull proclaimed the papacy as a divine monarchy — a theocracy — affecting every creature: "We declare, state and define that for every creature submission to the Roman Pontiff is absolutely necessary for salvation."[2] The symbol of this universal rule was the triple tiara, introduced by Boniface in 1300. He commissioned Arnolfo di Cambria to carve a statue of himself wearing that pretentious crown. The marvelous statue can be seen today in the museum of the Florence cathedral. In Rome's cathedral, St. John at the Lateran, there is a well-preserved fresco by Giotto, one of Dante's friends, showing Boniface wearing his high hat.

These medieval popes with their arrogance and greed contrast strikingly with the popes of recent memory: John XXIII, Paul VI, and the present pontiff, John Paul II, whose concerns for economic and social justice stand out as a bold assertion of gospel values: the Church as servant to the world, giving preference to the poor. The popes of our twentieth century have given outstanding witness to evangelical principles. John Paul II's recent encyclical letter *On Social Concern* is yet another courageous proclamation of the Church's compassion for the poor and of her promotion of economic justice for all, a concern so strongly articulated by Vatican II and by the American bishops in their recent pastoral letter on that topic. Even though some of the institutional practices of local churches as regards a just wage and benefits for lay employees still do not reflect these teachings, the official word is out — it has been since Pope Leo XIII in the nineteenth century! The Church's contemporary history — sad to say — is still tainted with economic scandals and injustices, although they are becoming less common. The Bride of Christ still has some outstanding warts and wrinkles.

In all fairness to the medieval Church, however, we should note how some of her economic practices arose. The issue of usury could be cited: it was originally intended to promote economic justice (the just price) and to protect Crusaders who had to borrow money in order to fulfill their sacred oaths. The Crusades brought about many changes in society in which the Church was deeply involved. Besides promoting the Crusades, an enterprise which we today would evaluate with far different criteria, the Church also encouraged certain institutions which developed from those "holy wars," such as the orders of the Templars and the Hospitallers, both modeled on the monastic reforms of the Cistercians. The protection of the crusaders and the promotion of Christian hospitality, the original purposes of these orders, were values flowing from the Christian virtue of *philadelphia,* love of one's brothers and sisters — an aspect of the fundamental virtue of *agape,* indiscriminate love for all. Unfortunately, that kind of love was not extended to the hated Saracens and Jews who held the Holy Land. Nonetheless, the Knights of the Templar Order expressed the noblest ideals of Christian brotherhood and chivalry in the mind of Dante. It is likely that Dante, a layman, was somehow affiliated with this religious order of celibate knights.[3] He certainly expressed a strong sympathy for them, manifested by his deep hatred for the two men who, out of greed and envy, effected their ruin: Pope Clement V and King Philip the Fair of France. (cf. *Purg.* XX, 91-93)

Dante's romantic reminiscences of the golden age of the Crusades are reflected in an episode in Paradise where he meets his ancestor, Cacciaguida, a knight who was killed in the Second Crusade about 1147. In Dante's mind he was a great Christian warrior, a martyr among the glorious soldiers of Christ in the heaven of Mars. Dante traced his family's claim of nobility to Cacciaguida, his great-great-grandfather. Although Dante has Cacciaguida declare that true nobility is a virtue of the individual and not a privilege inherited from blood descent, he nevertheless accepted with a certain pride his family's claim of "blue blood."

We know that Dante's family, the Alighieri, inherited land and privileges because of its noble lineage. This factor probably accounts for the modest wealth and real estate of the Alighieri family in both Florence and in the countryside. Besides, there is some evidence that Dante's father may have been a money-lender. Perhaps Dante was ashamed of his father's practice of usury, since he never mentioned him in his writings. In any case, his father died when Dante was only twelve.

The property and revenues which he inherited provided Dante with a rather comfortable and carefree existence as a young man and poet of leisure before his participation in Florentine political life, a topic which will be examined in a later chapter.

At present let us briefly explore Dante's participation in the life of the Church in Florence. As an infant he was baptized at the Easter liturgy in the cathedral of St. John the Baptist, the patron of Florence. The building stood on the site of the ancient temple of Mars, Florence's tutelary deity in Roman times. The graceful octagonal building, which dominated the city in Dante's time, still stands as the Baptistery in front of the majestic cathedral of *Santa Maria del Fiore,* which was under construction in Dante's time by Arnolfo di Cambria, the artist who had executed the exquisite marble facade of the baptistery. Throughout his life Dante cherished fond memories of his cathedral/baptistery, which he called "my beautiful Saint John." He refers to it with two significant adjectives: "my" and "beautiful."

His *bel San Giovanni,* was the spiritual birthplace of almost every Florentine and a place of dazzling beauty where both religious and civil ceremonies took place. On the interior cupola the entire biblical history of salvation from Creation to The Final Judgment is narrated in sumptuous mosaics. What an impression these colorful sacred images must have made on the sensitive Dante during his thirty-six years in Florence: the imposing, majestic figure of the cosmic Christ as the universal judge, the nine choirs of angels, the saints in Paradise, and the grotesque Lucifer with the damned in Hell. Many of those images may have affected Dante's concept of the other worlds. [4] Dante toward the end of his life made several allusions to his *bel San Giovanni,* hoping one day to return there to be crowned the city's poet. He expressed this hope in these nostalgic bittersweet words:

> If ever it happen that this sacred poem
> to which both Heaven and earth have set their hand,
> and made me lean from laboring so long,
> wins over those cruel hearts that exile me
> from my sweet fold where I grew up a lamb,
> foe to the wolves that war upon it now,
> with a changed voice and with another fleece,

> I shall return, a poet, and at my own
> baptismal font assume the laurel wreath,
> for it was there I entered in the faith
> that counts God's souls for Him, the faith for which
> Peter just turned himself into my crown.
> *(Par.* XXV, 1-12)

Dante's affection for his baptismal font reveals not only his gratitude for the gift of faith received there but also for his entrance into God's family, which is Christ's fold, the Church. Dante compares himself to a lamb to express his simple love for the Church which remained a constant in his life. His desire for worldly recognition as a great poet might seem out of place in this context, but we should note that he acknowledges that his sacred poem was not just his own labor: Heaven itself had cooperated in its accomplishment. Elsewhere Dante will attribute his poem to the gift of divine inspiration.

Another significant passage in which Dante refers to his baptistery is found in the meeting with Cacciaguida mentioned above. In the course of this encounter Cacciaguida predicts his great-great-grandson's impending exile, the terrible sufferings that he will endure from human injustices, and the honor that will finally come to him once he has proclaimed the bitter truth (the sacred poem) to the world. Cacciaguida foresees Dante, in the words of Umberto Cosmo, as "a victim designated for the highest purposes of Providence so that from the dust of his misery he might reveal himself as a prophet, apostle and soldier to a world put back on its hinges. Misfortune was the price of the glory which would come to him. This highly poetic situation is the most intimately personal of the whole poem . . . in which Dante's afflictions and pains oppress him with his feelings of revenge, his purposes of redemption, and with all the contradictions of both a Florentine attached to his *San Giovanni* and of a citizen of the world."[5]

Before Cacciaguida announces Dante's future woes and prophetic mission he recalls the Florence of the twelfth century. In his idyllic memories of the peaceful city before the vices of greed, luxury, ambition, lust and inner strife corrupted her citizens, we can read Dante's own disappointments and yearnings for a Florence and a peace that no longer existed. Some of the words of Cacciaguida's nostalgic encomium

of Florence should be quoted since they mirror Dante's ideal vision of
his beloved city:

> Florence, enclosed within her ancient walls
> from which she still hears terce and nones ring out,
> once lived in peace, a pure and temperate town:
> no necklace or tiara did she wear,
> no lavish gowns or fancy belts that were
> more striking than the woman they adorned.
> In those days fathers had no cause to fear
> a daughter's birth: the marriageable age
> was not too low, the dowry not too high.
> Houses too large to live in were not built,
> and Sardanapalus had not yet come
> to show to what use bedrooms can be put.
>
> . . .
>
> O happy wives! Each one of them was sure
> of her last resting place — none of them yet
> lay lonely in her bed because of France.
>
> . . .
>
> A mother, working at her spinning-wheel
> surrounded by her children, would tell tales
> about the Trojans, Rome and Fiesole.
>
> . . .
>
> To this serene, this lovely state of being
> within this comity of citizens,
> joined in good faith, this dwelling-place so sweet,
> Mary, besought by pains of birth, gave me;
> and then within your ancient Baptistry
> a Christian I became, and Cacciaguida.
>
> . . .
>
> And then I served Conrad the Emperor
> who later dubbed me Knight among his host,
> so pleased was he by all my gallant deeds.
> Along with him I fought against the evil

> of that false faith whose followers usurp —
> only because your Shepherds·sin — your rights.
> There the vile Saracen delivered me
> from the entanglements of your vain world
> the love of which corrupts so many souls —
> from martyrdom I came to this, my peace.
>   (*Par.* XV, 97-148)

In this stirring passage we can probably deduce from Cacciaguida's self-description how Dante saw himself and his mission in life: an individual, a Christian, a citizen of Florence, a hero of the Roman Empire, and a confessor and martyr of the true faith. Cacciaguida's discourse deserves extensive commentary, but a few observations might suffice here. Through this discourse Dante evokes the religious character of early Florence when the hours of public prayer were announced by the church bells and when women during the pains of child-birth invoked Mary. The poet extols the once simple Florentine way of life: no conspicuous display of wealth in clothing and jewelry, no overly large houses and no obsession with sexual pleasures — the very antithesis of Dante's Florence. It seems that Dante's Florence was a distant mirror of contemporary America in so many ways.

In his description of the earlier Florence Dante mentioned that wives did not have to fear long absences of their husbands who were away on business, purchasing and trading cloth in the fairs of French cities. Dante's Florence had become Europe's capital for the wool and leather industries as well as for the dyeing of expensive cloth. *Haute couture,* then as now, was a thriving business in Florence; the Gucci empire from Florence is a contemporary example.

Among the many virtues of the ancient Florentines evoked by Dante through his ancestor's speech was their civic pride in their Trojan and Roman origins. This pride was expressed by the imitation of those original Roman virtues of justice, moderation and heroism. Dante's admiration and love for his native city, the Church and the Roman Empire shine through his ancestor's speech. These loves were all interwoven, all of one piece. Dante's frequent outbursts of wrath in his *Comedy* against the Florentines, the popes and the civic leaders of his time are but deeply felt expressions of a lover's painful rage at the corruption of the objects of his love and devotion. Dante with deepest affection saw himself simultaneously as a son of Florence, of the Church and of the Empire.

Florence was not just a city: it was, in his words, "the sheepfold of St. John." Florence had once been a loving mother, like the Church, to Dante; but like the wicked popes and cardinals, she had become a cruel stepmother (cf. *Par.* XVI, 58-60). The epitaph which Dante supposedly composed for his own tomb describes Florence as the mother who bore him, but exiled him: "So little did she love him." Perhaps Dante's yearning for a loving mother stemmed from the loss of his mother when he was only six. His father soon remarried. Was his stepmother cruel? We do not know. Dante tells us nothing of her or of his father, but his desire to be embraced as a beloved son is often expressed throughout the *Comedy.* We detect this in the paternal/maternal figure of Virgil; in Beatrice, who often plays the maternal role; in Brunetto Latini, one of Dante's mentors; and in his beloved ancestor, Cacciaguida.

Dante's meeting with Cacciaguida in Paradise is described in terms of a father's encounter with a long lost son. It is compared to Aeneas' meeting with his father Anchises in the Elysian fields. There Anchises welcomed his son to the other world and predicted his future sufferings and his future glory as the founder of Rome:

> With like affection did Anchises' shade
> rush forth, if we may trust our greatest Muse,
> when in Elysium he beheld his son.
> "O sanguis meus, o superinfusa
> gratia Dei, sicut tibi, cui
> bis umquam celi janua reclusa?"
> (*Par.* XV, 25-30)

Cacciaguida's Latin words mean literally: "Oh blood of mine, oh over-flowing grace of God! To whom, as to you, was Heaven's gate ever opened twice?" This is the first and only time in the *Comedy* that a person greets Dante in Latin. The words *sanguis meus* are the very ones used by Anchises to greet his son Aeneas (cf. *Aeneid* VI, 835). The purposeful use of Latin, the language of the Romans and the sacred language of the Church, adds to the solemn character of the scene in which Dante is hailed as a new Aeneas with a "divine" mission for the Empire. Dante throughout the *Comedy* perceived himself as another Aeneas. We shall see later that he also saw himself as another St. Paul, who journeyed to the other world and received a divine mission for the Church.[6]

We should notice the context in which Dante's encounter with Cacciaguida takes place: the heaven of Mars, which is illuminated by the dazzling cross of Christ, the arms of which are populated with the glowing spirits of heroic warriors who promoted God's glory on earth. Among them are Joshua and the Maccabees of the Old Testament; Charlemagne, the first Emperor of the Holy Roman Empire; his nephew, the famous knight Roland, who fought against the Saracens; and many other heroes, such as Godfrey of Bouillion, leader of the First Crusade.

Dante's admiration for these warriors of God, and in particular for the Crusaders, raises the question of Dante's concept of a holy war for Christ — the fundamental "theology" of the Crusades. It also raises the question of Dante's appraisal of war itself and his active participation in local wars. Apparently Dante endorsed the medieval ideology of the Crusades: a justified enterprise to secure the holy places, especially Jerusalem, the central place both spiritually and geographically of the entire world for the medieval Christian. Jerusalem, besides being the place of God's Temple in the Old Testament times, was the place where Christ had died, was buried and had risen. For this reason it was the sacred goal of *the* pilgrimage which every medieval Christian aspired to make.

Since the Saracens and Jews prevented this sacred right and duty, a war against them was not only justified but became an expression of glorious witness and devotion to Christ. Thus an aura of sacred duty and even martyrdom surrounded the concept of the Crusades: a holy war to promote the triumph of Christ and His Cross. Dante expresses this ideology so clearly and forcefully in the triumphant spectacle of Christ's Cross in the heaven of Mars, described in canto XIV of *Paradise*.

By Dante's time, however, the idea of the Crusades was all but dead; it was more like an ideal from another age, a forgotten commit-ment, which revealed, according to Dante, the spiritual decadence and tepidness of his times. After the fall of Acre to the Saracens in 1291

European Christians were disheartened, and for the most part they finally admitted their failure. Many factors contributed to this spirit of defeatism, among which was the lack of that sense of a unified Christendom which existed at the beginning of the Crusades almost two centuries before. The rise of a nationalistic consciousness and other interests, such as the successful trading business with the East, turned public opinion against further warfare in that region. The Crusades had become for many Europeans, especially the Venetian merchants, an excuse for their ugly greed and barbarism. They were often merely a pretext for the most savage attacks even on fellow Christians in the East. The Crusades had degenerated into the very antithesis of the Christian gospel of love.

Dante does not allude to these perverse and immoral aspects of the once noble and holy experiment. Instead he severely castigates Boniface VIII more than once for not taking an interest in recovering the holy places. According to Dante, Boniface perverted the sacred ideology of a Crusade into a weapon to serve his sick pride and desire for revenge against his personal enemies. In Canto XXVII of the *Inferno* Dante tells the shocking story of a famous military leader, Guido da Montefeltro, who, having repented of his life of deceit and savagery, became a Franciscan friar only to be summoned by the crafty Boniface to give him advice on how to annihilate his enemies, the powerful Colonna family of Rome. The Colonnas, two of whom were cardinals, had denied the legitimacy of Celestine V's abdication of the papacy, which had led to Boniface's election as pope. Since the Colonnas refused to recognize Boniface as the legitimate pope, they had to be destroyed. Boniface called a "crusade" against them:

> And then the Prince of the New Pharisees
> chose to wage war upon the Lateran
> instead of fighting Saracens or Jews,
> for all his enemies were Christian souls
> (none among the ones who conquered Acre,
> none a trader in the Sultan's kingdom).
> His lofty papal seat, his sacred vows
> were no concern to him, nor was the cord
> I wore (that once made those it girded leaner).
> (*Inf.* XXVII, 85-93)

The wily Boniface offered amnesty to the Colonnas if they would only surrender to him. They were holed-up in their fortress-city of Palestrina, not far from Rome (the Lateran). Guido's evil counsel to the Pope was to "promise much and deliver little." After the Colonnas surrendered to the papal troops, Boniface razed their castle and city and then had all the captives sentenced to life imprisonment. So much for the good faith of Boniface! Among the prisoners was one of the greatest Italian poets of the Middle Ages, Jacopone da Todi, the spiritual Franciscan mentioned earlier. He was to spend many years incarcerated in a dark monastic cell of his native Todi. There he wrote his most ardent verses in mystical praise of God's love. It remains a mystery that Dante in his writings makes no allusion to this fellow poet and kindred soul who shared with him such contempt for Boniface. Perhaps Dante, in the spirit of St. Bonaventure, wanted to steer a middle course in his allegiance to the Franciscans by avoiding any suspicious association with the extreme Spirituals, who sometimes engaged in fanatical behavior.

Dante's independent, critical spirit comes across in his reference to Guido's Franciscan cord: "it once made those it girded leaner." Although Dante strongly supported the Franciscan movement, he had no tolerance for those friars who were lax in their commitment to poverty and austerity. The stereotype of the fat, jolly friar on our contemporary humorous greeting cards would not have amused Dante. His barbed comments on the obesity of his contemporary Franciscans did not conform, however, to St. Francis' admonition to his friars "not to have contempt for, nor to judge, those whom you see dressed in rich and colorful attire, who are accustomed to fine food and beverages." We will consider later Dante's admiration of Francis and Franciscan spirituality.

At present let us turn to Dante as a young Florentine and in particular his fulfillment of civic duties and loyalty, which usually required taking up arms for the cause of Florence. That Dante actually engaged in military activities and wielded a sword in battle is a matter sometimes disputed by Dante critics. Most, however, accept the testimony of Lionardo Bruni (1369-1444), an early biographer who reports that Dante, "Courteous, spirited and full of courage, took part in every youthful exercise; and in the great and memorable battle of

Campaldino, Dante, young but well esteemed, fought vigorously, mounted and in the front rank."[7] Bruni claims that he had a letter of Dante before his eyes in which Dante describes his active participation in the battle. The letter is no longer extant.

We do have, however, from Dante's pen a description of that battle at Campaldino against Arezzo, a neighboring city-state in Tuscany. Dante expressly states, "I saw the horsemen moving camp and joining battle." (cf. *Inf.* XXII, 1-12). In another passage he uses the same terms "I saw" in his description of a battle against Pisa, another Tuscan rival. (cf. *Inf.* XXI, 94-96) Was Dante merely an observer? In the judgment of most scholars today Dante, like any loyal citizen, engaged in those battles, even if he was not enamored of military glory or attracted by the pleasures of waging war. It seems to me inconsistent with Dante's artistic and sensitive temperament that he would be brandishing a sword on the battle field. Poets seem to belong in the more peaceful milieu of a garden or the countryside, but we have to recall an Aeschylus at Marathon, a Horace at Philippi, a Cervantes at Lepanto, and a St. Francis at Perugia.

St. Francis, according to his earliest biographer, Thomas of Celano (1190-1260), fought in Assisi's disastrous battle against Perugia and was taken prisoner. According to the same biographer Francis as a young man had dreams of being the heroic knight engaged in military adventures.[8] Chesterton's reflections on this phase of Francis' life are appropriate for an understanding of the young Francis and of the young Dante:

> War had broken out between Assisi and Perugia. It is now fashionable to say in a satirical spirit that such wars did not so much break out as go on indefinitely between the city-states of medieval Italy . . . But the citizens of the medieval republic were certainly under the limitation of only being asked to die for the things with which they had always lived, the houses they inhabited, the shrines they venerated and the rulers and representatives they knew; and had not the larger vision calling them to die for the latest rumors about remote colonies, as reported in anonymous newspapers.

> And if we infer from our own experience that wars paralyzed civilization, we must at least admit that these warring towns turned out a number of paralytics who go by the names of Dante and Michael Angelo, Ariosto and Titian, Leonardo and Columbus, not to mention Catherine of Siena and the subject of this story. While we lament all this local patriotism as a hubbub of the Dark Ages, it must seem a rather curious fact that about three quarters of the greatest men who ever lived came out of these little towns and were often engaged in these little wars. [9]

Perhaps we should agree with Chesterton's appraisal of Francis as "an ordinary young man" at that period of his life. According to Chesterton, Francis "acted out of an unconscious largeness, or in the fine mediaeval phrase *largesse,* within himself, something that might almost have been lawless if it had not been reaching out to a more divine law; but it is doubtful whether he yet knew that the law was divine. . . . It is true that there is not, as pacifists and prigs imagine, the least inconsistency between loving men and fighting them, if we fight them fairly and for a good cause." [10]

Whether Dante was actually a soldier at one stage in his life remains unclear, although the available evidence seems to support that opinion; but Dante in his extant writings never clearly identifies himself as a soldier nor does he exalt the image of the Christian knight except in the context of the Crusades. In his eulogy of St. Francis (cf. *Par.* XI) he praises Francis as the heroic lover of Lady Poverty, the imitator of Christ and the peaceful crusader who attempted to convert the Sultan, not to kill him. Dante's sympathies lay with Francis, the man of peace.

Dante's writings on world government contain many exhortations to peacemaking. We will consider them later, but they reveal a sincere and passionate apostle of peace, an architect of a peaceful order intended by God for human happiness on earth. Although not a pacifist in the current sense of the word, he promoted peace based on justice. His words often have the ring of Pope John XXIII's *Pacem in Terris,* the documents of Vatican II, the American bishops' pastoral letter on peacemaking, and most recently the teachings of John Paul II.

In many of his writings Dante shows a certain scorn for the military life and war. The following passage, identified by Mark Musa as an expression of Dante's *real* feelings about war, contains what most readers would consider vulgar, offensive language unworthy of such an intellectual and spiritual poet, but the very crudeness of it demonstrates, I believe, Dante's attitude toward war and the military life. It is a description of a contingent of devils in Hell and their military obedience to their captain:

> Before they turned left-face along the bank
> each one gave their good captain a salute
> with farting tongue pressed tightly to his teeth,
> and he blew-back with his bugle of an ass-hole.
> (*Inf.* XXI, 136-139)

No one after reading that passage can accuse Dante of not having a sense of humor, even if the vocabulary seems in bad taste. But for Dante the vulgar words are appropriate to the atmosphere of Hell. The names he gives to the soldier-demons are just as farcical, but they defy translation into English. Most English translations mollify Dante's scatological vocabulary in the *Inferno*; we should admire Musa's fidelity to Dante's tone and intentions. Musa is a genuine translator, not a traitor, proving that the famous proverb is not always true.

In spite of Dante's later cynicism and sarcasm on the subject of war and military life, he does seem to have been a typical Florentine in his youth — patriotic even to the point of doing battle against Florence's enemies. If Dante was a typical Florentine in his patriotism, was he also a typical Florentine in his religious life? That brings us to the topic of a typical layman's participation in the Church's life in medieval Florence. What was it like?

All the evidence points to a Florence that was exceptionally religious. Villani reports that the Florence of the early fourteenth century had 110 churches, 24 nunneries, 5 abbeys and 10 orders of friars. Although it could be said that every Italian city at that time was "exceptionally religious," Florence seems to stand out as the city in Italy — and in Europe — that was the most profoundly affected by the sweeping religious revival led by the Franciscans and Dominicans. As

early as 1210 the first Franciscans arrived in Florence amidst an
enthusiastic welcome from the people. Their small foundation in the
church of *Santa Croce* was greatly enlarged through contributions from
the faithful and from the Commune itself to become a major religious
and cultural center. *Santa Croce* with its great basilica and convent
became one of the largest and most impressive religious centers in all of
Italy. A statue of Dante (with scornful pose) stands before it today.

St. Francis visited Florence several times, and, according to one
tradition, composed the Rule for the Tertiaries there in 1221. Most
historians however contend that Francis never dreamed of creating a
"third order," but that it developed from the papal policy that sought to
place various associations of pious laity under the direction of important
religious orders. [11]

That Dante was a member of the third order of St. Francis is a
strong tradition, supported of course by the Franciscans, whose claim
on Dante is well known — especially on his bones. But that's another
story: the ongoing contention between the city of Florence and the
Franciscans of Ravenna over the remains of Dante. Most scholars
today deny that Dante was a Franciscan tertiary. [12] However, Franco
Tardioli in a recent book on Dante as a Franciscan argues from some
early commentaries on the *Comedy* and from evidence in the medieval
art of Assisi that Dante was not only a tertiary but had also been a novice
for some time at the *Santa Croce* convent. According to the author
Dante left *Santa Croce* before taking religious vows. [13]

While the question of whether Dante was a Franciscan tertiary or
novice is disputed, there is general agreement among the scholars that
he was deeply influenced by Franciscan spirituality and theology. Most
historians concede that Dante frequented the Franciscans' house of
studies — the *studium* at *Santa Croce* — and heard the preachers and
theologians there. Dante specifically mentions in his writings that he
attended lectures in the "schools of the religious." Besides the
Franciscans' school there were three other *studia* in Florence: The
Dominicans' at *Santa Maria Novella,* the Augustinians' at *Santo Spirito*
and the Carmelites' on the other side of the Arno. From our knowledge
of Dante's voracious appetite for learning, we could conclude that he
studied at some or at all of these schools which were open to laymen.

Strangely, there was no university in Florence, although there were several in Italy at that time: at Bologna, Salerno, Naples and Padua.

Laymen in Florence thus had some access to higher learning in the areas of philosophy and theology, the subjects taught at the *studia*. The same, unfortunately, can not be said about laywomen, although young girls were taught to read and write. Higher education was reserved for the boys, since girls were expected to become proficient only in domestic skills or in music and dancing. Boys needed more developed skills in literacy and numeracy since many became merchants or bankers. Some pursued higher education in order to assume professional roles as lawyers and notaries or to enter public life in their city-state.

It must be admitted, however, that a layman's proficiency in philosophy and theology was the exception in Dante's time. Villani's comment that Dante was "a great and learned person in almost every science, although a layman" confirms this. But Dante was exceptional: all the early biographers and commentators describe him as an avid learner, intensely curious about everything, endowed with extraordinary intelligence, prodigious memory and exquisite sensitivity. He had a passionate drive to excel in everything he put his mind to — an "achiever" and "perfectionist" in today's terms. There even seems to be a taint of pride and ambition in the young Dante's quest for universal knowledge.

But pride and ambition seem to be typical traits of the Florentines. Their enormous achievements in business, the arts and science bear witness to those traits. Another Florentine characteristic was their critical sense in spiritual and ecclesiastical matters. Many reform movements in the Church developed in and around Florence centuries before Dante and Dante knew this history. Both the laity and the religious of Florence had been deeply involved in various reforms of the Church and revivals of evangelical living for centuries.

This serious concern for reform in the Church, especially of the morally corrupt clergy and the lax, worldly monastic orders, was deeply felt by many popes, bishops, abbots and laypersons in the Middle Ages long before the great reforms effected by Pope Gregory VII in the late eleventh century. Many of these reform movements began in central Italy in or near Tuscany and found strong support among the laity of

Florence. Dante was well informed of this history, and in his writings praised the outstanding reformers from that earlier era, among whom were St. Romuald (950-1027) and St. Peter Damian (1007-1072). Both men were Benedictines, reformers and great contemplatives whom Dante meets in the heaven of the contemplative souls (cf. *Par.* XXII). Romuald had founded many reformed monasteries, among which was the famous hermitage at Camaldoli in the Casentino, the upper valley of the Arno. Dante spent much of his exile period in that region.

St. Peter Damian, a disciple of St. Romuald, spent much of his life as prior at the Camaldolese hermitage of *Santa Croce* at Fonte Avellana. In his conversation with Dante in Paradise (cf. *Par.* XXI, 52-135) he refers to that retreat "not far distant from your own country," i.e., Dante's Florence. It is very likely that Dante was a guest at that monastery and wrote part of the *Comedy* there. (A bust of Dante and an inscription in a cell there commemorates his sojourn.) Dante greatly admired Peter's spirit of reform, especially his ruthless invectives against the cardinals and corrupt clergy of the eleventh century, which in Dante's mind was a mirror of his thirteenth and fourteenth centuries. In his speech in Paradise Peter expresses compassion for the horses which had to bear such heavy loads — the fat cardinals! Peter's forthright condemnations of clerical corruption were shared by his friend Hildebrand, later to become Pope Gregory VII, and also by many laypersons who joined these communities in their efforts to reform the Church. Dante surely felt a strong affinity to Peter Damian, a highly cultured man, poet, talented writer in theology, energetic prophet and ardent contemplative. [14]

A contemporary of St. Romuald and St. Peter Damian was St. John Gualbert (995-1073), a Florentine and kindred spirit of these two reformers. He founded a congregation of reformed Benedictines at Vallombrosa, only 16 miles from Florence. It is puzzling that Dante does not mention him since he was a fellow Florentine and in Dante's time there were about 80 abbeys of his congregation throughout Italy. John had been a Benedictine monk in the Florentine abbey of San Miniato (mentioned earlier), but was disenchanted by the lax spirit there. He openly opposed the simony of his abbot and of the bishop of Florence who had him driven out of the monastery and the city. A popular uprising against the simoniac bishop resulted in his deposition.

The feisty Florentine laity thus showed their support for John and their impatience with the corrupt clergy and monastic leaders. Dante seems to have inherited this kind of critical spirit.

Many Florentine laypersons joined John in the communities he established as daughter houses of Vallombrosa. These foundations received strong support from a famous laywoman of the eleventh century, Countess Matilda of Tuscany. She encouraged the reform movement of Vallombrosa by bestowing generous donations on the congregation. Matilda is well known for her support of the papacy in its struggle with the German King Henry IV over the crucial question of imperial control of ecclesiastical appointments. Matilda was present with Pope Gregory VII in her castle at Canossa when Henry, her nephew, stood outside in penitential garb — that famous act of submission which was a turning point in the long medieval power struggle between the Church and the Empire. When Henry later decided to reverse his humiliation at Canossa and avenge himself, he attacked the papal territories. Matilda's troops defended the papal interests, but the city-states of Tuscany sided with the imperial forces.

Florence was the only city in Tuscany to remain faithful to Matilda. The Countess granted many political and economic privileges to Florence for its fidelity during that war with the German king. Thus was born a love affair between Matilda and Florence. Florence was to remain a stronghold of the Guelph party, the traditional supporters of the papacy against imperial claims. Florentines kept the memory of Matilda alive for centuries by naming their daughters "Contessa" or "Tessa." In Dante's time these were still very common names in Florence, a city still staunchly Guelph.

It's very likely that the Matelda in the Earthly Paradise (cf. *Purg.* XXXIII) was none other than the Countess of Tuscany. Some commentators argue that the woman in the garden of Eden is merely an allegory or symbol of the active life. But who, in Dante's mind, would better fulfill that role than the real woman, the Countess from Canossa, who had actively defended Christ's vicar on earth and who had distinguished herself by so many works of charity? Most of the early commentators, including Dante's own son Peter, interpret the Matelda in the edenic garden as Countess Matilda of Tuscany. She probably represented for Dante a regenerated humanity, a new Eve obedient to God's will, who responds to God's love by loving service.

All these memories of Matilda, loyalty to the papacy, concern for Church reform — when added to the enthusiastic reforms generated by the Franciscans and Dominicans — made of the Florentines in Dante's time a people profoundly interested and involved in the life of the Church. One might argue that Florence's alignment with the papacy was motivated by a mutual "back-scratching" strategy that served both Florentine and papal interests, but her traditional Guelphism may have included also a sincere fidelity to the Holy See for religious reasons. Such fidelity was the case with Dante who theologically defended the papacy's authentic responsibilities but who vigorously opposed the papacy's temporal rule.

Many people in Dante's time perceived him as an enemy of the papacy since after his exile from Florence he identified openly with the Ghibelline cause, which supported imperial claims to temporal rule and the interests of the high nobility. However, by Dante's time a clear-cut distinction between Guelphs and Ghibellines and their loyalties no longer existed. The terms had lost their original meanings and relevance. Furthermore, the Tuscan city-states seemed more interested in their own autonomy and development than in larger theological issues. Dante toward the end of his life repudiated any identification with either party, declaring himself "a party to himself."

Dante pursued a more theological approach to the Church. He considered himself a lamb in Christ's fold, the Church, under the pastoral guidance of Peter, the shepherd appointed by Christ. He fed in that pasture and found abundant nourishment, especially in the liturgical life of the Church. Documents from the thirteenth century describe the widespread practice of laymen and laywomen's daily attendance at all the Hours of liturgical prayer — the Sacred Offices — as well as at daily Mass. Their active participation in those liturgies may have been minimal, since the records describe them as "hearing" the Office and Mass — a term familiar to pre-Vatican II ears.

Perfect understanding of the readings and chants was accessible only to those who comprehended Latin, but ecclesiastical Latin was not so far removed from the vernacular spoken in Dante's Italy. My own experience in Italy in the years before the liturgical reforms of Vatican II

women could follow the Office with their beautifully illuminated "Books of Hours," but they were the exceptions rather than the general rule. Besides, one had to be very wealthy to own such a Book of Hours.

We might conclude by noting that laymen like Dante were more of an exception, even though the masses of illiterate laity received much spiritual nourishment from the Latin liturgy and sermons in the vernacular. The popularity of the new mendicant orders in the thirteenth century, the Dominicans and Franciscans, who preached in the vernacular, gave a new impetus to the laity who were hungering for a deeper spiritual life and a return to Gospel simplicity.

The organizations of many religious laymen and laywomen into third orders of the Dominican and Franciscan communities also contributed to the intense spiritual renewal of the thirteenth century. Although Dante probably supported this custom for laypersons to become tertiaries, it could be argued from a passage in his writings that he did not consider membership in any religious order of much relevance to a person's nobility of soul or eternal salvation. He plainly states that a married layperson can be just as "religious" as someone in a religious habit, since true religion is a matter of one's heart. In Dante's words, "It is not only those who adopt the habit or the way of life of St. Benedict, St. Augustine, St. Francis or St. Dominic that turn to religion; but anyone may devote himself to good and true religion while remaining in the married state, since God desires no religion from us but that of the heart. That's why St. Paul says to the Romans: 'It is not the man who is a Jew on the outside, whose circumcision is a physical thing. Rather, the real Jew is the person who is a Jew on the inside, that is, whose heart has been circumcised, and this is the work of the Spirit, not of the written law. Such a person receives his praise from God, not from man.' (Rm 2:28)"[18]

Besides the third orders a great number of lay organizations flourished in Dante's Italy. Such phenomena are probably evidence that the ordinary life of the Church, centered in the local parish, was not enough to satisfy the religious aspirations of many laypeople. Often the labor guilds in medieval cities functioned also as "quasi-religious" communities with their own patron saints, chapels and charitable projects. Florence in Dante's time had a highly developed network of such guilds — the wool merchants, cloth dyers, and many others — which regularly performed the corporal works of mercy and sponsored the building and maintenance of churches and abbeys. Besides these associations of craftsmen and professionals there were specifically religious groups known as confraternities, which led lives of prayer and active service to the community. We know that Dante enrolled in one of the guilds in 1295.

It was often difficult to determine the borderline between confraternity and guild.[19] Some of these confraternities had as their purpose to honor the Blessed Sacrament or to make reparation for outrages committed against the Sacrament by heretics. Many were devoted to personal penance for sins — the so-called "Brothers and Sisters of Penance." Still others were committed to honor some patron saint, a mystery of Christ or the Blessed Virgin Mary. Some were even organized to preserve the purity of the faith, but most were committed to practical works of charity. One of the famous confraternities in Dante's day was the Archconfraternity of Mercy, founded in 1240 and still active today. Evidence of the activities of these groups can be seen in a series of frescoes preserved in the tiny church of St. Martin, a few steps from Dante's home in Florence. The series, depicting the seven corporal works of mercy, is a marvelous summary of medieval practical spirituality.

Although there were many such confraternities loyal to the Church, there were just as many heretical and anti-clerical sects of laity, which flourished in the twelfth and thirteenth centuries throughout north and central Italy. Such a complex topic is beyond our scope here, but mention should be made of a "sect," apparently not heretical, which was an active confraternity in the Tuscany of Dante's time. It was known as the *Fideles Amoris,* the "Faithful Followers of Love." Dante scholars today are giving closer attention to this brotherhood and Dante's associations with it. We will examine this subject more closely in the next chapter.

This chapter has attempted to give some background for understanding the cultural and religious life of Dante's Florence. It has been far from exhaustive, but perhaps it has shed some light on the *genius loci* of Florence, on some of the typical Florentine traits, and on life in thirteenth-century Italy — all important subjects which help us to understand Dante and his world.

Chapter Two

POET OF LOVE

Early biographers of Dante describe a young man intellectually alive and intensely curious about all branches of knowledge. We know very little about his formal education as a boy. It seems that Dante from his teens through the rest of his life was for the most part self-taught. The biographers also describe his interest in music and art and his ability to draw well. But the more consuming interest, the passion which animated his life, was his love of poetry and his love for writing poetry; and the ultimate source of his inspiration was love itself. So perhaps the best words to describe the person of Dante — if anyone can be summed up in a few words — would be a poet of love.

The early deaths of both parents (his mother when he was only five; his father when he was twelve) could possibly be cited as factors which left a void in his affective life which he sought to fill through his early love affair (when he was not quite nine!) with the beautiful Beatrice of the same age. Even aside from the deaths of his parents, the sensitive Dante early in his life felt that most basic of all human needs: "to love and to be loved," as Augustine so succinctly expressed it in his *Confessions*.

Young Dante was taught his letters, perhaps by one of the local tutors. At an early age he was introduced to poetry since most of the texts used for instruction were poetic: Bible stories in verse form, the fables of Aesop, and even poetic paraphrases of great philosophers and theologians such as Boethius and Augustine. He soon acquired a taste for the great Latin poets such as Ovid and a lifelong love for Virgil. Not only the classical Latin poets captivated his imagination; he was stirred also by the popular Arthurian romances about knights and ladies, those famous love stories about Lancelot and Guinevere, Tristan and Isolde, and others.

There was also a trend among the Florentine literati of Dante's time to admire and imitate French literature, which had reached Florence through merchants and scholars who frequently traveled to France. Dante became well acquainted with this French culture. One of his mentors was Brunetto Latini, a Florentine scholar and statesman, whose most famous work was an encyclopedia written in French, called *Le Tresor*. Even if Dante was not a direct pupil of Brunetto, he greatly admired his work and expressed indebtedness to him as well as deep filial affection for him (cf. *Inf.* XV).

The influence of the French poetry of courtly love which flourished in *La Provence* was particularly visible in the Florence of Dante's youth. This popular literary movement, often called the troubadour tradition, had spread to Tuscany mainly by way of the Sicilian poets at Frederick II's court in the thirteenth century. It also developed through the influence of Guido Guinicelli and his school of poetry at Bologna. By Dante's time, writing verses in the vernacular and in the troubadour style was a respected art form, practiced especially by a group of poets known in Tuscany as the *Fideles Amoris* or the *fedeli d'amore,* the faithful followers of love.

Dante's verses soon attracted the attention of the leader of this group in Florence, Guido Cavalcanti, who became Dante's close friend in 1283, when Dante was eighteen. Guido, Dante's senior by ten years, greatly influenced Dante in his late teens and early twenties. Their common bond was the deep solidarity of poets who shared the same belief in the seriousness of their art. They were both attracted toward the same goal: to understand and praise love itself.

These faithful followers of love would exchange rhymes and invite responses from others in the group: a friendly competition which developed the artistic talents of all the poets in this fellowship. Besides verses celebrating love itself and its powerful effects on them, the *fedeli d'amore* focused their attention often on a lady whose physical and spiritual qualities they interpreted as miraculous graces from Heaven. The lady became an "angelic" figure and the object of the highest devotion — some would say even worship.

Needless to say, this outpouring of love poetry in France and Italy deeply affected the image and status of women in the Middle Ages. Women then were generally treated as men's slaves, and physical abuse of wives was common and even condoned by the preachers.[1] The *fedeli d'amore*, however, discovered in women qualities that incarnated the very beauty and wisdom of God. The lady of their lyrics often became an allegory of Divine Wisdom. Guido Cavalcanti in one of his sonnets enumerates the many stirring aesthetic experiences of his life and concludes with these words in praise of his lady: "She surpasses all these in wisdom, as much as heaven is greater than earth."[2]

Guido Cavalcanti, Dante and two other poets, Cino da Pistoia and Lapo Gianni, formed the nucleus of an elite brotherhood whose art became known as the *Dolce Stil Nuovo* — the sweet new style. These poets were not merely gentlemen of leisure whose nobility and family wealth permitted them the luxury of spending their time in a dream-like world contemplating the beauty of nature, women and love. Dante, Guido and Cino belonged to noble families, but by then these nobles had joined the bourgeois class of merchants, bankers and public servants. Guido was the most aristocratic of them all and Lapo, it seems, was not a nobleman at all; but all of them extolled the nobility of an individual's soul over nobility of blood based on superficial honors.

All of these poets were actively engaged in public life in some way. Cino and Lapo were notaries; Cino also taught law and Lapo was a judge. Dante, too, was to play an active role in the public life of Florence. Guido, Cino and Dante all suffered exile because of their political involvements. Therefore these members of a literary elite should not be thought of as so many aesthetes who shunned the real world and its pressing problems. They pursued their art because they were thoroughly convinced of its inherent worth and its ennobling influence on themselves and on society in general. They did not write verses merely for themselves as a closed clique: they purposely wrote in the vernacular to reach a wider public audience.

Their poetry then was not a form of escapism into a fantasy world of self-indulgence, although a hint of that can be detected in some of their sonnets and ballads. The young poet Dante seems to express this tendency in one of his early sonnets addressed to Guido:

Guido, I would wish that you, Lapo and I
were placed by an enchanter's magic wand
upon a little boat and taken by
every wind across the sea to wherever you and I would want to go.
I desire that no bad weather
or misfortune would impede our pleasant course,
but having but one mind among the three,
we might always be together and grow in our mutual desires.
And Monna Vanna and Monna Lagia too
and she who ranks the thirtieth on the roll
I would wish the enchanter to place with us,
and there we would always discourse on love,
and each of the ladies would be content,
just as I believe we would be.

(Rime LII)

There is an idyllic charm and beauty in this early sonnet, which reminds one of Baudelaire's *Invitation au voyage.* Guido's response to Dante's sonnet, however, was a sharp rebuke for Dante's lack of seriousness and indulgence in the merely pleasurable aspects of love. Dante's "chief friend" was also his mentor, who at times reprimanded Dante if he thought he had strayed from the path of rationality.

The identity of Dante's lady — "the thirtieth on the roll" — might suggest that Dante was a thirteenth-century Don Giovanni with a long list of female conquests. What seems to be the case is that at the time of Dante's love for Beatrice he composed a list of sixty of the fairest ladies in Florence, who served as "screen ladies" to divert the public's attention from his real lady: a familiar convention in the courtly love tradition. The lady chosen for the voyage would be the thirtieth on the list, which Dante has not preserved for us.

During these youthful years Dante not only wrote verses on love and praises of many ladies; the influence of the faithful followers of love was not the only one in his life. He also assiduously pursued studies in classical literature, philosophy and theology. His emotional life also reached an intense pitch for it was during these same years that his love for Beatrice was developing into one of the most sublime hymns of praise to a woman and to love in all of world literature. This hymn is the

Vita Nuova, The New Life, a work which Dante completed probably in 1295, five years after Beatrice's death.

The *Vita Nuova* is a landmark in world literature for many reasons, and its interpretation has had a long, complex history in literary criticism. It broke ground as a genre in vernacular literature since it combined poetry and prose narrative into one work. It is a delightful mixture of beautiful lyrics and an intensely emotional story of a young man's turbulent love life. Although it had much in common with some of the romances popular at that time, it would certainly disappoint a modern reader looking for a romance that caters to erotic interests.

Modern readers generally find the work difficult and enigmatic: a strange juxtaposition of dreams, interpretations of these dreams, visitations from the god of love, and rapturous ecstasies. There are also real persons encountered in the streets and churches of Florence, reflections on the nature of love, laments over the death of Beatrice, and several digressions on various subjects. The work seems to end abruptly as if the author left it unfinished to go on to something better.

What is the meaning of it intended by its author? Hundreds of books and articles have attempted to discover it. Dante, the supreme artist, often conceals his art, but not for the purpose of remaining obscure or aloof. I think he wants to lead his readers into a fuller participation in the action and meaning of the text. He gives enough clues which should enable the attentive reader to make the important connections and find the intended meanings. This may appear as the technique of modern mystery writers, but Dante's art is more subtle than that. His art makes great demands on the reader, requires a vast culture and respects the intellectual and aesthetic sensibilities of the reader. Dante may seem at times to preside as a pedant far above the inferior crowds, but in reality he is with them, speaking their own language and communicating extraordinary experiences which he assumes the reader can and wants to share with him. Dante was well aware that art and poetry are multi-dimensional and yield several levels of meaning to the reader who seeks to find them.

But to understand the meaning of Dante's *Vita Nuova* requires a wide range of knowledge: the facts about Dante's life, medieval life and culture in general, the literary tradition of courtly love in particular, Florentine history and customs, etc. One of the most important areas of research should also be the many intellectual and spiritual influences on Dante during those years before the final composition of the work. This work came about after years of philosophical and theological progress as well as emotional turmoil. It includes many of his earlier verses and seems to be a retrospective meditation on that formative period of his life: his youth and early adulthood.

During those formative years he immersed himself in the study not only of the classical Latin writers — Cicero, Virgil, Ovid and others — but also of the Greek philosophers, particularly Aristotle. He also delved into the classics of Christian literature. His knowledge of the Bible, Fathers of the Church and medieval mystics was phenomenal at this stage of his life. The works of Augustine, Boethius, Dionysius, Bernard of Clairvaux, Thomas Aquinas and Bonaventure shine through the pages of his work, even at this early stage. Often literary critics show too little concern for the influence of these Christian sources on Dante.

One of the great American Dante scholars of our era, Charles Singleton, has given an interpretation of the *Vita Nuova* which does justice to the biblical, patristic and mystical sources of Dante's work. Singleton is not the first or only critic to draw attention to these sources, but his research and his analysis of Dante's work seem to get at the very heart of the matter: the *Vita Nuova* as a mystical, Christ-centered meditation on the meaning of love and death — a truly Christian reflection which Dante derived from his lived experience of love for Beatrice and his loss of her in death.

Dante's *Vita Nuova* in many ways resembles St. Augustine's *Confessions,* the first spiritual autobiography in Christian literature. Dante, like Augustine, writes a "book of memory" in which he describes his inner life as well as some significant events of his external life. He has come to see into — to intuit — what was really happening within himself and outside himself during those years when Beatrice filled his soul. If we look at Augustine's *Confessions* we see a story of his discovery of God, of His beauty and of His saving grace. From beginning to end Augustine's work is an extravagant outpouring of praise — a "confession" or "profession" in that original sense of pure praise of God. But in another sense it is also a confession of his sins, which God's mercy has forgiven. Augustine expressed both simultaneously:

in confessing his sin he confessed praise of the God who forgave him. His self-discovery was God-discovery — a single movement of the soul. Augustine upon making this discovery sang to the Lord a "new song." He had become a new man, and in his words, "The new man is the new life (*vita nova*)."[3]

Was Dante's *Vita Nuova* also a confession of sin? Another great American Dante scholar, Mark Musa, thinks so. In the conclusion of his illuminating essay Musa states: "The greatness of the *Vita Nuova* lies, not in the poems included by their author in the work, but in the purpose which he formed them to serve. Certainly it represents the most original form of recantation in medieval literature — a recantation that takes the form of a re-enactment, from a new perspective, of the sin recanted."[4] That sin, Musa observes, was Dante's emotional self-indulgence, his self-centeredness, "the canker that the heart instinctively tends to cultivate." According to Musa, Dante has gone far beyond his fellow troubadours' treatment of the lover's glorification of his own feelings and the glorification of the Beloved. Dante's *Vita Nuova* would be an unparalleled indictment of his misguided obsession with his own feelings — especially his hysterical self-pity. It would be a recognition of his own failure at one point in his life to recognize the true — the divine — meaning of the beloved one. But in that very recognition of failure lies the greatness of this work of Dante.

In the *Vita Nuova* Dante does give us a glimpse of the divine dimension of Beatrice, but he understands that he still has to write much more profusely about this wonderful new insight. In that sense this work is a failure, but a magnificent failure which became the fertile seed of his greatest book of praise — the *Comedy*. He buried the precious seed — the memory of his dead Beatrice — knowing that it would bear abundant, life-giving fruit in the harvest of his masterpiece.

In contrast with Musa's stress on the recantation theme (not the only message of the work, as he clearly states) we read how forcefully Singleton argues that the *Vita Nuova* is not a book of recantation: "The work ends facing God as no other beginning in troubadour love had ever done or would ever do --without recantation. The unique achievement of the *Vita Nuova* as a theory of love is the seeing how love of woman may be kept all the way up to God."[5] The work then would not be a cry of guilt — a *mea culpa* — over his love for Beatrice. It is rather an account of his spiritual progress from *amor* to *caritas,* from *eros* to *agape,* i.e., from imperfect, human love to perfect, divine love. Musa too recognizes this twofold nature of love when he analyzes the figure of the god of love who sometimes represents the "lesser aspect" and at other times the "greater aspect" of love.[6]

The *Vita Nuova,* according to Singleton, is a discovery of Beatrice in terms of the Incarnation: a manifestation of God's love for us mediated through the human. In that sense the work is a theological one written in a very personal vein and summing up all the essentials already expressed by biblical, patristic and medieval Christian mystics. John, Paul, Augustine, Bernard and Bonaventure are cited as sources for Dante's meditation; but the originality of the work is Dante's appropriation of the theme of courtly love with its glorification of the beloved lady and his final transformation and transcendence of it — not his repudiation of it or his guilt-ridden recantation.

Dante was well aware of the recantation theme in the courtly love tradition. He knew the many stories of troubadours who repented in their last years of their glorification of adulterous love and turned to the cloister and to God. He refers to this recantation and repentance as "lowering one's sails" and finding repose in the safe port of God's mercy:

> The noble soul surrenders itself to God in this stage (i.e., old age) and awaits the end of this life with great desire. It seems to leave the inn and return to its proper dwelling place; it seems to leave the road and return to the city; to leave the sea and return to the harbor. How wretched and vile are you who with raised sails race to this port and then, where you ought to repose, you suffer shipwreck from the wind and you lose yourselves right at that point to which you have been traveling for so long.
>
> Certainly Lancelot did not wish to enter with raised sails, nor did our most noble Italian Guido of Montefeltro. These nobles did well to lower their sails from worldly pursuits and in their old age they turned to religion and put aside every worldly delight and enterprise.
>
> (*Conv.* IV, XXVIII, 7-9)

We should note that Dante in his *Inferno* cites the romantic story of Lancelot and Guinevere's adulterous affair as the occasion of Francesca and Paolo's adulterous sin and their place in the circle of the carnal sinners. Tristan of the Arthurian romances is there too and "all those knights and ladies of ancient times." (cf. *Inf.* V, 66-72). At the end of Canto V Dante the poet describes Dante the pilgrim in the drama (we should always keep this crucial distinction in mind when reading the *Comedy*) as so moved with pity for these ancient lovers that he swoons and falls like a corpse. Dante is obviously thinking of that earlier stage of his life when he was absorbed in his own self-pity. Canto V then is a judgment and indictment of the courtly love theme with all its obsessions with self-gratification. It seems that in the *Vita Nuova*, written before the *Comedy*, he is already rejecting the troubadours' preoccupation with self, but he does not repudiate love for a woman as something sinful in itself. Rather, he discovered its sublime worth, its transcendent value and its power to reveal God's loving presence within his life.

In this respect both critics, Singleton and Musa, agree, although they apparently contradict one another. Yes, the *Vita Nuova* is a recantation of certain aspects of courtly love, mainly its sinful self-absorption. It does apply, in a most subtle, artful way, the surgeon's knife to that consuming cancer of the soul. But at the same time it preserves the troubadours' glorification of the woman by transcending it — by seeing in the woman a real, earthly manifestation of divine presence within the physical and the human. Dante repeatedly in the *Vita Nuova* perceives Beatrice as a miracle, a wonder, an angel — a Christ-like figure who reveals the divine immanence in the created world. She is the image of God's invisible wisdom and love.

This incarnational theology, so clear to Dante and to medieval mystics, seems to have gotten lost somewhere in later centuries. The rich symbolism and allegory of medieval art and poetry was lost by the sixteenth century when editors of the *Vita Nuova* began to read blasphemy and idolatry into Dante's work and felt the need to change Dante's words. Beatrice could no longer be called Dante's "salvation" or "blessedness," since orthodox faith and theology recognized only Christ as our salvation. Those editors failed to read Dante's very orthodox and profound use of analogy in his evaluation of Beatrice as a figure of Christ.[7] Could those sixteenth-century inquisitors have also been suffering from some latent misogynism derived from the theological bias against any daughter of Eve, the archetypal sinner and temptress?

Our twentieth-century recovery of that biblical, patristic and medieval insight into God's immanence in created reality can be attributed partly to the works of a man who was so similar to Dante in his universal interests — Pierre Teilhard de Chardin, poet, scientist and mystic. In his *Le Milieu Divin* he sings, like the poet Dante in his *Vita Nuova,* of that charity which animates our human love for one another, bringing us by that same movement of communion with others into communion with Christ. Teilhard de Chardin found Christ at the heart of human love, in human flesh, and in the entire material universe. His works are hymns of praise for the God-filled material universe and worship of that God who is present in it all. There is no place for recantation in a truly Christian love for the world and for other human beings. It is interesting to note that his prose poem *L'Eternal Feminin* is dedicated "to Beatrice."

Beatrice as a figure or image of Christ is one of the main themes of the *Vita Nuova.* Singleton maintains, as do many other commentators, that the image of Christ permeates the pages of Dante's "Book of Memory." Christ would be the principle or inner form which controls the outward form of the work. In particular the memory of Christ on the Cross stands at the very center of this work and the image of the Savior shines through all its pages. [8] Let us consider now some of the passages in which Dante describes Beatrice in terms of Christ. The following one, in which Beatrice is compared to Christ and Giovanna, the lady of Dante's friend Guido Cavalcanti, is compared to John the Baptist, reveals the mystical meaning of Beatrice and also gives us an example of how Dante combined prose and poetry in this work:

> I saw coming toward me a gentlewoman, noted for her beauty, who had been the much-loved lady of my best friend. Her name was Giovanna, but because of her beauty (as many believed) she had been given the name of Primavera, meaning Spring, and so she came to be called. And, looking behind her, I saw coming the miraculous Beatrice. These ladies passed close by me, one of them following the

other, and it seemed that Love spoke in my heart and said: "The one in front is called Primavera only because of the way she comes today; for I inspired the giver of her name to call her Primavera, meaning 'she will come first' (*prima verra*) on the day that Beatrice shows herself after the dream of her faithful one. And if you will also consider her real name, you will see that this too means 'she will come first,' since the name Joan (Giovanna) comes from the name of that John (Giovanni) who preceded the True Light, saying: 'I am the voice of one crying in the wilderness: prepare the way of the Lord.'"

After this, Love seemed to speak again and say these words: "Anyone of subtle discernment would call Beatrice 'Love' because she so greatly resembles me." . . . Later I wrote this sonnet:

> I felt a sleeping spirit in my heart
> awake to Love. And then from far away
> I saw the Lord of love approaching me,
> and hardly recognized him through his joy.
> "Think now of nothing but to honor me,"
> I heard him say, and each word was a smile;
> and as my master stayed awhile with me,
> I looked along the way that he had come
> and saw there Lady Joan and Lady Bice
> coming toward the place where I was standing:
> a miracle that led a miracle.
> And, as my memory recalls the scene,
> Love said to me: "The first to come is Spring;
> the one who is my image is called Love."

(*Vita Nuova*, XXIV)

This is a remarkable passage in which the figure of Love (obviously the "greater" or divine aspect of love) proclaims the Christ-like nature of Beatrice. She is compared here to Christ, the Lord and True Light, and she is called the image of Love itself.

Dante in another passage expresses the resemblance between Beatrice and Christ when he describes Beatrice's death in terms of Christ's death. In his poetic version of the event he writes:

> Now captured by my false imaginings
> and somehow in a place unknown to me,
> I was the witness of unnatural things:
> of ladies passing with dishevelled hair,
> some weeping, others wailing their laments
> that pierced the air like arrows tipped in flame.
> And then it seemed to me I saw the sun
> grow slowly darker, and a star appear,
> and sun and star did weep;
> birds flying through the air fell dead to earth;
> the earth began to quake.
> A man appeared, pale, and his voice was weak
> as he said to me: 'You have not heard the news?
> Your lady, once so lovely, now lies dead.'
>
> (*Vita Nuova*, XXIII)

This scene corresponds very closely to the description of Christ's death in Matthew's Gospel: the darkness, the earthquake and other apocalyptic details derived from the Hebrew prophets' descriptions of a universal calamity and grief (cf. Jr 4:28). Dante's emotionally-charged description of his sorrow over Beatrice's death reminds us of the marvelous fresco called *The Lamentation* by his friend Giotto in the famous Arena chapel in Padua. There we see the frenzied grief of the women surrounding the dead body of Christ and the angels in the dark sky expressing the same extravagant pathos. This theme of pathos over the death of Jesus was a familiar one in the art, liturgy and religious poetry of Dante's time. [9] Jacopone da Todi's verses in the *Pianto della Madonna* (Our Lady's Lamentation) and the famous Latin hymn *Stabat Mater* are among the lyrical masterpieces on that theme.

In another passage Dante begins by quoting from the *Book of Lamentations*, a biblical work which Dante and his age attributed to Jeremiah: "How the city sits solitary that was once full of people! How she has become a widow, she that was great among the nations!" He applies this biblical lament over Jerusalem to his own lament over Beatrice's death. He then reflects on the day, month and year of Beatrice's death, showing how the number nine keeps appearing. Beatrice died on the ninth day of the month, in the ninth month of the year and she departed "in that year of our Christian era (1290 in the year of Our Lord) in which the perfect number had been completed nine times in that century in which she had been placed in this world."[10] He then demonstrates how this number nine corresponds to Beatrice herself:

> If anyone thinks more subtly and according to infallible truth, it will be clear that this number was she herself — that is, by analogy. What I mean to say is this: the number three is the root of nine for, without any other number, multiplied by itself, it gives nine: it is quite clear that three times three is nine. Therefore, if three is the sole factor of nine, and the sole factor of miracles is three, that is, Father, Son, and Holy Spirit, who are Three in One, then this lady was accompanied by the number nine so that it might be understood that she was a nine, or a miracle, whose root, namely that of the miracle, is the miraculous Trinity itself. Perhaps someone more subtle than I could find a still more subtle explanation, but this is the one which I see and which pleases me the most.
>
> (*Vita Nuova*, XXIX)

The number nine, besides expressing an analogy with the three divine persons, also corresponded to the death of Jesus in the ninth hour, as the Scriptures state. Dante in other works (cf. *Conv.* IV, XXIV, 6) alludes to Christ's death at that hour. We might note too how variations of the numbers three and nine were so important liturgically in Dante's time. Besides the official hours of prayer — Terce, Sext, and None — we know that Mass was celebrated at the sixth hour to commemorate Christ's crucifixion and at the ninth hour to recall His death at that hour.[11]

But the death of Christ in Christian faith is never isolated from His glorious resurrection and ascension. In the *canzone* cited above, immediately after the scene of grief over Beatrice's death, Dante continues:

> I raised my weeping eyes to look above
> and saw what seemed to be a rain of manna:
> angels who were returning to their home;
> in front of them they had a little cloud
> and sang 'Hosanna' as they rose with it.
> Then I heard Love: 'I shall
> no longer hide the truth from you.
> Come where our lady lies.'
> My wild imaginings led me to see
> my lady lying dead;
> I looked at her, and then ladies
> were drawing a veil over her face.
> She had an air of joyful resignation;
> it was as if she said: 'I am in peace.'
>
> .   .   .
>
> and when I was alone,
> I raised my eyes toward Heaven, and declared:
> 'Blessed is He who sees you, lovely soul!'
> (*Vita Nuova* XXIII)

Singleton notes that this vision of Beatrice's assumption into heaven is similar to the miraculous death of Galahad, who dies before the Grail and is assumed into heaven by angels. [12] Dante may have been influenced by the Grail legend, so popular in his time. Often the Holy Grail was understood in a Eucharistic sense. In the original story by Chretien de Troyes the Grail is called "a holy and spiritual thing, whose Host alone sustains and preserves life." Here in Beatrice's elevation angels sing the same song chanted right before the elevation of the Host at Mass. We might note the allusion to manna and the white color of Beatrice's soul. Later we shall see that Beatrice's glorious arrival in the earthly paradise (cf. *Purg.* XXX) is described in a similar way: she is announced by the same chant of the angels and she is clothed in white. There Beatrice as Christ in the Eucharist is much more clear, but perhaps even here Dante is evoking the elevation of Christ in the Host.

Later in the *Vita Nuova* Dante refers to Beatrice's assumption as the event "when the God of justice called this most glorious one to glory under the banner of that blessed Queen, the Virgin Mary, whose name was always uttered with the greatest reverence by the blessed Beatrice."[13] Dante's lady Beatrice is never far removed from Mary, Our Lady. In fact the resemblance is profound and striking at times. One thinks of the many medieval versions of Mary's Assumption in art and literature: Christ coming with angels and bearing away Mary's soul, depicted as a little child clothed in white. One such representation, perhaps seen by Dante, is a mosaic by Cavallini (ca. 1291) in the church of Santa Maria in Trastevere in Rome. It is very similar to Dante's description of Beatrice's assumption.

The assumption of Beatrice, as well as Mary's and Christ's ascension into heaven, all have this in common: they express God's victory over death and the glorification of His faithful ones. The death and glorification of Beatrice is thus the destiny planned by God's love for all those "who have lived and died in Christ." St. Paul's stirring words come to mind:

> In the same spirit of faith we also speak because we believe. We know that God, Who raised the Lord Jesus to life, will also raise us up with Jesus and take us together with you into His presence. . . .
>
> We know that when this tent we live in — our body here on earth — is torn down, God will have a house in heaven for us to live in, a home He Himself has made, which will last forever. . . .
>
> We are ruled by the love (*agape*) of Christ. . . . No longer then do we judge anyone by human standards. Even if we judged Christ at one time according to human standards, we no longer do so. When anyone is joined to Christ, that person is a new being; the old is gone, the new has come. All this is done by God, Who through Christ changed us from enemies into His friends and gave us the task of making others His friends also. Our message is that God was making all humanity His friends through Christ.
>
> (2 Cor. 4:14; 5:1; 5:14-19)

Paul's faith vision — the same as John's in his gospel and letters — is the Christian vision of death and also of love: two of the main themes in Dante's *Vita Nuova*. It sees another human person as one beloved by God and destined for eternal life after death. A beloved one in this life is loved with this *agape,* which is God's gift to all.

This *agape,* I believe, is the central theme of the *Vita Nuova.* This is the "new life" of the Christian who is now a "new being." This is the great discovery that Dante made in the course of his relationship with Beatrice. He no doubt struggled with the sensuous kind of love (*eros*) and realized its ambiguities and deficiencies. He also recognized the limitations of the courtly concept of spiritual and Platonic love. This inner struggle, I believe, is transferred to the figure of the god of love who in the *Vita Nuova* plays a dual role of *eros* and *agape,* but it is the truly Christian love, *agape,* which ultimately fills the heart of Dante. That is the underlying inspiration of the work: Dante's way of surpassing his fellow *fedeli d'amore.* It is "the victory which is our faith," as St. John expressed it.

Since God is Love, as John states, all those whom we love "in God," "in Christ" or "in His Spirit" — whatever way we express it — are loved with "good" and "perfect" love. Thus the dichotomy and tension between "secular" and "sacred" love is overcome. The troubadours' love for the lady, which stopped at the creature without moving on to the love of the Creator, was therefore radically deficient. In fact it amounted to idolatry. Dante understood this. His faith opened to him another vision: creatures lead us step by step to the knowledge and love of God.

The idea of progress, movement and ascent to God through steps or degrees of knowledge and love was most familiar to Dante, as it would have been to any medieval scholar in search of knowledge about self, the world and God. For the Western tradition this pattern of spiritual progress was well established by St. Augustine; in the Christian East a similar pattern can be found in the writings of Origen, Gregory of Nyssa, Dionysius, to name only a few. Augustine gives a marvelous description of the soul's ascent to God in his *Confessions,* a work well known by Dante.

Augustine describes this ascent as a three-stage process which begins by contemplating the created world outside himself. Then he turns inward and finally soars above himself by the gift of the Spirit, the Love that carries him into the mystical experience of God. This three-stage movement is described by Augustine particularly in the final "books" of his *Confessions*. These books (X-XIII) are among the most stimulating and rewarding writings in all of Western spirituality. The psychological insights into the inner world of a soul's hunger for absolute Beauty, Truth and Goodness are unparalleled, I believe, in all of Christian literature. Augustine's unutterable mystical joy in finding God, Who is Love, is a joy which he has shared with countless fortunate readers over the centuries.

The great writers on mystical experience in the Middle Ages — Hugh and Richard of the St. Victor community, their contemporary St. Bernard of Clairvaux, and later St. Thomas and St. Bonaventure — were all spiritual heirs of St. Augustine. They all express in their writings the same basic process of three stages in the soul's ascent to God. Sometimes there are subdivisions into six stages, but the fundamental pattern remains the same.

Augustine's journey, which begins with the classical Pauline text about contemplating the invisible qualities of God made manifest through the visible creatures of this world (Rom 1:20), proceeds interiorly into the soul's faculties of understanding, memory and will. There the interior light of God's gift — grace, the Spirit — illuminates the soul and carries it beyond itself — upwards — into God Himself, the soul's rest and peace.

Of the many memorable passages from Augustine's analysis of this ascent one of the most quoted is the following:

> We are told of Him alone (i.e., the Holy Spirit) that He is your free gift. It is in Your gift that we find our rest. It is in Him that we enjoy You. The place where we find rest is the appropriate one for us. To it we are raised by love. To it Your Spirit lifts us up, lowly creatures as we are, from the gate of death. It is in goodness of will that we find our peace. A body inclines by its own weight towards the place that is fitting for it. Weight does not always tend towards the lowest place, but to the one that suits it best, for though a stone falls, flame rises. Each thing acts according to its

weight, finding its right level . . . When things are displaced,
they are always on the move until they come to rest where
they are meant to be.

In my case love is the weight by which I act. To
whatever place I go, I am drawn to it by love. By Your gift,
the Holy Spirit, we are set aflame and borne aloft, and the
fire within us carries us upward. Our hearts are set on an
upward journey, as we sing the song of ascents. It is Your
fire, Your good fire, that sets us aflame and carries us
upward. For our journey leads us upward to the peace of the
heavenly Jerusalem; it was a welcome sound when I heard
them saying, 'We will go into the Lord's house.' There, if
our will is good, You will find room for us, so that we shall
wish for nothing else but to remain in Your house forever.

(*Confessions* XIII, 9)

This theme of our final peace and happiness in God concludes
Augustine's *Confessions,* as he summarizes the three-step journey in a
few sentences:

All these works of Yours we see. We see that together they
are very good, because it is You Who see them in us and it
was You Who gave us the Spirit by which we see them and
love You in them.

We see the things which You have made, because they
exist. But they only exist because You see them. Outside
ourselves we see that they exist and in our inner selves we
see that they are good. But when You saw that it was right
that they should be made, in the same act You saw them
made. . . . We hope that we shall find rest when You admit
us to the great holiness of your presence. But You are
Goodness Itself and need no good besides Yourself. You are
forever at rest, because You are Your own repose.

What man can teach another to understand this truth?
We must ask it of You, seek it in You; we must knock at

Your door. Only then shall we receive what we ask and find
what we seek; only then will the door be opened to us.

(*Confessions* XIII, 34-38)

This "Augustinian journey" can also be found in the works of St.
Bonaventure, which were known by Dante. Some even claim that
Dante as a boy heard Bonaventure preach at Santa Croce in Florence.
Bonaventure condensed into an extraordinary little summa of Christian
spirituality, *The Soul's Journey into God*, all the riches of the Scriptures,
Augustine and the medieval theologians. In this wonderful synthesis
Bonaventure integrated psychology, philosophy, theology and biblical
wisdom. In the words of Ewert Cousins, "Bonaventure achieved for
spirituality what Thomas did for theology and Dante for medieval
culture as a whole."[14]

Bonaventure, like Augustine, proceeds along a three-stage
journey which leads into God. Bonaventure summarizes the ascent in
this way:

By praying in this way, we receive light to discern the steps
of the ascent into God. In relation to our position in creation,
the universe itself is a ladder by which we can ascend into
God. Some created things are vestiges, others images;
some are material, others spiritual; some are temporal,
others everlasting; some are outside us, others within us.
In order to contemplate the First Principle, who is most
spiritual, eternal and above us, we must pass through his
vestiges, which are material, temporal and outside us. This
means to be led in the path of God. We must also enter into
our soul, which is God's image, everlasting, spiritual and
within us. This means to enter in the truth of God. We must
go beyond to what is eternal, most spiritual and above us,
by gazing upon the First Principle. This means "to rejoice in
the knowledge of God and in reverent fear of his majesty."
(Ps 85:11)

This threefold division, then, corresponds to the three
days' journey into the wilderness (Ex 3:18) and to the
threefold intensity of light during a single day: The first is

like evening, the second like morning, the third like noon. This division reflects the threefold existence of things: in matter, in the mind and in the Eternal Art, according to which it was said: Let it be made, he made it; and it was made (Gn 1:3). It reflects also the threefold substance in Christ, who is our Ladder: bodily, spiritual and divine.

.   .   .

By all of these we should dispose ourselves to ascend into God so as to love him with our whole mind, our whole heart and our whole soul. In this consists both perfect observance of the Law and Christian wisdom.

(The Soul's Journey into God, I, 2-4)

This summary of the soul's ascent into God may have been the basic model Dante followed in the structure of his three-stage journey described in the *Comedy.* We should note that the first stage, which begins with the creatures of this world, is already a discovery within matter of the "Eternal Art of God," Christ, the primordial sacrament, Who contains all that has existence. Bonaventure often asserts this "sacramental" character of all creatures: "For every creature is by its nature a kind of effigy and likeness of the Eternal Wisdom." He claims that all creatures should lead us "to know, bless and love God in all of them."[15]

This intuition that the created world is a sacrament which reveals God's grandeur, beauty and goodness is a theme that inspired many religious poets throughout the centuries. One thinks of the Hebrew psalmists, of St. Francis of Assisi and so many others whose contemplation of nature issued in rapturous praise of the Creator. Dante's *Vita Nuova* is a book of praise which belongs to that tradition. Closer to our own time we see this theme expressed so vigorously in the sonnets of Gerard Manley Hopkins, a Christian poet whose "inscape" — that mystical illumination and sudden perception of the deeper order and unity which gives meaning to the external forms — grasps the sacramental presence of God in created beauty.

Hopkins in many of his poems expresses this experience of transcendent beauty which flames out "like shining from shook foil." This beauty and grandeur "flashes off" the clouds, the stars, the trees, flowers, fish, the fire of music and especially from human bodies and faces. His sonnet "To What Serves Mortal Beauty?" is a typical expression of it. There he notes how beauty is dangerous: it makes the blood dance. The music of Purcell and the beauty that Pope Gregory saw in the "lovely lads" from England are given as examples. Hopkins observes that this beauty, however, led to a nation's conversion, since Gregory sent missionaries from Rome to England as a result of his insight. Hopkins claims that we should love "world's loveliest — men's selves. Self flashes off frame and face." He exhorts us to meet this beauty, love it as "heaven's sweet gift," but "then leave, let that alone" and wish "God's better beauty, grace."[16]

This same intuition concludes his "As Kingfishers Catch Fire," where he describes "The just man" as always living and moving in the presence of God: he "acts in God's eye what in God's eye he is — Christ — for Christ plays in ten thousand places, lovely in limbs, and lovely in eyes not his to the Father through the features of men's faces."[17]

In both these sonnets the poet is making the Bonaventurian journey into God through the three-stage process: outside of us, within us and above us. Hopkins, like Bonaventure, perceives Christ actively present in this process. Christ, who "plays to the Father through the features of men's faces" reminds us of the description of Divine Wisdom in the Book of Proverbs: "I was with Him forming all things, and was delighted every day, playing before Him at all times, playing in the world; and my delights were to be with the children of men." (Pr 8:30)

That Christ is present in the created world and more personally in His brothers and sisters is the fundamental truth revealed by Jesus Himself and expressed by Paul so often, as in his famous "I live, now not I; but Christ lives in me." Hopkins sees Christ in the bodies and faces and eyes of human beings, who are members of Christ's mystical body. In one of his sermons he comments on this:

> For grace is any action, activity, on God's part by which, in creating or after creating, he carries the creature to or towards the end of its being. . . . It is Christ in his member on the one side, his member in Christ on the other. It is as if

> a man said: That is Christ playing at me and me playing at
> Christ, only that it is no play but truth; that is Christ *being*
> *me* and me being Christ."[18]

This mystical, sacramental view of the world and of human beings
pervades Hopkins' poetry. He resolves the tensions and temptations
(the dangerous attractions which set the blood dancing) to self-
centeredness and creature worship by a loving renunciation of the self
and others, by giving the gift back to its source. In his "The Leaden
Echo and the Golden Echo" he states: "Give beauty back, beauty,
beauty beauty back to God, beauty's self and beauty's giver."

This is the same mystical return to God which Dante experienced
in his relationship to Beatrice.[19] He was ravished by her beauty, which
set his blood dancing, but he came to see in her, as his fellow poets the
fedeli d'amore also saw in their ladies, a revelation of Divine Wisdom.
But Dante went beyond their praise of the creature to the praise of God.
The concluding sonnets of his *Vita Nuova* describe that experience of
his "new life." Later in life, after a certain beclouding, or perhaps even
total loss of that vision, he will rediscover Beatrice and express it more
maturely and more magnificently in the concluding cantos of *Paradise*,
where he will finally give all that beauty back to God.

Let us now consider the conclusion of the *Vita Nuova*. The penulti-
mate sonnet describes his distress over Beatrice's death, but his prose
commentary on it expresses his insight into the new meaning of
Beatrice, who is now in God's presence beholding the face of Christ, the
ultimate goal of Dante's journey. The pilgrimage theme which dominates the *Comedy* is introduced here by Dante, as he painfully perceives
the pettiness and provincialism of his self-pity and overcomes it by the
truly Christian vision of Beatrice, glorified now "in Christ."

In his prose digression on the topic of pilgrimage Dante describes
three kinds of pilgrims who "travel in the service of the Most High":
those who are called "palmers" since they cross the sea to the Holy
Land and bring back palms: "pilgrims" who travel to the tomb of the
Apostle St. James in Galicia; and "romers" who travel to Rome. Then in
his sonnet to the pilgrims passing through Florence he expects them to
sympathize with him:

Ah, pilgrims, moving pensively along,
thinking, perhaps, of things at home you miss,
could the land you come from be so far away
(as anyone might guess from your appearance)
that you show no signs of grief as you pass through
the middle of the desolated city,
like people who seem not to understand
the grievous weight of woe it has to bear?

If you would stop to listen to me speak,
I know, from what my sighing heart tells me,
you would be weeping when you leave this place:
lost is the city's source of blessedness,
and I know words that could be said of her
with power to humble any man to tears.

(*Vita Nuova* XI)

Mark Musa offers some excellent comments on this sonnet and the prose passage which narrates Dante's initial "reaction of defiance" toward the pilgrims and then his final realization that they are engaged in a serious, religious journey which later would become his own pilgrimage as the Christian "Everyman" through Hell, Purgatory and Paradise in the *Comedy.*

Musa remarks: "The protaganist's (i.e., Dante's) first feeling of pique would seem to have given way to the solemn realization that the pilgrims' spiritual goal is more important than his grief or that of the people of Florence; his provincialism which was like the social reflection of his self-centeredness would have given way to a recognition of new vistas."[20] The new vistas which Dante will discover will be described in his visions of Christ in Paradise, the eternal Rome, the goal of his pilgrimage. The earthly pilgrimage to see the imprint of Christ's face on the veil of Veronica in Rome would become for Dante a "figure" of his spiritual journey to the beatific vision in Paradise.

Dante in his final sonnet describes the miraculous nature of Beatrice and his own nature as a "pilgrim spirit" to whom Love has given a "new intelligence," enabling him to "make the journey upward spiritually":

> Beyond the sphere that makes the widest round,
> passes the sigh arisen from my heart,
> a new intelligence that Love in tears
> endowed it with is urging it on high.
> Once arrived at the place of its desiring
> it sees a lady held in reverence,
> splendid in light; and through her radiance
> the pilgrim spirit looks upon her being.
>   (*Vita Nuova* XLI)

In his final words of prose commentary Dante announces that his praise of Beatrice is inadequate, that she is a mystery which leads into the mystery of God:

> After I wrote this sonnet there came to me a miracu-
> lous vision in which I saw things that made me resolve to say
> no more about this blessed one until I would be capable of
> writing about her in a nobler way. . . . Accordingly, if it be
> the pleasure of Him through whom all things live that my life
> continue for a few more years, I hope to write of her that
> which has never been written of any other woman. And
> then may it please the One who is the Lord of graciousness
> that my soul ascend to behold the glory of its lady, that is, of
> that blessed Beatrice, who in glory contemplates the
> countenance of the One "who is through all ages Blessed."
>   (*Vita Nuova* XLII)

Dante realizes that this flash of inspiration will require years of reflection until he will be able to write about it "in a more noble way." And so the *Vita Nuova* ends unfinished — though with the beauty, one might say, of Schubert's "Unfinished Symphony." But the majestic symphony of his *Paradiso* will be more like the finale of Beethoven's "Ninth" or the final hymn of Handel's "Messiah."

Reading these selections from the *Vita Nuova* has introduced us to Dante, the young man and poet; it has also introduced us to the remote world of medieval culture: the world of the troubadour love poets — the *fedeli d'amore* — to whom Dante was so indebted but whom he transcended as a *Christian* poet. That is not to say that his fellow poets were not Christian, but Dante in his art went beyond them by discovering in his youthful experience of love for a woman a dimension which can only be described as the Christo-centric mystery: the sacramental or incarnational presence of the divine within the human. Singleton in the final chapter of his essay on the *Vita Nuova,* called *Beatrice Dolce Memoria,* shows how Dante's memory of Beatrice is similar to "the sweet memory of Jesus," celebrated in the famous medieval hymn, *Jesu Dulcis Memoria,* in which Christ is the central person in the memory of every Christian. For Dante Christ and Beatrice were discovered as united in one memory.

True, this discovery came after the death of Beatrice and was somewhat short-lived, as some of his subsequent works reveal, but yet it was a flash of light or perhaps a "spark which produced a great flame," to use Dante's phrase. The great flame was his masterpiece, the *Comedy,* which perhaps should be read first, as T.S. Eliot suggests. [21] But Eliot also recommends that we read the *Vita Nuova* for the light it can throw on the *Comedy,* since it can help us more than any of Dante's other works toward a fuller understanding of the *Comedy.* Thus they are really complementary works which shed light on one another.

Although the *Vita Nuova* is often relegated to the category of "quaint" and dreamy love poems — in the manner of the Pre-Raphaelites — it is much more. In many ways it defies specific classification from a literary point of view; but it belongs more, as many critics claim, to the tradition of Christian mysticism. Dante's personal experience of love for a particular woman raised for himself the question of the meaning of Beatrice and of love itself, which thereby led him to a deeper consciousness — what we might call the Christ-consciousness. This deeper experience should not be relegated to the isolated experience of a medieval poet such as Dante. It can and should be, I believe, the lived experience of every Christian, especially today when human love is so trivialized and the sacred character of the human person is so ignored and debased by materialistic philosophies and shallow psychologies.

Dante came to understand in his late twenties that his initial attraction toward the physical beauty of a nine-year old girl was actually a fundamental attraction toward the Final Cause of all beauty and love. He discovered that physical attraction and human love can only be explained and made meaningful by some higher love. And Dante, as his *Comedy* certainly demonstrates, arrived at that highest love.

Dante's reflections on this process of sublimation, to use a modern term, invites and compels us to look into the meaning of our loves — a reflection which may be difficult and even painful, like any re-birth, but yet necessary and rewarding. If we make that conscious attempt, following Dante's lead, we too may recover that sense of wonder before the "miracle" of the beloved person and the much greater wonder before the transcendent beauty of God's love for us. Dante's world and spiritual experience will then not be so strange and foreign to us. It might even uncover how empty and superficial our twentieth-century culture really is and provide a cornucopia of spiritual nourishment to fill that void.

Dante's intuition into the meaning of Beatrice and of love itself will remain throughout the rest of his life the source of his inspiration as a poet. She and love together (we recall how Dante identified her as the image of love) will be his Muse, the fount and life-giving spring of his poetic art. For some years after the *Vita Nuova* — years of emotional and moral crises, of disappointments and fiascoes in political life, of the most dreadful personal disasters such as the loss of family, reputation, property and his native city — the vision of Beatrice will fade and even disappear at times. But fortunately (we should say, through the mysterious action of divine grace) the vision will be retrieved and will give birth to a truly "beatific" vision.

This mysterious action of divine grace was discovered by Dante toward the end of his life as the hidden source of his inspiration as a poet. But before that discovery, at various stages in his life he theorized on poetic art and inspiration, even though he never dedicated an entire work to these subjects. We do have in his *De Vulgari Eloquentia* (abbreviated henceforth to DVE) some reflections on the art of poem-making, although that work has as its main purpose the defense of the Italian language. It was written in Latin for fellow scholars and proved to be an epoch-making work. It "broke ground" with the established literary tradition which held that serious and noble themes must be expressed in Latin and in accordance with fixed rules and models from the classical art of rhetoric.

Dante's primary purpose in this work is to defend and justify the use of the modern Italian language — the vernacular — as a worthy medium for high poetry and prose: a truly courageous and adventurous enterprise at that time in history. But Dante was adventurous — he made breakthroughs by discovering and exploring new worlds and new futures. In this audacious work Dante's encyclopedic mind probes into the origins of language itself, beginning from Adam in the Biblical accounts and ending with an analysis of the evolution of the Romance languages in southern Europe. His philosophical analysis of human language, which employed empirical methods learned from Aristotle, is very interesting and in many ways very modern; but what concerns us here is his theory of poetry.

Dante found in the classical Latin tradition (Aristotle's *Poetics* was unknown to him) a work which discussed the art of poetry. It was Horace's *Ars Poetica,* a work which Dante highly valued at this stage of his life (circa 1305, shortly before the beginning of the *Comedy*). In his DVE Dante refers to Horace as "our master" and later in his *Comedy* mentions Horace together with Homer, Ovid and Lucan as "the beautiful school" of poets under the leadership of the "highest poet," Virgil (cf. *Inf.* IV, 89). Although Dante shows little evidence of having been influenced by Horace's poetry, he does seem to subscribe to Horace's theory of poetry, even though he finds it inadequate.

Horace's poetic theory was derived from an ancient philosophical tradition, namely the Stoic concept of the orator and poet as the wise man and man of virtue. According to Horace, knowledge and wisdom are equivalent to moral philosophy. Horace defines the great poet as one who possesses not only a natural talent (*ingenium*), but also the technical skill (*ars*) of expressing it. The poet should use both these gifts for a higher purpose: to teach and celebrate the highest ideals: *salus* (military heroism), *venus* (love) and the *honestum* (moral virtue).

Dante found these three ideals admirably expressed in the poetry of Virgil, considered by Dante the greatest of all poets. Dante quoted the sixth book of the *Aeneid* where Virgil described true poets as those "beloved of God and sons of the gods, raised by glowing virtue to the sky." Dante by quoting Virgil thus held that natural genius and technical skill were not enough for the true poet: he must "first drink of Helicon," i.e., the fount of inspiration supplied by Apollo and the Muses. Only with the aid of such inspiration can the poet "imitate the eagle and soar to the stars."[22]

Poetic inspiration then was necessary for the singing of the three great themes of poetry which Horace and Virgil celebrated in their works. In his DVE Dante paraphrased those three ideals as *probitas armorum* (bravery in war), *amoris accensio* (the joy or flame of love) and *directio voluntatis* (rectitude of the will). These three themes corresponded to the Stoics' "ends" or purposes of human existence: "the useful," "the delectable" and "the virtuous."

Horace, as a typical Stoic moralist, claimed that a poet should not only delight the reader but should elevate his moral sensibilities by blending poetic sweetness with useful, profitable teaching. He was a spokesman for a theory of moralistic art which endured for centuries even into Dante's time and far beyond. Dante subscribed to this classical tradition of moralistic, didactic poetry and never completely abandoned it, although he departed from it in some remarkably original ways. We should perhaps say that he perfected it.

In his famous letter to Can Grande della Scala, which explains his purposes for writing the *Comedy,* he specifically mentions that "the branch of philosophy which regulates the work in its whole and in its parts is morals or ethics, because the whole was undertaken not for speculation but for practical results." He also states there that his primary goal is "to remove those living in this life from the state of misery and lead them to the state of happiness." Thus Dante was eminently "practical," even as a poet.

Dante followed the classical tradition described by Horace not only in his moralistic aims, but also in his choice of subjects. He wrote poetry about love, virtue and at times even about warlike bravery, although that theme is never a major one in his works. However, Dante departed from the classical tradition by writing "high poetry" in the vernacular language, as his much-admired French predecessors and his Italian masters such as Guido Guinicelli and Guido Cavalcanti had done. He also took the daring step of writing about real, historical persons rather than only about legendary and mythical characters, as the classical tradition dictated. In this respect he was really a pioneer of modern literature. He even wrote about persons living in his own time.

Another bold, and perhaps his most adventurous enterprise, was his writing "theological" poetry. Today we would probably call this "doing theology by poetry." We might even say that Dante perceived poetry as his particular "charism" in the Church, to use Pauline terms. In Dante's age poetry was generally held in very low esteem, as his masters in theology, Augustine and Thomas, evaluated it. [23] Dante by writing theological poetry was thus inviting ridicule and scorn.

But perhaps this is the unique achievement of Dante: to celebrate the beauty of truth. St. Thomas Aquinas had defined beauty as the "Splendor of truth." Dante's poetry revealed that splendor. He took truth (whether philosophical or theological) and transformed it as a poet into beauty; or, expressed differently, he discovered in the truth the "raw material" for creating the beauty of poetry. Dante was unique in so far as his intellectual thirst for truth coincided with his passionate sensibility and love for beauty. [24] One thinks of John Keats' famous verse: "Beauty is truth, truth beauty — that is all ye know on earth, and all ye need to know."

Many scholars have identified this coincidence as Dante's particular genius. In the words of Weatherby: "It is perhaps Dante's greatest accomplishment that he is able to represent the full ramifications of Catholic theology in his cosmological symbols." He further comments that "Dante's task as a poet is to translate these concepts (i.e., the language of pure theology) into images without diminishing their notional force. Somehow he must make us see in symbols what in fact can only be understood or known." [25]

This task of the poet — his unique genius — has been described in many ways. Dante called it his "high fantasy" in the closing verses of *Paradiso,* a phrase best translated today as "imagination," in the sense of creative imagination. Poets throughout history have referred in one way or another to this indescribable soul of poetry, most often identified simply as inspiration or creativity. We should perhaps recall the etymology of the word poet: it is derived from the Greek *poetes,* a maker, based on the verb *poiein,* to make or create. Dante in his DVE defines poetry as "a *fictio* (the Latin for making or creating) of verses which are *poita* (the Greek for the same concept), according to rhetorical and musical art." We might also recall here that St. Paul described Christians as a new creation: "a poem (*poiema*) of God" (cf. Ep 2:10). Poetry then is a highly creative activity, similar to God's creative art. Often Dante refers to nature as God's art or as God's daughter, and to human art as the "granddaughter" of God. (cf. *Inf.* XI, 100-105)

Jacques Maritain in his masterly work, *Creative Intuition in Art and Poetry,* defines poetry as "the free creativity of the spirit and the intuitive knowledge through emotion, which transcend and permeate all arts, inasmuch as they tend toward beauty as an end beyond the end."[26] Maritain's admiration for Dante's poetic genius occupies a large portion of this work. He attempts a description of Dante's "genius" in these words: "Complex as the obscure reality meant by this word may be, genius has essentially to do with the fact of poetic intuition taking shape in the inaccessible recesses of the soul at an exceptional degree of depth. When it comes to designating the particular quality which characterizes those creative regions, we are at a loss to find an appropriate name. The least defective term I am able to suggest is creative innocence. This creative innocence, which is one with unimpeded power and freedom of poetic intuition, is, I think, the most profound aspect of Dante's genius."[27]

Maritain continues to describe two meanings of innocence. One would be the child-like naivete whose simplicity and confidence, like the charity described by St. Paul, "believes all things." The other would be integrity, an untouched original purity, which is "an amazement without end before the face of love unveiling its miraculous and terrible ambiguity . . . and a pure abiding feeling of spiritual fidelity, an unbroken process of deeper knowing and purifying love. Shelley states that Dante 'understood the secret things of love' more than any other poet . . . While Dante's love for God his Savior, for 'Him Who is the lord of courtesy,' transfigures the woman he once desired, his love for this transfigured woman is the medium through which divine love penetrates the creative center of his poetry. The entire *Commedia* was written to bear testimony to the purification of love in the heart of a man."[28]

Love as the creative source of Dante's poetic inspiration has caught the attention of many Dante scholars. Francis Fergusson in his excellent introduction to Dante has singled out a brief, but most important, passage in Dante's works which seems to summarize this underlying source of all Dante's writings. It even appears to be the motivating energy throughout all the stages of his life:

> I am one who, when
> Love inspires me, takes careful note,
> and then gives meaning to what
> He dictates within my heart.
> (*Purg.* XXIV, 52-54)

This one tercet, Fergusson believes, is the final definition of Dante's poem-making.[29] It applies to his romantic youth, his rationalistic phase, and to his final change of heart and spiritual maturity, expressed in the *Comedy*. In all three major phases of Dante's life, love, defined by Dante as a "movement of the spirit," is the underlying wellspring of his poetic inspiration. Dante's formulation of "Love dictates within my heart" probably came from a mystical treatise on love, attributed to Richard of St. Victor, which stated that "Only he can speak worthily of love who puts together exteriorly the words that the heart dictates interiorly."[30]

Even during the middle period of his life, when his intellectual pursuit of Lady Philosophy consumed him, love was still the driving power and hidden source of his energy. But it is only in his final stage, when he was writing the *Comedy,* that love will acquire its fullest meaning as God's love, which is the life and movement drawing all creatures back to Himself.

The human creature Beatrice, encountered in childhood and youth and remembered thereafter, would become for Dante his way back to the wonder and innocence of his experience of "new life." Often commentators on the meaning of Beatrice refer to how Dante has transformed her into a symbol of divine grace, revelation, wisdom, theology, faith, the Church — or even his alleged lost vocation as a cleric — but we should always keep in mind that for Dante Alighieri the woman Beatrice Portinari was always a real individual of both physical and spiritual beauty. She was once a young Florentine whose dignity as a baptized Christian already gave her a spiritual beauty that surpassed imagination. After her premature death she was still a living woman, but one transfigured into glory.

This metamorphosis was not an invention of Dante: it was a basic tenet of Christian faith in the destiny of a baptized Christian who "has lived and died in Christ." It was the fundamental insight given by Christ, received by John and Paul and the others who wrote the New Testament, and handed on through Christian tradition. It was expressed in the creeds of the Church, especially in the words, "The Communion of Saints."

One of the greatest medieval scholars of our century, Etienne Gilson, has given an eloquent expression to it in these words:

> In order to understand Dante's attitude towards Beatrice, as, for that matter, that of Beatrice towards Dante, one need only remember that not all the saints are in the calendar. Like so many other Christians, Dante thinks that, if he has a personal chance of salvation, it consists not in the intercession of the great saints, men and women of the whole Church, but in that of his own saint. Now let us not forget that Dante *knows* that Beatrice will live henceforth as a saint among the saints. Why, then, should she not be to him what to so many Christians those beloved beings are, to whom they *know* that they can pray, and to whom they do pray? As a means to the discovery of Love, how should they not first think of those whom they love still, and by whom they are loved? In this man's past, the mother whom he lost when so young — at about the age of six — is too indistinct a figure for him to think of turning to her. For him there is really no woman elect of God to whose personal intercession his love entitles him but this *Beatrice beata* whom, with that instinct which makes so many Christians pray to their mothers, Dante has made his mediator. If he undertakes a journey to the lands beyond the grave, what blessed soul does Dante hope to meet first to receive him on the threshold of heaven and lead him in? None but Beatrice. And she is, in fact, there. [31]

Beatrice, Dante's own patron saint, will be the one to save him eventually from his near despair and damnation. Dante had become like a drowning man who is saved by clutching the hand of salvation: Beatrice. He will be lost in a dark forest of sin and terror, and she will send him help. His *Comedy* will be the story of his salvation through her; it will be his penitential psalm of remorse for having betrayed his saintly Muse and for having offended the God of Love, Whose instrument she was.

The story of Dante's salvation calls to mind the wonderful words of the Church's Easter Proclamation, the *Exsultet: O felix culpa!* (O happy fault!). Dante's guilt and remorse became a source of inspiration for the *Comedy,* his new song in which he proclaims the sheer happiness and grace of conversion and salvation. But before considering the wonderful beauty of this grace, we should first explore the depths of darkness and decay into which he had sunk. This we shall do in the following chapter, which will attempt to describe Dante's periods of emotional, moral and intellectual crises as well as the turmoil and catastrophes which affected Florence, the Church and medieval society.

Chapter Three

IL TROVATORE TRAVIATO

The years between 1295 (the probable date for the completion of the *Vita Nuova*) and 1307 (the probable year for the beginning of the *Commedia*) were years of multiple crises in Dante's life. The death of Beatrice in 1290 had been a major crisis; the *Vita Nuova* described his grief and sense of loss as well as his faith-interpretation of her death. But, as happens with many believers, the faith vision of reality often fades into the background, crowded out by many preoccupations and obsessions. Like the seed in Jesus' parable, it can take root for a time but be choked and overpowered by other cares and interests. Later in his *Paradiso* Dante will reflect on such cares and worldly pursuits and warn all humanity about the snares of all these vanities from which he had been finally delivered. As he enters the realm of the truly wise in the heaven of the sun, he addresses Everyman and includes himself as one who was once trapped in those earthly entanglements:

> O senseless strivings of you mortals,
> how useless are those reasonings of yours
> that make you beat your wings in downward flight!
> Men bent on law, some on medicine,
> some on the priesthood, others in pursuit
> of governing by means of force or fraud,
> some planning theft, others affairs of state,
> some tangled in the pleasures of the flesh,
> some merely given up to indolence,

> and I, relieved of all such vanities,
> was there with Beatrice in high Heaven,
> magnificently, gloriously welcomed.
>   (*Par.* XI, 1-12)

Dante in this passage, while not disparaging the professions *per se,* looks upon the exclusive pursuit of earthly goals as so many vanities in comparison with the one transcendent goal of divine wisdom. Dante refers specifically to the "affairs of state" and "pleasures of the flesh" as some of the vanities which impede the hearts of mortals, and it seems that these very vanities were among the earthly cares which preoccupied him, at least during a certain period of his life.

That period of his life is often summed up by Italian critics in one word: *traviamento,* which means deviation, perversion or corruption. It comes from the verb *traviarsi,* meaning to go astray, to lose one's way by straying from the right path. The verb is the basis of *la traviata,* the "fallen woman," a term familiar to us through Verdi's opera of that name, whose tragic heroine, Violetta, was caught up in carnal and other transitory pleasures. Dante in the opening words of his *Comedy* describes himself as a man who has strayed from the right path (*la diritta via*) and found himself lost in a dark forest. He then was a *traviato.*

But he was also a *trovatore,* the Italian translation of the French *troubadour,* a word which literally means "one who finds" in both languages. We might recall another famous opera by Verdi, *Il Trovatore.* These two Italian words — *traviato* and *trovatore* — both titles of operas by Verdi, have suggested the title of this chapter. I beg the indulgence of both Verdi and Dante for this juxtaposition and this play on words used to describe Dante, the troubadour (the "finder") who becomes lost.

The starting point of the *Comedy* recreates Dante's own psychological and moral condition — the result of more than ten years of various personal crises. The complexity of these many crises and Dante's own complex personality make it impossible to simplify into neat categories the many aspects of Dante's life in those critical years. Aware of the pitfalls of classifying and analyzing a person's life, we might reduce the areas of Dante's *traviamento* to three: moral, intellectual and social-political. It seems best not to speak of a "religious" crisis in the sense of a complete loss of faith. Dante was never an apostate, heretic or agnostic in the accepted meanings of those words today, although he seemed to have lost for a time the intensity and fervor of faith: that evangelical "single mindedness" or purity of heart, the loss of which could be described as a religious crisis. However, I would prefer to call this a "spiritual" crisis, which affected all aspects of his life: the moral, emotional, intellectual and professional.

Much has been written about the exact nature of Dante's *traviamento*. The critics' assessments of Dante's detour from the true path have varied over the centuries: some stressing his moral degradation, in the sense of carnal sins; others citing his absorption in intellectual pursuits or in political affairs. There seems to be some truth in all these interpretations of Dante's aberrations.

As to his propensity toward "sins of the flesh," we have the testimony of the early biographers that Dante, like most young men, was attracted to physical beauty and engaged in amorous adventures. Boccaccio, a Florentine writer born during Dante's lifetime, knew many of Dante's contemporaries and wrote a "biography" which is generally regarded by Dante scholars as trustworthy and factual, although the accuracy of all the details is sometimes disputed. In his life (or, more exactly, his eulogy) of Dante, Boccaccio praises the many virtues of his fellow Florentine man of letters, but he also comments on some of Dante's vices. His words about Dante's carnal lust are worthy of our consideration and they also reveal Boccaccio's humor and perhaps even a sense of guilt for a vice that he calls "in a certain sense necessary." The following passage follows some extravagant praises:

> Amid so great virtue, amid so much learning, as we have seen was the portion of this wondrous poet, licentiousness found a large place; and this not only in his youth, but also in his maturity. Although this vice is natural, common, and in a certain sense necessary, it not only cannot be commended, but cannot even be decently excused. But what mortal shall be the just judge to condemn it? Not I. O little strength! O bestial appetite of men! What influence cannot women have over us if they will, since without caring they have so much? They possess charm, beauty, natural desire and many

other qualities that continually work in their behalf in the
hearts of men. . . .

And did not Solomon, to whose wisdom none ever
attained save the Son of God, forsake Him who had made
him wise, and kneel to adore Balaam in order to please a
woman? . . . Among so many and so great ones, then, our
poet may pass on, not excused, but accused with a brow
much less drawn than if he were alone. [1]

Boccaccio in other passages of his biography had exposed some of
Dante's other faults, namely his rage and bitterness, but hastened to
beg Dante's pardon, thinking that Dante might be looking down on him
"with scornful eye from some high region of heaven." Boccaccio thus
expresses the opinion of his contemporaries that Dante indeed had
been a sinner but that he was saved and among the blessed. The earliest
portraits of Dante, namely the famous one by his friend Giotto and
another one by Nardo di Cione, show him in a placid, contemplative
pose among the blessed of Paradise. It's amusing to note that for
Boccaccio the "blessed" Dante is still scornful in heaven.

It must be stated clearly, however, that we have no direct information about Dante's love affairs. Boccaccio had described Dante's love
for Beatrice as chaste and noble, in no way indecent or immoral.
Another early biographer, Lionardo Bruni, who wrote later in the
fourteenth century, sought to supplement and improve on Boccaccio's
biography, which he considered a bit frivolous and superficial. He tends
to mitigate Boccaccio's stress on Dante's amorous appetites by writing:
"In his youth Dante associated with young lovers and he too was filled
with a like passion, not through evil desire, but out of the gentleness of
his heart." In describing Dante's marriage to Gemma Donati, which
took place after Beatrice's death, he refers to marital love as "natural,
lawful and allowable," and implies that Dante's marriage was based on
that kind of love. He does not allude to any marital unhappiness, as
Boccaccio repeatedly does in his biography, but instead compares
Dante to Socrates, "the noblest philosopher that every lived," who also
had a wife and children and held public offices in his day. [2]

But what about Dante's many love poems, written before, during
and after these critical years, which have such strongly erotic

overtones? Some critics interpret the erotic images as metaphors for Dante's love of philosophy, as Dante often leads the reader to believe in his prose commentaries on some of them. Other critics, Francis Fergusson among them, claim that "good metaphor emerges from experience."[3] He cites as an example Dante's *Canzone* VI, which seems to express very violent passion:

> If I had grasped the beautiful tresses
> That have been my lash and whip,
> Seizing them before tierce
> I should have spent with them vesper and evening bells:
>
> And I should be neither pitying nor courteous,
> But like a bear when he plays.
> And if love thereby scourges me,
> I should take more than a thousand vengeances.
>
> Still into those eyes whence issue the sparks
> That set on fire the heart I carry slain
> Should I look, close and fixed,
> To avenge the flight he made me take:
> Then should I give her with love peace.[4]

A Freudian analyst might detect some latent (or even blatant) sadomasochism in that poem with its allusions to whips, lashes, scourges and rough play; but there are also references to the more gentle aspects of love, expressed through the eyes and heart, and leading to peace. Perhaps Dante is expressing here two aspects of human love: animal passion and gentle, spiritual affection. No doubt Dante throughout his life experienced that conflict and struggle which often accompanies human love: that strange mixture of two kinds of love: "concupiscence" and "benevolence," as the medieval Scholastics described it.

One of the most revealing admissions of this conflict can be found in a letter Dante wrote about 1306 to one of the feudal nobles who befriended him during his exile, Lord Moruello, Marquis Malaspina. In this letter he excuses himself from any neglect of duty because he has been held captive by love, who, "raging like a despot expelled from his fatherland, returns to his native soil after long exile, slew, expelled and enchained all opposition in me. He slew the praiseworthy determination which gave me the strength to hold myself aloof from women, those instruments of his enchantment; and the unbroken meditations wherein I was pondering on things both of heaven and of earth, he relentlessly banished as things suspected; and finally, that my soul might never again rebel against him, he chained my free will; so that I must turn not whither I would, but whither he wills. Love, therefore, reigns within me, with no restraining influence."[5]

Those words are followed by a *canzone,* the famous "Mountain Ode," which describes with the cold images of a stormy mountainous region the servile passion within him for a pitiless lady who is beautiful but cruel. Dante describes himself as powerless and dead, like "snow that seeks the sun." These and similar images depict the poet's subjection to passion and his losing battle against the slavery which the beauty of a woman imposes on him.

There is also a series of odes, called the *Pietra* group, which are addressed to a woman whose cold, unyielding aloofness is compared to a stone (*pietra* is the Italian word for stone or rock). Dante, the frustrated, passionate lover, transformed this experience into the cold, quiet music of poetry in these beautiful odes. The scholars debate whether Pietra was a real woman, but the powerfully passionate tone of these poems suggests a lived experience.

The many odes, ballads and sonnets in which Dante expresses his passionate sighs and frustrated love focus on many women, whose names are sometimes mentioned specifically: there is a Violetta, a Lisetta, a Fioretta — perhaps all from the list of sixty "screen ladies" of Florence, mentioned earlier. Then there are the ladies with more metaphorical names: the "gentle" lady, the "strong" lady, the "mountainous" lady, or simply *La Pargoletta,* the little girl. Critics continue to discuss whether these were real women, but the evidence that Dante left us in his writings seems rather persuasive that he is describing real persons and lived experiences. Without passing judgment on Dante's sexual mores, we should not expect Dante to be more than human, with everything that the word "human" implies. Besides, it is only in the final stage of his earthly journey that he describes the "transhumanizing" experience of his ultimate ascent to Paradise. For most of his life, the "great power" of erotic love seems to have disturbed him and held him captive at times — many times in fact.

His best friend, Guido Cavalcanti, seems to be addressing Dante's disordered passions in this sad sonnet which he wrote to him:

> I come to you many times a day
> and find that you are thinking too vilely;
> then do I mourn for that noble spirit of yours,
> and for the great virtues that are taken from you.
> The great crowd used to displease you,
> you used to avoid the vulgar people:
> you spoke of me, indeed, most cordially,
> who had accepted all your poems.
> Now because of your vile life I do not dare
> to show that what you say could please me,
> nor do I come to see you face to face.
> If you read this sonnet many times,
> the vulgar spirit that is pursuing you
> will depart from your degraded soul. [6]

This is strong language from a close friend. It was most likely written after Dante had composed his *Vita Nuova;* and even though we do not know the exact circumstances of it or the exact meaning of "vile life," it nonetheless suggests that Dante was entangled in some kind of degrading lifestyle which brought on this serious rebuke.

This "vulgar spirit" and "degraded soul," reprimanded by Guido could possibly refer to the phase of Dante's life reflected in his famous (or perhaps infamous) sonnets to his friend and distant cousin, Forese Donati. They are part of a *tenzone,* a literary combat or duel, which could be dated between 1293 and 1296. The discovery of this *tenzone* caused a stir among the critics in the last century: some pious admirers of Dante were unwilling to attribute such crude sentiments and language to Dante, but today the *tenzone* is generally considered authentic. In these sonnets Dante attacks Forese as a glutton, a negligent (or impotent) husband, a thief, a bastard, and as a nocturnal street prowler.

He alludes to Forese's wife, Nella, who suffers from constant chills even "in the middle of August" because she is left alone in a cold, empty bed. Forese responded by references to the sins of Dante's father: possibly usury or heresy. He accuses Dante of, among other things, being a beggar because of his unpaid debts. Just how much veracity there is in these mutual accusations is a matter of dispute, but we know how some truth often lurks beneath friendly banter. Nonetheless, the tone and topics of these sonnets are a jolt to those who know Dante mainly through his serious works. From the *tenzone* one gets the impression that Dante was immersed in an "eat, drink and be merry" way of life, since the "barroom brawl" tone of these poems suggests that Dante, together with Forese, was engaged in certain nocturnal activities which usually remain unmentioned in more genteel circles.

Dante later meets Forese in Purgatory on the terrace where the souls cleanse themselves of the sin of gluttony. According to Umberto Cosmo, it is "the most explicitly autobiographical episode" of the entire *Comedy*. Dante up until this point had always observed the canons of "high poetry," which banned the poet from making direct, concrete references to his personal life, family and friends. In fact he never mentions his parents, wife or children anywhere in his works, but here he abandons his own poetic theory and speaks very explicitly of his intimate friendship with Forese and recalls details of a specific period of their youth together in Florence.

The dialogue between Dante and Forese is one of the most tender and moving exchanges in the whole *Comedy*. It exudes the most exquisite and delicate sentiments of friendship, of nostalgia, and of mutual forgiveness. The meeting of the two friends who review their past with transformed and purified emotions is a testimony to the healing power of divine grace. Both men have tasted the grace of repentance and are on their way, drawn by a joyful gravity toward God.

Dante at first does not recognize Forese because of his shriveled, emaciated appearance; but then he identifies him by his voice and cries: "What grace has been bestowed on me!" Dante, whose memory is rekindled by the spark of Forese's voice, addresses him in these touching words:

> "When death was on your face, I wept," I said,
> "and now the grief I feel is just as great,
> seeing your face so piteously disfigured.
> In God's name tell what strips you so bare.
> Do not ask me to speak, I am benumbed!
> And one speaks ill whose thoughts are somewhere else."
> (*Purg.* XXIII, 55-60)

Forese responds by explaining how his present pain is actually a divine grace which makes him and the other souls "sing while we lament." He even calls the pain a "solace" by which they are led, as Christ was, to cry *Eli* (i.e., "My God"), when He sacrificed himself on the cross. Dante responds:

> Forese, since that day when you
> abandoned our world for a better life,
> less than five years from your last day have passed!
> If, when you knew that moment of sweet grief
> that weds the soul to God again, you were
> close to your death, able to sin no more —
> how have you climbed so high up on the mount?
> I thought, surely, to find you down below
> where souls who wasted time must pay with time.
> (*Purg.* XXIII, 76-84)

Forese then responds that it was his sweet widow, Nella, whom he greatly loved, who by her tears and prayers shortened his stay on Purgatory. He then contrasts Nella, so "dear and pleasing to the Lord" and "unique in doing good" with the other Florentine women, who are "bold-faced and now walking our city streets as they parade their bosom to the tits!" As one contemporary commentator recently wrote, "The topless made its world premiere in thirteenth-century Florence!"[7]

Forese's moralistic reflections on the degradation of the Florentines and their need to reform are then abandoned as he asks Dante, his "brother," to tell him about himself. Dante answers with these revealing, and at the same time enigmatic, words:

Whenever you recall
what we were like together, you and I,
the memory of those days must torture you.
From that life I was called away by him
who leads me here — just a few days ago,
when his sister (I pointed to the sun)
was shining full. Still wearing this true flesh
I came into and through the darkest night
of the true dead with this soul as my guide;
from there, sustained by him, I came up here
climbing and every circling round this mount
which straightens in you what the world has bent.
He says that I shall have his company
until I am where Beatrice is —
and from then on, without him I must go.
(*Purg.* XXIII, 11 5-129)

"That life together," from which Dante was rescued by Virgil, who had been commissioned by Beatrice to save him, was certainly much more sinful than the mere writing of some coarse, abusive sonnets. It was a way of life whose memory "tortures" both Dante and Forese. Was it merely overindulgence in food and drink? Was it carousing together in pursuit of women of the night? Some of the earliest commentators, who knew personally the contemporary circumstances and the persons in Dante's life, speak about some serious moral disorders. Benvenuto da Imola, writing about 1375, mentions that Dante lived with Forese *familiariter* for some time. Commenting on this particular passage of *Purgatory,* Benvenuto describes this period of Dante and Forese's life together as spent in "lascivious loves and other vain things." They were pursuing "immoral delights."

Another famous commentator, shortly after Benvenuto, was Giovanni Bertoldi da Serravalle, a Franciscan friar and later bishop. His historical knowledge about Dante and his times is highly valued by Dante scholars. Serravalle's comments on this passage are even more specific than Benvenuto's insofar as he asserts that Dante and Forese "were associates in certain lascivious things which they did together (*insimul*) and to one another (*invicem*)."[8]

There is no reason to believe that the good friar, learned theologian and bishop, was guilty of calumny. He was a respected man of wide culture, who taught theology in Florence for many years in the late fourteenth century. At the request of English bishops at the Council of Constance in 1414 he translated Dante's *Comedy* into Latin. He also wrote a commentary on the entire *Comedy* and promoted Dante's book as one which "should improve the life of any person who studied and understood it."[9] He often lauded Dante's call for spiritual reform as an antidote for the evils that plagued the Church then.

Gilson thinks that Serravale's remarks are true to the meaning intended by Dante in this passage, even though certain "virile commentators and full-blooded he-men" refuse to believe it.[10] Gilson considers this passage to be of capital importance for the correct interpretation of Dante's moral crisis, since it describes that very life of debauchery, that dark forest of "actual sins" from which Dante was rescued by Virgil at Beatrice's bidding. It is the story of his sin, repentance and conversion. In Gilson's words, "The choice between Forese Donati and Beatrice had to be made. Dante chose Beatrice."[11]

Most commentators even today do not take seriously the possibility that Dante for a time participated in a liaison with another man. And yet we know from Dante's own account that the sin of sodomy was rampant among the literati of his day. In the circle of the sodomites in Hell he meets his beloved mentor, Brunetto Latini, who informs Dante that "all here were clerics and respected men of letters of great fame; all befouled in the world by the one same sin."[12] Homosexual activity was so prevalent in medieval Florence that the German word for it was *florenzen*.[13] It is no secret any more that many of the geniuses associated with Renaissance Florence — men like Leonardo da Vinci and Michelangelo — were homosexuals.[14]

Modern biographies about great men and women who have contributed to the arts and sciences throughout the centuries do not conceal the fact that they were homosexuals and often were forced by society to live double lives. The notoriety of the Oscar Wilde case no longer shocks the public. The number of biographies about great literary figures who were also homosexual persons is increasing at a rapid rate. Today the once "unmentionable vice" has been the subject of much sympathetic study as well as heated controversy, revealing how the mystery of human sexuality — whether it be heterosexuality, bisexuality or homosexuality — is still such a complex and puzzling phenomenon.

It is impossible on the evidence available to us about Dante's sexual orientation, or orientations, to make any definite pronouncements, let alone moral judgments. This is not to ignore the Church's teaching on the morality of homosexual acts with its fine distinction between orientation and activity. It is simply to refrain from judging Dante and the exact nature of his *traviamento*. Dante confesses his sins both indirectly in this passage just discussed and even more directly and publicly — although still in veiled, general terms — in the great encounter with Beatrice on the summit of Mount Purgatory. At any rate, whether Dante engaged in sexual sins with many women, or with men also, is still and will probably remain a matter of conjecture; and perhaps we have already given too much attention to an area of Dante's personal life, which his own discretion had left a guarded secret. He confesses to having abandoned the right path and to having lost himself in a dark forest, a metaphor which "covers a multitude of sins" — if St. Paul would pardon this popular misuse of his famous phrase.

From the complex and ambiguous world of Dante's loves, passions and sins let us now move on to a brief consideration of his participation in public life. The reasons for his entrance into an active public life are probably multiple: his closest friends — the *fedeli d'amore* — were actively involved, and participation in the life of the Commune was practically inevitable for an educated young man of Florence at that time. It could perhaps be argued that Dante felt the attraction of political power and prestige and had such ambitions, which stem from self-aggrandizement and pride. [15] But Dante's motives were most likely of a nobler caliber, as his later masterpiece on political philosophy, the *De Monarchia,* will reveal. It seems that Dante's political interests and involvement flow mainly from his profound sense of community, of civic responsibilities and ultimately from his passionate concern for justice and peace.

Justice and peace were not the hallmarks of Florentine politics at that time. On the contrary, it was a time of intense turmoil when political factions and powerful families constantly warred against one another, at times with barbaric violence. Riots would sometimes break out in the streets where a prominent member of one family could have his nose cut off, thus setting off a series of revengeful acts leading to even more chaos. [16] Usually, however, the battles were conducted through plots, conspiracies, fines and expulsions from the city. There were strong tensions between the families of "old money" with their banking empires throughout Europe and the "new money" families whose wealth was obtained through the thriving wool and silk industries and international trade. These two poles formed factions known as "the Blacks" and "the Whites," controlled respectively by two influential families: the Donati and the Cerchi. These factions actually represented a split in the Guelph party, which had come to dominate Florentine politics.

The Guelphs could be described as the party which supported the political and economic independence of Communes vis-a-vis the old feudal system with its imperial jurisdiction and control. Guelphs normally gravitated toward the Papacy, as we have seen, since they received support from the Popes in the ongoing power struggle with the Empire, supported by the Ghibellines. In Dante's time there existed a certain *entente* (in Dante's mind, more of an "unholy alliance") between the Pope and Florence. It was a marriage of convenience, by which both sides gained economic and political advantages. Boniface VIII's greed for Florentine money and his interest in controlling the Florentine banking system as his source for operating, among other things, the Roman curia were matched by the Florentines' desire to prosper in trade and banking and to be protected militarily by papal troops.

This oversimplification of the Guelph/Ghibelline conflict, which had perdured for centuries in Western Europe, is mentioned merely to provide some background for understanding the very complicated political situation of Dante's Florence. Boniface certainly played a crucial role in the political and economic life of Florence. He sided with the Blacks because he wanted to place Florence and all Tuscany under his control. His schemes and strategies were often enforced under threat of excommunications and interdicts which he at times imposed on Florentine political leaders and on the city. His political and economic ambitions were openly criticized by Dante, and we might identify this defiance as the basic cause for Dante's fiasco in Florentine political life and his expulsion from the city altogether.

Beginning in 1295 Dante served on the People's Council of the Commune of Florence and on the council for the election of the two priors of the city. In 1296 he was a member of "the Council of the Hundred," which dealt with crucial civil and economic issues. Later, in 1300, he was elected one of the six priors, an office whose term lasted only two months (an indication of how fluctuating the situation was). During these years of increasing unrest in Florentine politics, caused by the open conflict between the Blacks and Whites, Dante, courageously at public meetings, opposed the Florentines' reliance on papal military intervention to settle their political differences and turmoil. But with the support of Boniface and his military forces (supplied by the French army under Charles of Valois) the Blacks finally emerged as victors and the Whites were expelled from the city. At that time might meant right. The Blacks, through a *coup d'etat* with the help of the French troops completely took over Florence.

Shortly before the *coup* Dante had been sent with three other envoys from the Commune to Pope Boniface to request a change in papal policy and to protest the various intrigues and plots of the Blacks. It was during his absence from Florence in 1301 that the Blacks and French troops staged their *coup*. The Blacks in Dante's absence found him guilty of graft, embezzlement, opposition to the Pope, disturbance of the peace and several other crimes. All these charges were trumped-up, of course. The only one that bore any truth was his opposition to the Pope's military intervention, but that was not a crime in Dante's mind. Dante was sentenced *in absentia* to two years of exile and permanent exclusion from public office. Other penalties were confiscation of property and exorbitant fines to be paid for his "crimes." Since Dante refused to appear to answer these unjust charges or to pay the fines, a second sentence was imposed on him in 1302 which banned him from ever returning to Florence with the addendum that if he should, he would be burned alive. Dante never returned to his beloved native city.

It is no wonder that Dante for the rest of his life carried within himself a deep-seated hatred for Boniface, whom he considered the ultimate, albeit indirect, cause of his public downfall and miserable exile. In Dante's eyes Boniface was the enemy of true peace, the traitor to his sacred office, the tricky manipulator of kings and cities, the unscrupulous despot consumed by an insatiable lust for power and money. It is no surprise that he reserved a hot hole of torment for him among the damned in Hell.

Dante's banishment from Florence was a radical, perhaps the most radical, crisis in his life. An eminent Florentine lawyer in the thirteenth century, Accursius, had described exile as a kind of secular excommunication "insofar as it excludes from the common good." For Dante it was a most bitter experience that lasted for the rest of his life. His wanderings took him to many cities, mainly in Northern Italy, and perhaps even to Paris and to Oxford, as some historians claim.

We know that he was received as a guest in the castles of several Ghibelline lords who welcomed this distinguished poet, able diplomat, and opponent of papal arrogance. He found refuge first with the powerful della Scala family, the lords of Verona. He also spent time in Bologna at the university where he most likely joined his old friend Cino da Pistoia, fellow poet and political exile as well. No doubt he continued his studies there. He probably also stayed for a time in Padua.

Although it is impossible to retrace exactly Dante's travels through Northern Italy, we know that he was also a guest of the Malaspina family in Lunigiana and that he lived for a while in the mountains of Casentino where he probably stayed at monastic foundations and the castles of noble patrons. The powerful Guidi family in that region offered him hospitality for some time. Later — about 1314 — he took shelter again with the della Scala family in Verona. Can Grande, the reigning lord then, befriended Dante, who repaid his hospitality and support by dedicating the *Paradiso* to him. Dante's final years were spent at Ravenna, where Guido Novello da Polenta, a nephew of the infamous Francesca da Rimini, offered him asylum. Shortly before his death he was sent by Guido on a diplomatic mission to Venice where he contracted some fatal malaise. He died soon afterwards in Ravenna on September 14, 1321.

During the early years of his exile Dante was associated with his fellow exiles, the White Guelphs of Florence, and conspired with them in various strategies to regain admission to their native city. Dante, however, disapproved of their bellicose machinations; and in his quarrel with them called them "wicked and stupid." He did not take part in their military attack on Florence in 1304 which failed miserably. Dante by then thought of himself as a "party of one," even though he sought and accepted asylum and support from the Ghibelline nobles in Northern Italy.

In order to understand more fully the abysmal misery of the exile we should turn to Dante's own accounts of it. He makes several references to it in his works, the most famous being the passage in which his ancestor Cacciaguida, met in Paradise, predicts his exile in these words:

> As Hippolytus was forced to flee from Athens
>   by his devious and merciless stepmother,
>   just so you too shall have to leave your Florence.
> So it is willed, so it is being planned,
>   and shall be done soon by the one who plots
>   it there where daily Christ is up for sale.
> The public will, as always, blame the party
>   that has been wronged; vengeance that Truth demands,
>   although, shall yet bear witness to the truth.
> You shall be forced to leave behind those things
>   you love most dearly, and this is the first
>   arrow the bow of exile will shoot.
> And you will know how salty is the taste
>   of others' bread, how hard the road that takes
>   you down and up the stairs of others' homes.
> But what will weigh you down the most will be
>   the despicable, senseless company
>   whom you shall have to bear in that sad vale;
> and all ungrateful, all completely mad
>   and vicious, they shall turn on you, but soon
>   their cheeks, not yours, will have to blush from shame.
> Proof of their bestiality will show
>   through their own deeds! It will be to your honor
>   to have become a party of your own.
>
>   (*Par.* XVII, 46-69)

The tercet describing the salty taste of others' bread and the descent and ascent of others' stairs is perhaps the most poignant in the entire *Comedy*. It reveals the humiliating pathos of Dante the exile, who is forced to beg his food and lodgings. The "despicable and senseless company" are Dante's fellow White Guelphs from whom he had broken shortly after his banishment.

The reference to the one who plots his exile there "where Christ is daily up for sale" is Boniface VIII, whose simony was condemned by clergy and laity alike in Dante's time. Boniface's place in Hell will be among the simoniacs, but the reference to divine vengeance in this passage is usually understood as the disgraceful last days of Boniface on earth. Boniface's collusion with King Philip the Fair of France had turned sour in 1303, the result of Philip's usurpation of ecclesiastical powers and his dispute with Boniface over the taxation of the clergy.

This situation led to a vehement verbal battle between the Pope and the French monarch. Philip's lawyers accused Boniface of being a false pope, of having murdered his predecessor Celestine V, of heresy, simony, and of every sexual perversion. Philip, in order to depose Boniface, called a general Council at which nearly all the French clergy confirmed the twenty-nine charges. Before the Council, however, Philip made an attempt to kidnap the pope and carry him off to face the Council. This attempt was the infamous incident at Anagni, where Boniface was residing at the time. His old enemies, the Colonna family, in the person of Sciarra Colonna, also took part with the French in this ignominious assault, which included over a thousand soldiers. The Anagni townspeople defended the pope, who died shortly afterwards in Rome. But despite all Dante's hatred of Boniface, he was outraged by this attack, which he described with the words: "I see the *fleur de lys* enter Anagni and in his vicar Christ made captive." (*Purg.* XX, 86-87)

Boniface's death in 1303, however, did not reverse Dante's fortunes as an exile, even though it offered some hope at the beginning. The next pope, Benedict XI, tried to bring peace to Florence by restoring the Whites, but the Blacks turned down the truce offered by the Pope's legate, who eventually placed Florence under yet another interdict! Dante and the Whites were disappointed by this failure and even more disappointed when the good pope (the only one in Dante's maturity not placed by him in Hell!) died that same year (1304) as a result of eating poisoned figs served by a young man dressed as a nun, according to the chronicler Villani. [17]

Dante expressed the sufferings of his exile also in his *Convivio,* a work he began a few years after Pope Benedict's death. There he refers to his exile as "going through almost every region to which this tongue of ours (i.e., Italian) extends, a stranger and almost a beggar . . . like a ship without sail and without rudder, wafted to diverse havens and inlets and shores by the parching wind which woeful poverty exhales." (*Conv.* I, III, 5) The image of the storm-tossed ship reappears throughout his works. Dante's uprootedness and vulnerability are well conveyed by this metaphor, which also expresses the many dangers and privations of exile.

Dante's wanderings in Italy from court to court, begging his bread, are also portrayed in the tragic figure of Romeo, whom Dante meets in Paradise. Dante describes him as a "man of lowly birth, a pilgrim-soul," who attached himself to the court of Raymond, Count of Provence. Romeo managed admirably the funds and affairs of the court, but was unjustly accused by envious courtiers of embezzlement. He left the court, assumed again the pilgrim's garb, and set off to wander again. It is a sad picture of Dante's own life of exile:

> Within this pearl there also radiates
> the radiance of Romeo who accomplished
> fair, noble deeds that went unrecompensed;
>
> . . .
>
> but when those envious tongues convinced his lord
> that he should call this just man to account,
> this man who had rendered him twelve for ten,
> Romeo, proudly, old and poor, departed.
> And could the world know what was in his heart
> as he went begging, door to door, his bread —
> though praised today, he would be praised still more.
> (*Par.* VI, 127-142)

Dante also makes allusions to his exile in his letters, ten of which are extant. Among them are letters to Cino da Pistoia and to a relative in Florence, probably his brother-in-law, who was a religious. The letter to Cino bears the salutation, "To the exile from Pistoia, a Florentine undeservedly in exile wishes health through long years and the continuance of fervent love." In it Dante exhorts his dear friend to arm himself with patience "against the darts of Nemesis." He advises him to read the philosopher Seneca's *Remedies Against Fortune,* but especially recommends in his conclusion that he keep in mind Christ's words in St. John's Gospel: "If you were of the world, the world would love its own." I think it is noteworthy that Dante's concluding exhortation is taken from Christ's farewell discourse to His disciples in which He predicts their persecutions and rejection by the world.

The second letter, written seven years later (about 1315) and believed to be addressed to his relative who was a priest, begins with the simple salutation: "To a friend in Florence." In it Dante mentions that "it rarely happens that an exile finds friends." He also refers to the offer of pardon extended by Florence if he should "pay a sum of money and submit to the stigma of oblation." This "oblation" was a public ceremony in which the repentant exile was offered to St. John the Baptist, the patron of Florence. Dante calls these conditions "ridiculous and ill-advised." The famous concluding paragraphs should be quoted in full:

> This then is the gracious recall of Dante Alighieri to his native city, after the miseries of almost fifteen years of exile! This is the reward of innocence manifest to all the world and of the sweat and toil of unremitting study! Far be it from one familiar with philosophy to submit himself to such a senseless act of abasement as the oblation, like a prisoner in bonds, after the fashion of Ciolo and other infamous wretches who submitted to it. Far be it from the preacher of justice, after suffering wrong to pay with his own money those who had wronged him, as though they had deserved well by him.
>
> No, my father! I will not take this path of return to my fatherland. If some other can be found by yourself or by others, which does not detract from the fame and honor of Dante, that will I accept with no lagging feet. But if no such path leads back to Florence, then will I never enter Florence again. What then? May I not gaze upon the face of the

sun and stars? May I not contemplate the most precious
truths wherever I may be under any sky, without first
returning to Florence, disgraced and dishonored in the eyes
of my fellow citizens? Assuredly, I shall not lack for bread.

(*Epistula* IX)

Dante's exile — twenty years of wanderings, countless deprivations, indescribable sufferings — proved to be, however, the occasion,
if not an important contributing factor or cause, of Dante's monumental
masterpiece, *The Divine Comedy*. Many literary critics and poets have
made this observation over the centuries. Carducci thought that a
statue should be erected in every Italian town to Conte de' Gabrielli, the
lord mayor of Florence who issued the sentence of exile against Dante.
Our thoughts might turn to the many men and women in history who left
the world enduring spiritual treasures which they composed while
suffering the deprivations of exile or imprisonment: Socrates, the
Second Isaiah, St. Ignatius of Antioch, St. Perpetua and St. Cyprian of
Carthage, St. Athanasius, St. John Chrysostom, Boethius, St. John of
the Cross and many others. Closer to our time, Edith Stein and Dietrich
Bonhoeffer could be cited. And even now there are many who are
suffering for the sake of justice and holiness.

The remembrance of these holy men and women of the past who
through their exiles and sufferings discovered the hidden God and left
us inspiring written accounts of that discovery brings to mind a great
religious writer of the last century — John Henry Newman — who in
many ways was a kindred soul of Dante. Newman's spiritual experience
of exile, although not imposed by some external authority, was deeply
felt at various times in his life. The metaphors of exile and homecoming,
loss and gain, sickness and health, recur often in his works to express
the intellectual, spiritual and emotional crises of his life.

In his *Apologia Pro Vita Sua* Newman refers to his departure from
the Anglican Church and from his beloved Oxford as an uprooting and a
voyage on the open sea. Entering the Roman Catholic Church was for
him "like coming into port after a rough sea," but the pain of losing so
many beloved persons, places and things was real and bitter. To
remember it was almost as painful, as he writes in his *Apologia*: "I am
about to trace, as far as I can, the course of that great revolution of

mind, which led me to leave my own home to which I was bound by so many strong and tender ties." Recalling this past experience is "a cruel operation, the ripping up of old griefs, and the venturing again upon the *infandum dolorem* of years, in which the stars of this lower heaven were one by one going out."[18]

The allusion to the *infandum dolorem* — the unspeakable grief — comes from Virgil's *Aeneid* where Aeneas renews his grief over the Fall of Troy by retelling it to Dido. This same Virgilian passage was used more than once by Dante in his *Comedy*. It is interesting that Newman sees a parallel with his own spiritual exile in the story of Aeneas who leaves his fallen Troy behind to follow the mission given him by the gods to found Rome, a greater Troy. Dante had understood his mission in life along the very same lines: he was another Aeneas who suffered the loss of his homeland, experienced the perils of exile and wanderings, and finally found his spiritual home in "that Rome where Christ is a Roman."

Newman also expressed his experience of exile in an historical novel, *Callista: A Tale of the Third Century,* in which the main characters, St. Cyprian of Carthage, Agellius and Callista, are auto-biographical reflections of his own exile. The exiled Cyprian proclaims: "It is the compensation of my flight from Carthage that I am brought before the face of God." Callista and Agellius, who follow Cyprian into exile, also find a "fairer Paradise." After their voyage they "come home to their father's house." In this story Newman was describing his own spiritual exile and journey to his ultimate goal: the knowledge of God in his conscience and heart. All the halfway houses, such as Oxford and Rome, were symbols and anticipations of home; his real home was in the invisible world of spirits, before the face of God. The same basic pattern and intuition can be found in Dante, who discovered through his exile that the Christian can never be completely "at home" in this world, that he is always a pilgrim and wanderer on his way to his true home in God. His *Comedy,* in essence, is the autobiographical account of this journey which began first in exile.

During his exile Dante certainly had strong feelings of hatred and vengeance, as any brooding political exile of his time would have had; his horror and disgust over human injustice sometimes erupted into outbursts of righteous indignation. This dark side of his complex personality is evident in many of his writings, but he seems to have overcome the temptation to be utterly consumed by self-pity, anger, bitterness and revenge. A superficial acquaintance with his *Inferno* has led many readers to think that Dante was frozen in his self-righteousness and gloated over the punishments of the damned, especially his personal enemies, such as Boniface VIII. That, unfortunately, is the most popular image of Dante that endures even to this day. However, more often in the *Inferno* Dante shows pity and compassion for the damned by weeping and even fainting.

There can be no doubt that Dante suffered from hatred, hurt pride, frustrated ambitions, guilt and self-doubt during his years of exile. To these could be added poverty and the ignominy of begging food and shelter. To be homeless, as so many people today know, is a most lonely, desperate experience, inexpressible in words. Dante endured this for twenty years, but during this time he was also transfigured by the rediscovery over and over again of the memory of Beatrice and by all the graces which that rediscovery brought with it: hope, comfort, inspiration, repentance, salvation and peace.

During this twenty-year dark night of the soul, apart from his major works such as his monumental *Comedy*, he was able to pen the beautiful canzone *Tre Donne*, in which he pleads for peace and reconciliation with his beloved Florence. It concludes with these moving words:

> Song, go hawking with white-winged birds,
> Song, go hunting with the black hounds,
> From which I am forced to flee
> Though peace is in their power to bestow;
> Not knowing what I am, they treat me so.
> To Pardon's room the wise man locks no door,
> For pardoning is the beautiful victory of war.
>
> (*Rime* CIV, 101-107)

Dante's request for pardon and peace was denied repeatedly by Florence; but to the very end he desired peace for Florence — an end to the *black* hounds' hunting down the *white* birds — and hoped to return to a peaceful Florence. We notice in the words of this ode Dante's sincere humility as he appeals to a higher wisdom, the practical wisdom of mercy and pardon, which alone can bestow peace.

To speak of Dante's humility might raise some eyebrows or bring a smile to the lips of some readers. Dante's pride, especially his wounded pride, during this period of his life seems to be the overriding trait of his personality. But by his own admission (cf. *Purg.* XIII, 136-138) he was guilty of pride in his life and will have to cleanse himself of it on the first terrace of Purgatory. That honest admission of sin reveals a sincere humility and the need for repentance in Dante's later years. But what about the early years of his exile when bitterness, resentment and hatred could possibly have crippled and paralyzed this man who had risen to such heights in politics and in literary circles? The passages quoted above from his letters manifest deep disappointment, resentment and hurt pride — natural reactions to the devastating blow of banishment — but Dante recovered somewhat and resumed his formal writing in an important work which would remain, however, unfinished: his *Convivio,* usually translated as *The Banquet.*

Dante's purpose in writing this work has been discussed by scholars for centuries. Some think that Dante was attempting to rehabilitate his reputation in the eyes of the Florentines, that he was trying to reestablish himself in their good graces. The *Convivio* would then be an *apologia pro vita sua* of sorts, a work intended to display himself as a man of mature virtue and learning, rather than as a romantic poet who had been dawdling and wallowing in passionate sighs of unrequited loves, as many of his poems may have suggested. Dante would want to convince the public that he is a man of reason and philosophy, not a victim of passions and emotions. He would want to display the public *persona* of a man dedicated to and in love with reason, virtue and learning rather than the *persona* of a poet dedicated to romantic love. For that purpose in the *Convivio* he chooses several of his love poems, his *canzoni,* and interprets them allegorically as expressions of love not for a real woman but for Lady Philosophy.

This device may strike us as a sign of Dante's pride — perhaps even dishonesty — and may lead us to believe that Dante was hypocritically playing the role of an intellectual who condescends to share his superior riches of intelligence and learning with the uncultured masses. The *Convivio* would then be his over-compensation for the disgrace and failure which he had suffered and a vindication of his real worth and dignity in the eyes of the public.

There may be some truth in these interpretations of Dante's motives, but I think we should be open-minded and attentive first to Dante's own words at the beginning of the *Convivio*. There he states clearly the purpose and nature of his work: it is an invitation to philosophy, expressed metaphorically as a banquet where the natural desire of humans to know — as Aristotle had expressed it — could be nourished at the table of wisdom. And here Dante's humility is nowhere more striking, as he declares that he himself "does not sit at the blessed table" but "at the feet of those who sit there." He gathers gratefully and with great delight the crumbs that fall from them; and "moved with pity," shares them with the unfortunate masses who are prevented for one reason or another from partaking at the feast. Dante mentions some of the reasons that keep the majority of people away: family and civic responsibilities, the lack of a school (or great distance from one) and for some people sheer laziness.

Dante then is humbly confessing that he is not a philosopher in the technical sense of the word, but that he has garnered some wisdom which he wants to communicate to the vast majority who are deprived of this necessary food. Philosophy, according to Dante, is a practical wisdom, indispensable for laypersons who want to attain their temporal goal of living happily in this world. Since most laypersons could not conveniently frequent the schools of the clerics and religious where philosophy was taught in Latin, Dante is providing in the vernacular a work accessible to them. I think we should accept Dante's statement of purpose as his sincere desire to give to ordinary people an introduction to philosophy which otherwise would have been denied them.

Philosophy at the time was mainly the province of the clerics and religious, who were able to read Latin. Together with theology it was vigorously and enthusiastically taught at the several *studia* that existed in Dante's Florence. As mentioned earlier, Dante most likely frequented those schools in Florence before his exile; after his exile he seems to have continued his enthusiastic study of philosophy and theology on his own — wherever he could find the books. Whether he actually sat at the feet of the learned masters and doctors at Paris and Oxford is still debated, but his works reveal a profound knowledge of Albert the Great, Thomas Aquinas, Bonaventure, as well as of the many learned debates which took place among the Scholastics at Paris and elsewhere in European universities.

Another reason for his writing the *Convivio* could have been his sheer excitement and enthusiasm in discovering "the joy of philosophy." Repeatedly in this work Dante sings the praises of his new-found object of love. Always the poet, he expresses it through beautiful images: philosophy is his Lady now, the *Donna gentile,* who occupies all his thoughts and imagination. Perhaps we can all identify in some way with Dante's exhilaration over a new discovery. I can recall my own fascination for a time with British romantic poetry, and later in life with French romanticism and still later with French impressionism in art, music and poetry. These transitory "passions" captivate our attention and affections for a time, and leave lasting impressions on us.

Augustine in his *Confessions* reviews many objects of enthusiastic love which preoccupied him during various phases of his life: Virgil's *Aeneid,* the theater, an intimate male friend, a female lover, Cicero's writings, Neo-Platonic philosophy, Manichaeism, and so on. Augustine's list almost reads like Dante's own spiritual biography. In his *Convivio* Dante expressed this fundamental human attraction for what seems good and beautiful in these words:

> And like a pilgrim who is travelling on a road where he has never been before, who believes that every house which he sees from afar is the inn, and finding that it is not, directs his belief to another, and so from house to house until he comes to the inn; even so our soul, as soon as she enters upon the new and never-yet-made journey of life, directs her eyes toward the goal of her supreme good, and therefore whatever she sees that appears to have some good in it, she thinks to be it.
>
> And because her knowledge is at first imperfect, through having no experience or instruction, little goods appear great to her. . . . And so we see little boys intensely longing for an apple and then going on further, longing for a little bird, and further on longing for fine clothes, and then a horse, and then a mistress, and then small riches, and later

great riches, and then more and more. This happens because in none of these things does the soul find what she is
ever seeking, and she believes she can find it beyond.

(*Conv.* IV, xii)

After Beatrice's death Dante found the remedy for his ailing soul in
the consolation which his discovery of philosophy gave him. He began
with Boethius' famous *De Consolatione Philosophiae* and with Cicero's
treatise on friendship, *Laelius sive de Amicitia,* which gave consolation
to Laelius, who had lost his friend Scipio. Dante's enthusiasm increased
as he explored the various philosophical schools and made the discovery
of Aristotle, "the master of those who know." These years of passionate study and love for philosophy drove every other thought from his
mind and heart and even expelled for a time the memory of his former
love, Beatrice.

And yet during these years when Dante experienced what may be
called "a crisis of pure philosophism,"[19] he wrote the *Convivio* as a man
who had already been won back by the heavenly Beatrice. The memory
of his saint in heaven broke through in the midst of his new passion for
philosophy, and her presence in the *Convivio* is quite visible. The
memory of the woman Beatrice, the poet's true Muse, who is now "the
blessed Beatrice" in Paradise, recurs again and again throughout this
unfinished work. The work's second treatise, which is actually the
beginning of the work's content since the first treatise is a general
introduction, opens with one of Dante's earlier *canzoni* (written about
1293) and perhaps the most important and beautiful canzone of the
entire work: *Voi che intendendo il terzo ciel movete.* The ode, written a
few years after Beatrice's death, describes the conflict within Dante's
heart between his old love for Beatrice and his new love for Lady
Philosophy, which struggles against the old. The new passion fills him
with anguish, as he recalls the "humble thought which continues to
speak to me of an angel, crowned in heaven." His tormented soul,
always moved by some kind of love, exclaims: "O Love, true lord,
behold your handmaid; do what you will!"

This paraphrase of Mary's words to the angel at the Annunciation
may seem almost blasphemous, or at best bombastic, since Dante uses
it in the context of his momentary betrayal of Beatrice for his new love;

but understood in the wider context of his concept of love as the spiritual movement of any human soul for what appears good and beautiful — the classical meaning of *eros* — it simply expresses that basic, innate attraction. He will eventually come to realize that there is only one *eros,* but the physical absence of Beatrice seeks for some mediation, some present object of love.[20] Beatrice, who has been transported above the highest spheres, now seems so distant and inaccessible to Dante; and he needs some intermediary to nourish this ultimate *eros* within him.

Philosophy becomes the substitute and the bridge to the one who is now so far away. Dante even calls philosophy "the daughter of God" and "the queen of the universe." And so "that blessed Beatrice who lives in heaven with the angels and on earth within my soul" is now replaced by another *donna gentile* who takes pity on Dante and befriends him in his "widowed" life. And yet in this same work he maintains that "that glorious Beatrice still held the fortress of my mind."[21]

This inner conflict between the love in his past and his present love is the radical struggle which constitutes this crisis in his life. In the third treatise of the *Convivio* he delves into the meaning of wisdom, the object of the philosopher's love, and discovers that wisdom is found in her perfection only in God:

> Philosophy is a loving converse with wisdom, which is found in God most of all, since in Him dwell highest wisdom and highest love and highest act; and it cannot exist elsewhere except insofar as it proceeds from Himself. Therefore divine philosophy is part of the divine essence. . . . and she exists in Him in a true and perfect way — as it were, in an eternal marriage.
>
> In the other intelligences she exists in lesser degree, almost like the beloved lady (*druda*) of whom no lover has complete enjoyment, but in whose aspect he finds satisfaction for his enthusiastic desires. . . . O most noble and excellent heart who perceives in the spouse of the Emperor of Heaven not only his spouse, but his sister and most loved daughter!
>
> (*Conv.* III, XII, 12-14)

Hans Urs von Balthasar considers this the key passage of the Convivio. [22] He translates the word *druda* as "prostitute" and observes "that philosophy is prostitution as long as it is still on the way to the highest love." The word *druda,* which is so crucial here, has several meanings in Dante's works: it can simply mean "lover" or it can have the pejorative connotation of sinful lust, as it sometimes has in the *Comedy* (cf. *Inf.* XVIII, 134; *Purg.* XXXII, 155). Here it seems to be an ambiguous term which aptly expresses the ambiguous nature of Lady Philosophy. Philosophy can be the object of a wholesome, noble love; but when it becomes one's exclusive passion without any reference to its true home in God it becomes a prostitution and a form of idolatry. Thus to abandon Beatrice, who is now in God, for the love of wisdom (philosophy) would be a prostitution and Dante apparently senses this as he writes the *Convivio.* Most likely he abandoned that work primarily because he realized this truth which he must develop and sing about later in his *Comedy.*

But abandoning the *Convivio* did not mean for Dante a repudiation of philosophy itself. Philosophy as the pursuit and love of wisdom would remain for Dante even to his last breath the naturally good and necessary pursuit for every human soul — the innate *eros* which draws us toward God. However, Dante realizes at this stage in his life that this *eros* is inadequate, that human philosophical power cannot on its own reach its proper goal. Only God's love, His divine *"eros"* for His intelligent creatures, can accomplish this. God took the initiative — through the mediation of His grace — by assuming a likeness with us in Christ and by coming to us personally as our Wisdom.

Dante the philosopher always remained the faithful Christian, even throughout his "philosophical" crisis. The Christian revelation, mediated by the Scriptures and the Church's creed, is always the ultimate norm of truth in Dante's mind. The memory of Christ as the eternal Wisdom of God, the Word of St. John's Gospel, is always present to him. He concludes the third treatise of the *Convivio* with these words: "Open your eyes and see that before you were made she (i.e., Wisdom) loved you, guiding and ordering the whole process of your life; and after you were made, in order to direct you straight, she came in your own likeness to you." This seems to be a clear reference to God's incarnate Wisdom, Christ; but could it also refer to Beatrice as another manifestation on earth of that divine grace found in its fullness in Christ alone?

Dante seems to think so, since in his *Comedy* Beatrice will appear as one of three heavenly ladies — a sort of "Blessed Trinity" — who mediate God's "maternal" love for Dante and save him from the tragedy of sin. Dante will describe this rescue mission (cf. *Inf.* II, 64) as the initiative of Divine Love who moved Mary to take pity on him. Mary in turn sent St. Lucy, one of Dante's patron saints, to St. Beatrice, who, moved also by the same love, descended into Hell to seek Virgil's help in saving Dante. Virgil, we should note, represents human wisdom and philosophy, although Dante never forgets that he is a real human person.

We should notice that in this respect the *Convivio* and the *Commedia* differ fundamentally. In the *Convivio* Dante is more concerned with philosophical abstractions such as the idea of man, the nature of the human soul, the ideas of contemplation and morality. Philosophy is allegorized as a lady; she is not a flesh and blood lady as Beatrice is. In the *Convivio* Dante explicitly states that he is following "the allegory of the poets," which employs a mythological figure such as Orpheus in Ovid's poetry to be an allegory of the wise man's power to calm the animal passions and to move others toward a rational, virtuous way of life. Thus Orpheus, a fictional character, is an allegory of the philosopher who uses the sweet force of reason to tame the savage beast within the human heart. [23]

But Dante is also aware of another kind of allegory, which he describes in the same passage as "the allegory of the theologians," the kind used by the biblical authors. This type of allegory is quite different: it is based on real, historical persons and particular events, not on universal ideas and abstractions. In the *Comedy* this is the dominant kind of allegory, the one in which the literal meaning prevails. In the *Comedy* real persons act and interact.

Beatrice, the real woman, comes to life again in the *Comedy*, as Dante discovers that the only real mediation between him and God is His *incarnate* grace. Dante realized that he could not be saved by philosophy alone: his salvation was a work of divine grace, operating through real historical persons: Christ, who is Wisdom Incarnate and His personal envoys (not substitutes): Mary, Lucy and Beatrice. Virgil, too, the philosophical poet, has an important role to play in the drama of Dante's salvation.

The entire *Comedy,* which develops this fundamental insight, will center continuously on the rediscovery of Beatrice, whose eyes, smile and laughter are focused on perfect beatitude: God. In the *Convivio* the eyes and smile of the beautiful Lady Philosophy will sometimes flash like lightning and lead the poet upwards, but those momentary flashes of light and comfort will be eclipsed by the superior light of Beatrice, "the work of faith." The final eclipse of Lady Philosophy will happen later in his life, but even during the writing of the *Convivio* the Beatrician memory will keep intruding like a half-remembered dream into Dante's heart and lift him occasionally into a rapturous experience of sweet joy:

> I contemplated in thought the kingdom of the blessed. . . . I climbed upwards in thought when I say 'where I saw a lady in glory' in order to let it be understood that it was because I was certain and am certain, through her gracious revelation, that she was in heaven. Hence by thinking often of it, as I was able, I used to go, as it were, into an ecstasy. The effect of this thought gave such a sweetness that I became desirous of death in order to go there.
>
> > (*Conv.* II, VII, 6)

The poet Baudelaire described his youth as "only a dark storm, crossed here and there by brilliant suns." The young Dante found some brilliant flashes of light in philosophy and in momentary ecstatic memories of Beatrice, but the dark forest and the stormy sea would envelope him for some years before his final rescue by the supernatural light of Beatrice. His perdition in the dark forest and stormy sea (images he employs at the beginning of the *Comedy* to describe the crises of his life) will be the prelude to his descent into Hell, followed by his ascent of the mountain on which Beatrice in the splendor of a brilliant dawn will come to him — but as the jealous lover who had been betrayed. In that most poignant scene Beatrice will accuse Dante of having abandoned her for others. She will refer to his aberrations as "that school which you have followed" (*Purg.* XXXIII, 86).

This accusation seems to be a clear allusion to Dante's transitory infatuation with philosophy, a "doctrine which teaches mankind's ways, which are just as far away from those divine as earth is from the highest sphere," as Beatrice sharply declares. This rebuke from Beatrice concerning Dante's "school" should be understood in the light of the previous canto (cf. *Purg.* XXXII, 79), where Dante had described the "school of Christ" as the disciples Peter, James and John who witnessed Christ's supernatural revelation on the mountain in the company of Moses and Elijah.

These condemnatory words of Beatrice about the "school" and "doctrine" which Dante once followed — a human teaching contrasted with the divine ways — raise many questions about the relationship between philosophy and theology, reason and faith, nature and grace. The medieval Scholastics debated this relationship for centuries and their discussions were profound and often very heated. The famous controversy between St. Bernard and Peter Abelard comes immediately to mind. This issue preoccupied Dante who, as a scholar, was quite knowledgeable of these debates; but they held a particular interest for him since he was so enamored of classical learning and so concerned for the eternal salvation of the great luminaries of pagan culture, such as Plato, Aristotle and his beloved Virgil.

Although Dante was neither a philosopher nor a theologian "by profession," he possessed exceptional clarity in speculative matters; as a poet he expressed it through images and persons who made abstractions "come alive." Jaroslav Pelikan's assessment of Dante's contribution to these questions is an excellent summary of these debates:

> The most influential presentation of this doctrine of the relation between reason and revelation was probably not that of any of the theologians with whom we have been dealing (namely, Augustine, Peter Lombard, Abelard, Bonaventure, Thomas Aquinas), but that of Dante Alighieri. Although his epitaph acclaimed him as "Dante the theologian, not lacking in any doctrine," it is evident that this was "a poetical eulogy," for he was not a theologian in the technical sense. On the other hand, although "the Thomism of Dante is an exploded myth," it is no less

evident that he "was at home in the intellectual world of the Latin Middle Ages," so that it is quite proper to speak of the "Augustinism" of Dante.

The identification of the role of Virgil in the Divine Comedy as, among other things, that of reason leading to revelation and of nature being completed but not abolished by grace is, despite the objections of some Dante scholars, warranted by the words of the poem as well as by its very structure. "I can speak to you," Dante had Virgil say, "only as far as reason sees; beyond that, you must wait for Beatrice, for that is the business of faith." In that realm the natural reason represented by Virgil was no longer able to be of service, since he could "see no further"; and only the grace of revelation, represented, at least in part, by Beatrice, could suffice.[24]

As Pelikan notes, Dante presents this relationship between reason and faith (human philosophy and divine revelation) in terms of the persons Virgil and Beatrice, two of Dante's guides in his journey to God. Dante, however, had already dealt with this question extensively in his *Convivio*. There in his description of the structure of the universe he compares theology, "the divine science," to the highest heaven, the Empyrean, the dwelling place (beyond any "place") of God:

> The Empyrean heaven, in its peace, resembles the divine science, which is full of peace and suffers no conflict of opinions or of sophistical arguments, because of the most excellent certainty of its subject, which is God. And speaking of it He says to His disciples: 'Peace I leave with you; my peace I give to you' (John 14: 27), when He gives and leaves to them His doctrine, which is that science of which I speak.
>
> Solomon has said of it: 'There are sixty queens and eighty concubines, and young handmaids without number. My Dove, my perfect one, is unique.' (Song of Songs 4:8-9) He calls all the sciences queens and lovers (*drude*) and

handmaids; but this one he calls "Dove" because it is without the stain of debate, and he calls it "perfect" because it makes us see the truth in which our soul finds rest.

(*Conv.* II, XIV, 19-21)

Etienne Gilson in his extensive commentary on this passage observes that theology is equated with Christ's teaching. [25] For Dante theology is simply the pure word of God transmitted to us through the Scriptures. It brings us the unshakable certainty of divine revelation. When we think of all the fierce theological debates that have disrupted the Church and divided Christians over the centuries we wonder if Christians have recognized that peace which Christ intended by His gift of revelation. We are amazed at the theological controversies that continue to unsettle the Catholic Church today, not to mention the many theological differences among the various Christian churches. And then there are the endless and turbulent debates between fundamentalists and liberals over the meaning of the written word of God.

Gilson observes how Dante's conception of theology differs from St. Thomas Aquinas'. Although Dante was deeply influenced by Thomas, he often disagreed with his teaching. Dante knew the Thomistic doctrine of the subordination of all the sciences to theology, summarized in Thomas' dictum that "All the other sciences are handmaids to the queen, which is theology." But Dante purposely avoids this judgment and declares that all the sciences are queens. For Dante theology is "the unique Dove" who reigns in splendid isolation beyond the limits of this world by virtue of its perfection and supernatural dignity. Although some Dante scholars argue that Dante and Thomas are saying the same thing, there is a definite difference between them.

By exalting theology beyond any human science Dante does not thereby debase human wisdom and philosophy. He actually elevates philosophy, classifying her as a queen and as a collaborator far prouder and more independent than one might imagine her to be. [26] Dante goes so far as to declare that philosophy is a wonder — "a miracle of its own existence" — because it enables us every day to see and deem possible the miracles of Christ, which we do not see. Let us examine the extraordinary passage in which Dante asserts that philosophy can actually help us toward the act of faith:

> She (i.e., Philosophy) is useful to all people . . . by helping our faith, which more than anything else is useful to the whole human race, since it enables us to escape from eternal death to attain eternal life. Philosophy helps our faith in this way: since the principal foundation of our faith is the miracles accomplished by Him who was crucified, the Same One who created our reason and willed that it be inferior to His powerful works which were done by Him and by His saints, and since many are so obstinate, uncertain, and doubtful and thus unable to believe any miracle without some visible experience of it, this lady (Philosophy) is something visibly miraculous, by which the eyes of men can daily have experience of miracles. She also makes other miracles believable to us. It is evident that this lady, with her wonderful aspect, helps our faith. And thus I say that from eternity she was ordained in the mind of God to bear witness for the faith of those who live in this time.
>
> (*Conv.* III, VII, 15-17)

Such extraordinary praise of philosophical wisdom cannot even be found in all the pages of St. Thomas. The biblical passage which forms the basis for Dante's words is Proverbs 8:3, "From eternity I was ordained and from ancient times before the earth was," a passage which the theologians of Dante's time interpreted as a reference to Christ, the Eternal Wisdom and Word of God. But Dante applies it to philosophy, calling it a miracle, predestined by God to render the miracles of Christ more credible to sceptics! Dante then goes far beyond Thomas in his positive assessment of this humble handmaid of theology, as Thomas would have her be.

We should note, however, that Dante in his exaltation of the wonderful aspects of philosophy and human reason often expresses extreme caution and reserve. He realizes the weaknesses and limitations of human philosophy. We might cite as an example of his reserve his treatment of the immortality of the soul. This topic was forced on

Dante by the ever-recurring memory of his Beatrice. It is a subject that both philosophy and theology had studied for centuries. Dante generally accepted the Scholastics' doctrine that it was a rational certainty, consistent with the nature of man, as Thomas clearly taught. But he disagrees with Thomas by asserting that it is not *perfectly* seen in this life through reason. For Dante, reason enables us to see it, but somewhat obscurely. The following passage illustrates his position:

> The infallible teaching of Christ makes us certain, that teaching which is the way, the truth and the light (John 16:6): the way, because by it we go without obstacle to the happiness of that immortality; the truth, because it is not subject to any error; the light, because it illumines us in the darkness of the ignorance of this world.
>
> This teaching, I say, makes us certain of it more than all other reasons, because He who gave it to us is He who sees our immortality and sets its bounds. We cannot see it perfectly so long as the immortal in us is mingled with the mortal. But we see it perfectly through faith; and through reason we see it with a shadow of obscurity because of the mingling of the mortal and the immortal. And this should be a most potent argument that both are in us. And thus I believe, affirm and am certain of passing after this life to another and better one, to the abode where that glorious lady (Beatrice) lives, of whom my soul was enamored.
>
> *(Conv.* II, 8)

Dante, then, was well aware of both the strengths and weaknesses of his Lady Philosophy. When it came to questions dealing with eternal realities, such as God, the angels and the human soul, he realizes that human reason and philosophy are aiming too high. He humbly admits the limited resources that we humans possess, and often replies to such questions with a simple "only God knows it and it seems presumptuous of me to discuss it." *(Conv.* II, V, 17)

It would be interesting to explore in more detail Dante's philosophical thought in his *Convivio,* but that subject would require many chapters and even books. We should notice, however, how practical a man Dante was, even though he was strongly drawn toward speculative philosophy. On the one hand he affirms the superiority of the contemplative life over the active life, and on the other hand he claims that the noblest of human sciences is not metaphysics but ethics. For Dante metaphysics is *in itself* the highest and most perfect of the sciences; but as far as we are concerned — in this world and in this earthly life — the practical science of ethics holds the first place. He maintains throughout his writings that man has two distinct goals, and thus two beatitudes: an earthly and an eternal.

As a man of tradition he follows the patristic and scholastic interpretation of St. Luke's narrative about Mary and Martha as symbols of the contemplative and active lives. He agrees with the traditional interpretation that the words of Christ point to the superiority of the contemplative (cf. *Conv.* IV, 17). Dante also agreed with Aristotle that the highest felicity in life, even if rarely experienced, is the practice of contemplation.

But Dante also asserts that contemplation in this earthly, mortal life is not quite complete or perfect. He explains this by recourse to another biblical passage, Mark's version of the holy women who went to Christ's tomb on the first day of the week. He gives a very intricate allegorical interpretation of this narrative, seeing in the three Marys symbols of the three philosophical schools of the active life — the Aristotelians, the Stoics and the Epicureans. The tomb represents this world, the place of mortal realities. The women seek the Savior, who is Beatitude, but they do not find Him there.

The angel clad in white, whom they meet there, is the soul's nobility, derived from God, who speaks through our reason and tells the three philosophies that beatitude is not to be found there in the tomb. He goes before them in Galilee, interpreted as the brightness of contemplation (Dante had found a curious derivation of *Galilee* from the Greek word *gala,* meaning "milk" or "whiteness"!). The conclusion of all this fanciful, allegorical interpretation is:

> It thus becomes apparent that our beatitude is to be found, as it were, in an imperfect form in the active life, that is to say, in the functions of the moral virtues; then, as it were, in a perfect form in the functions of the intellectual virtues,

these two classes of function being the easy and direct way
to the attainment of supreme beatitude, which, moreover,
cannot be enjoyed on earth, as is evident from what we have
said.   *(Conv.* IV, 22)

It is important for us to notice here that supreme happiness —
beatitude — is something transcendent. It is associated with perfect
contemplation, the "face to face" eternal vision of God. This passage
asserts that Christ the Savior is not only the way to it, but also the goal.
We should also recall that Dante called Beatrice his "beatitude" in the
Vita Nuova. In the *Convivio* she is always thought of as being among the
blessed in that eternal abode of contemplation, the Empyrean, where
true theology is experienced. So linked together in Dante's mind are
Christ, Beatrice, beatitude, contemplation and theology that we have to
conclude that for Dante man's highest goal and happiness lie beyond this
mortal life.

That is not to say that Dante does not see any value or any
happiness in this earthly existence. Quite the contrary! In fact, Dante
on this point differs significantly from St. Thomas by asserting a certain
autonomy and independence of man's temporal goal of happiness in this
life. He certainly follows Thomas in affirming the importance of ethics,
human virtues, the active life and human felicity, but he also strongly
asserts a self-sufficiency of the moral life and the purely natural and
human goal of happiness in this life in a world regulated by that highest
human virtue: justice. [27] Dante mentions this autonomy in his *Convivio,*
but this subject, which is related closely to the role of earthly government, receives a more detailed treatment in his great work *De
Monarchia,* which we will consider in a later chapter.

In this chapter we have briefly investigated some of the crises in
Dante's life before he began to compose the *Comedy.* His works up until
then reflect certain disorientations of a moral, intellectual and political
nature. His works sometimes express a partial recovery from certain
detours and aberrations. His *Convivio,* which deserves more attention
than we could give it, remains an important work for understanding
Dante's spiritual and intellectual growth through this period of his life.
Together with the *Vita Nuova* it helps us to understand the various

crises through which Dante passed on his way to his ultimate vision, expressed in the *Comedy.*

We have not referred to all the passages of the *Convivio* in which Christ and Beatrice are explicitly mentioned, but we have observed how the remembrance of Christ and of Beatrice kept recurring. The *Jesu Dulcis Memoria,* the sweet memory of Jesus, which inspired the *Vita Nuova,* was also present to Dante during the writing of the *Convivio.* I would conclude by observing that the memory of Beatrice, which brought with it the memory of Christ, was never completely forgotten by Dante, in spite of temporary lapses and periods of *traviamento.*

Dante will explore those dark moments and the effects of his sins in the first two phases of his journey to God — his *Inferno* and *Purgatorio.* In the *Inferno* those three types of crises seem to be reflected in certain persons he meets there: his erotic sins in Francesca (cf. Canto V); his political ambitions in Farinata (cf. Canto X); and his intellectual pride in Ulysses (cf. Canto XXVI). In Purgatory he will allude to his own sins of pride and ambition (cf. Cantos XI, XII, XIII) and before entering the earthly Paradise to encounter Beatrice he will have to pass through the wall of fire which purifies lust.

In the next chapter we shall focus on that most dramatic meeting with Beatrice in the earthly Paradise where her role as divine revelation so clearly unfolds. We will then see the role which she assigns to Dante as prophet to a corrupt world and to a corrupt Church. But since a prophet is essentially one who communicates God's word to the world, we will first investigate Dante's knowledge of and attitude toward God's Word, especially as it is revealed in the Scriptures, the books we call the Bible. This, then, will be the main topic of the next chapter: Dante as a man of the Bible, a man of biblical faith.

Chapter Four

MAN OF BIBLICAL FAITH

The Bible's influence on medieval life was simply all-pervasive. It was *the* book. Meditation on the Bible was an essential part of the monastic day (the *lectio divina*). Biblical texts were the core of the official prayer life of the Church (the *Officium divinum,* or "Liturgy of the Hours"). It was studied in the cathedral and monastic schools and later in the great universities as the basic source of all theology. The *Sacra Pagina* was truly the "soul of theology." Scenes from the Old and New Testaments were sculpted on the exteriors of churches and public buildings, painted on the interior walls, portrayed in stained glass windows. Key biblical stories were performed in the mystery plays for the instruction and entertainment of the general populace. Itinerant minstrels sang the great biblical themes of the Fall, the Redemption and the Final Judgment. The preaching was generally biblically inspired and the education of children in their ABC's usually began with the psalms and poetic paraphrases of the Bible. In brief, one could not escape the ubiquitous presence of the Bible in daily life, especially in the culturally alive city of Florence in Dante's time. Everyday language, as a result, reflected a strong influence of biblical phrases and images. The gap between the literary clergy and religious on the one hand and the masses of illiterate laity on the other has often been greatly exaggerated, especially as regards knowledge of the Bible in the Middle Ages.

By Dante's time literacy among the laity was more common than we generally presuppose today. We have evidence that thousands of boys and girls in early fourteenth-century Florence were taught to read and write.[1] Children were taught the psalms, the important themes of the Bible in verse form, and the difference between biblical truths and pagan myths. The "bestiaries," in which real and imaginary animals symbolized Christ, the virtues and the vices, were also read by children and adults. Contrary to many exaggerations about widespread medieval ignorance, it should be noted that the religious and biblical education of the laity was highly developed in medieval Florence, even though it could not be compared to the vast knowledge of the Bible held by the clerics and religious.

Dante, however, in his insatiable quest for knowledge, was an exception, as we have already observed. He was definitely a bibliophile, and the book which he knew and loved the most was the Bible. As a poet he was infatuated with the classical poets of the Latin tradition, especially Virgil, and as a philosopher he revered his "master of those who know," Aristotle; but as a theologian and Christian he venerated the Bible, as we have observed already, as the very words of God. He quotes the Bible more than any other book and often refers to its "divine authority" and to its inspiration by the Holy Spirit. For Dante "the whole of the divine law is enshrined in the Old and New Testaments." The Bible was his source of the "infallible and supernatural truth necessary for our salvation."[2]

When questioned by St. Peter in Paradise about the source of his faith, Dante responded:

> The bountiful rain of the Holy Spirit showering
> the parchments, Old and New, is to my mind
> unquestionable certainty of Faith,
> so accurate that any other proof
> compared to it would sound most unconvincing.
> (*Par.* XXIV, 90-96)

Further on in this same dialogue with Peter, Dante specifically mentions Moses, the Prophets, the Psalms, the Gospel and the writings of Peter, too, who "was once kindled by the Holy Spirit's tongue." He refers to all these writings as "the source, the very spark which ignites into a living flame and like a star in Heaven lights my mind."

There are numerous passages in Dante's writings where he asserts the primacy of God's word. Here is another, placed in Beatrice's mouth, where the Scriptures are placed first, followed by the papal magisterium:

> Christians, you have the Testaments, the Old and the New;
>   as guide you have the Shepherd of the Church:
>   they should be all you need to save your soul.
>   (*Par.* V, 75-78)

We have seen that as a young man Dante immersed himself into the study of philosophy and theology, an avocation which consumed most of his time and energy for the rest of his life. From his own testimony we know that he frequented the schools of the religious, many of whom had been educated at Paris. His impression, however, of the learning that went on in these schools was sometimes critical, as this comment reveals: "A true philosopher is not the one who is a friend of wisdom for utility, as are the lawyers, doctors and almost all the religious, who study not for wisdom, but to acquire money and dignity." (*Conv.* III, II) Dante, however, seems to have pursued wisdom for its own sake and found in the schools abundant nourishment for his hunger.

In the schools he imbibed a broad biblical culture, the fruit of a revival of biblical studies which had reached a high point in the twelfth century with the Victorine school in Paris, but which flourished in a new way with the great Dominican and Franciscan masters who entered the intellectual mainstream of the European universities. Dante no doubt heard the learned Dominican teacher (and former student of St. Thomas at Paris), Fra Remigio dei Girolami, at the Dominican *studium* of Santa Maria Novella in Florence and also the fiery, prophetic Pier Giovanni Olivi and his disciple Ubertino da Casale at the Franciscan *studium* of Santa Croce. He thus had personal contact with the scholars and preachers who carried the teachings of Aquinas, Bonaventure and many others to Florence. He not only became acquainted with the thought of Thomas and Bonaventure, who had taught at Paris, but also came to know the many currents of philosophical and theological speculation which flowed at the University of Paris in the thirteenth century. From the passages of Dante's works which we have seen already it is evident that he possessed a remarkable knowledge of the major philosophical and theological disputes of the golden age of Scholasticism, which included a very sophisticated knowledge of biblical interpretation and exegesis.

The relationship between the Bible and Scholastic theology is a vast theme, far beyond our scope here, but a brief summary might be in order. Modern critics and historians of Bible study in the Middle Ages often notice two quite divergent tendencies in medieval biblical interpretation: a strict, naive literalism (what we usually call biblical fundamentalism today) and an excessive allegorism, with its multiple spiritual, moral, mystical and often fanciful meanings. Medieval theologians, however, did not generally see a profound chasm between the literal and spiritual meanings. They usually took the literal sense seriously and employed it as a basis for their theological reflections and speculations. Thomas Aquinas, for example, maintained a balanced method of biblical interpretation by stressing the primary importance of the literal or historical sense as the foundation for further meanings. [3]

This general method of interpretation can be traced back to the early Church Fathers (Origen and Augustine and many others), to the New Testament writers themselves, and further back to the Old Testament writers and their commentators in the Jewish tradition. Dante was well aware of the many abuses of Scripture and the possible errors concerning its spiritual senses. In his *De Monarchia* he quotes Augustine on this subject: "This Doctor in his *Doctrina Christiana* says of the person who tries to give the Scriptures a sense different from that intended by the writer: 'He makes the same mistake as a person who leaves the main road and then only after a long detour reaches the place to which the road was leading.' " Dante concludes that those who pervert the Scriptures for their own ends are guilty of a serious sin: "What an unsurpassed crime — to abuse the intention of the Holy Spirit! It is not against Moses that they sin, nor against David, Job, Matthew or Paul, but against the Holy Spirit speaking through them. For although those who write down the divine word are many, they all do so at the dictation of the one God who has condescended to display His good pleasure towards us by employing the pens of many people" (*De Monarchia* IV, 8-11).

By the time of Dante a fourfold interpretation of the Scriptures was already a commonplace among the great Scholastic theologians and their students in the thirteenth century. Although an individual theologian's terminology for the four senses of the Bible differed somewhat from another's, a basic pattern was in place and it was generally accepted. Some theologians often discovered more than four meanings, or sometimes less or even only one. But basically their method of biblical interpretation was summarized in the following familiar dictum, which was a rhyme in the original Latin:

> The letter teaches the facts;
> allegory what you should believe.
> The moral sense teaches what you should do;
> the anagogical where to direct yourself. [4]

This fourfold interpretation of the Scriptures had already been firmly established in the ninth century by Rabanus Maurus, a famous German Benedictine scholar whose works were widely studied in Dante's time. Rabanus' summary of the four senses is expressed in a more imaginative way: "In the house of our soul *history* (i.e., the historical sense) places the foundation; *allegory* erects the walls; *anagogy* puts the roof on; *tropology* depicts with various decorations both the inside through the affections and the outside through the effects of good works." [5]

These succinct summaries of the four biblical meanings formed the basis for Dante's interpretation of Scripture as well as the basis for his own method of writing in the *Comedy*. This brings us to the astounding claim of Dante (although he never put it in so many words) that he wrote as God wrote! In this respect he boldly parted company with his revered master in theology, St. Thomas Aquinas, who held that the fourfold interpretation applied solely to Scripture and not to other literature. But Dante applied the four senses to his own poetic creation, the *Comedy*. The discovery, or perhaps the appreciation, of this audacious aspect of Dante's poetic art is best expressed, to my knowledge, by Charles Singleton, who has repeatedly noticed throughout his studies and commentaries that Dante *imitated* God's way of writing. [6]

For Dante God is the artist *par excellence,* the divine poet who by creation wrote a book — the universe — and by another creative act (another act of salvific love for His creatures) wrote the Scriptures, which express the meaning of that universe and His plan for us. God's two words — His two volumes — both reveal Himself to his creation. The second volume was also intended for our salvation, a scope which Dante expressed as the scope of his own masterpiece, his supreme creation, the *Commedia.* Dante was fully convinced that he was given this mission: the vocation to write as God wrote for the salvation of the world.

Dante's famous letter to Can Grande della Scala, whose authenticity is disputed by only a few scholars today, reveals his purpose in writing the Comedy and also gives the reader a clear indication of how to interpret the work. Dante clearly states that he wrote it "to remove mankind from misery to happiness," and gives the fourfold meaning of the Scriptures as the key to understanding his own work:

> For the clarity of what will be said, it is to be understood that this work (the *Comedy*) is not simple, but rather it is polysemous, that is, endowed with many meanings. For the first meaning is that which one derives from the letter, another is that which one derives from things signified by the letter. The first is called "literal" and the second "allegorical" or "mystical." So that this method of exposition may be clearer, one may consider it in these lines: "When Israel came out of Egypt, the house of Jacob from people of strange language, Judah was his sanctuary and Israel his dominion." (Psalm 113)
>
> If you look only at the letter, this signifies that the children of Israel went out of Egypt in the time of Moses; if we look at the allegory, it signifies our redemption through Christ; if we look at the moral sense, it signifies the turning of souls from the sorrow and misery of sin to a state of grace; if we look at the anagogical sense, it signifies the passage of the blessed souls from the slavery of this corruption to the freedom of eternal glory. And although these mystical meanings are called by various names, in general

they can all be called allegorical, inasmuch as they are
different from the literal or historical. For "allegory" comes
from *alleon* in Greek, which in Latin is *alienum* (strange) or
diversum (different).   (*Epistula* X)

Even if this letter is not accepted as authentic — and I think the
arguments against it are very weak when compared with the ac-
cumulated reasons and the consensus of so many renowned Dante
scholars today — there are sufficient passages throughout Dante's
writings that confirm the belief that he was conscious of employing this
method of interpretation, which essentially asserts that *real* history
(the facts) is the basic content of biblical stories and that the literal sense
of these events contain in themselves meanings which God intended for
us and for our salvation.

We should note also that medieval biblical exegetes were aware of
anthropomorphic expressions about God in the Bible and of the biblical
writers' use of parables and metaphorical language to express spiritual
truths.[7] We cannot expect to find in medieval biblical scholarship the
progress made in the Renaissance in the field of philology and
knowledge of the original biblical languages, even though many biblical
scholars in the Middle Ages knew and revered the "Hebrew truth."[8]
Nor can we expect to find in medieval scholarship a detailed and
profound knowledge of literary forms, a science that has reached such
refinement only in twentieth-century biblical criticism. We tend to smile
condescendingly at the often naive, literal interpretation of some
medieval exegetes in the thirteenth century when they made serious
inquiries into how Jonah resisted the digestive system in the belly of the
great fish.[9] But such rigidly naturalistic and literal interpretations of
Scripture still flourish among fundamentalists (both Catholic and Protestant) today.

What is essential, however, for us to notice and admire is the
medieval scholar's sense of real history, of the reality of God's concrete
involvement in human history, which reached its climax in the Incarnation. The medieval scholar flatly rejected any Gnostic or Manichaean
denial of the reality or goodness of the material world or God's mingling
with such crass and crude "messiness."[10]

It is the great merit of several twentieth-century Dante scholars, such as Erich Auerbach, Charles Singleton and Robert Hollander, to have recovered this understanding of Dante's central technique of allegory: the allegorical method of interpreting the Scriptures, which was the traditional method not only of the biblical writers themselves, but also of the Church Fathers and the great medieval scholars. Dante not only accepted this method, but gave it as the key to understanding his own greatest work. This daring, innovative step seems, in my opinion, to be one of the most original aspects of Dante's work — an aspect which often escapes the attention of today's readers of the *Comedy*.

The faith expressed in the prologue of St. John's Gospel about the Incarnation comes to mind here: "The Word became flesh and pitched His tent among us." This same faith was proclaimed later in the Nicene Creed which stated that He became man "for us and for our salvation." The reality of human history and the real entrance of God's creative Word into that history in the most concrete way is the original and consistent faith of the Church, expressed in her Scriptures and in other normative documents of her faith tradition down to our own times. The Vatican II document on Divine Revelation expressed this relationship between the Incarnation and the Scriptures in these few, dense words:

> In sacred Scripture, therefore, while the truth and holiness of God always remain intact, the marvelous "condescension" of eternal wisdom is clearly shown, "that we may learn the gentle kindness of God, which words cannot express, and how far He has gone in adapting His language with thoughtful concern for our weak nature." For the words of God, expressed in human language, have been made like human discourse, just as of old the Word of the eternal Father, when he took to Himself the weak flesh of humanity, became like other men.
>
> (*Dogmatic Constitution on Divine Revelation*, III, 13)

The centrality of the mystery of the Incarnation in Dante's interpretation of the Bible is evident in all his major works. We noticed it in the *Vita Nuova* where the memory of Jesus crucified and risen shone through its pages as Dante remembered the death and exaltation of Beatrice. We have observed already that Beatrice is a "Christ figure" in that work and that Dante's allegorical method in that work disclosed significant likenesses between Beatrice and Christ, particularly in reference to the mystery of His death and resurrection, the central event which revealed Him as Savior and source of our eternal blessedness.

The critical studies over the centuries on the various meanings of Beatrice are extremely numerous. In fact no other person mentioned in Dante's works has received so much attention and so many different interpretations from the Dante scholars. Investigation into the meaning of Beatrice still occupies a central position in twentieth-century criticism. At this stage of Dante criticism some of the conclusions that are generally accepted are that she was first of all a real, historical person; that she acquired in Dante's works several allegorical meanings, such as divine wisdom, revelation and grace as well as Christian faith and theology; and that she occupied in Dante's mind, poetry, and life a preeminent place that is reflected in his three most important works: the *Vita Nuova,* the *Convivio* and the *Commedia.*

Without commenting on all the meanings of Beatrice, many of which we have observed already — ideal woman, angel of God, miracle, Christian saint — we should always keep in mind that for Dante Beatrice transcended them all in so far as she was a "figure" or "shadow" of Christ Himself. In this respect he followed the technique of the biblical writers, the Church Fathers and the medieval exegetes in their allegorical method. In the manner of the Church Fathers Dante perceived the universal history of humanity as the gradual unfolding of God's plan.

In this all-embracing vision the persons and events of the Old Testament were figures (shadows, types or allegories — the terms were more or less synonymous) of the Christian dispensation. Even certain persons in Roman and Greek history (Virgil and Cato of Utica, for example) were types or figures of the Christian reality in one way or another. But the one historical person who revealed to Dante the Christian mystery most concretely and personally was undoubtedly Beatrice.

Beatrice, whose allegorical meaning was vaguely announced in the *Vita Nuova,* acquires splendid clarity in the *Commedia.* If we compare the two works we will no doubt notice the development in Dante's mind and heart of a spirituality which integrates many elements from the humanistic traditions of the French and Italian troubadours, neoplatonic philosophers, Greek and Latin poets and esoteric seers with the biblical tradition of the Gospels and St. Paul. Scholars have explored and analyzed for centuries the multiple literary sources for Dante's idea of Beatrice, but we should not allow their many valuable insights to obscure from our sight the real flesh and blood girl of Florence who became in Dante's life the person who led him to God. She was for Dante a veritable *iter ad Deum,* a road to God. In this sense Beatrice bears a profound likeness to the Incarnate Word, who is the way to the Father. The deepest meaning of Beatrice thus unfolds for us in "the Christian Incarnational art of Dante," to use a felicitous phrase from Hollander. [11]

In the many passages which we cited from the *Vita Nuova* we clearly saw how Dante's biblical faith had interpreted the death of Beatrice in terms of Christ's death and resurrection. Dante gave us with moving poetry based on biblical revelation the truly Christian meaning of the death of a loved one. He translated into poetry St. Paul's profound theology of death. Paul had taught Dante that we know Christ no longer in His mortal flesh but rather in His risen, glorious life and that every believer who dies in charity is now "in Christ" and a new creature. For Dante Beatrice had passed from death to life, from mortal flesh to glorious Spirit: she is now in Christ, a glorious member of His body. She had passed from the shadow or image to the reality. Dante followed her with his memory, visions and above all with his biblical faith which saw her as a blessed lady in Heaven gazing on the source of all blessedness. Her new life in Christ had become his new life: his *Vita Nuova.*

In this respect Dante had transcended the love poets of his time — and perhaps of all time — by integrating his passionate love of a woman with his biblical faith which had God as its ultimate object of love and adoration. For Dante, Beatrice always remained a creature, even though in the extravagant language of love poetry she was called his "blessedness" and "salvation." But the language of love is always hyperbolic. Dante knew that Beatrice was only an analogy of Christ, Who is the Creator and supreme Lover of humanity, leading us through

His death and resurrection to the blessed vision of God. Dante's love for Beatrice never became an obstacle on his way to God, nor did he sacrilegiously and idolatrously worship her — a mistaken criticism made several times against him.

In his *Vita Nuova* and even more so in his *Commedia* Dante achieved a marvelous harmony and integration of faith and reason, grace and nature, divine revelation and human wisdom, *agape* and *eros*. He was able to place the tragic event of the death of a young woman whom he passionately loved into the broader perspective of his biblical faith which interpreted events in this visible world as so many signs revealing the invisible plan of God. His microcosm — the little world of thirteenth-century Florence with his love for a young Florentine girl who died prematurely — was understood in the light of God's macrocosmic, universal love which gave to the world in a very limited time and place in its history a unique revelation which sheds light on all history for all times and places. This revelation — the sum and substance of all biblical stories — culminated in the death and resurrection of Jesus and remains for us Christians today the unique vision and pattern in which we understand our own little lives, our loves, tragedies, joys and eventually our death and future resurrection.

Dante, barely known and appreciated by our modern culture, can shed so much light on our own lives today, especially at times when we are confronted with the apparently tragic and meaningless death of a person whom we love and admire. When such a person dies, particularly if that person was very young, we touch the very mystery of death and in a sense we do experience death. We might recall here how the loss of his young sister Mary affected John Henry Newman. Mary's passage from this world strengthened Newman's sense of exile in it; her death did for him what falling in love does for other people: it opened his heart and helped him toward a deeper understanding of love. His vulnerable heart experienced a pain which was fruitful. Through the pain of Mary's death he felt the divine touch which made him more aware of the hidden realities of God. His faith became more "real." The visible things of this world became for him veils of the invisible world of God. In Newman's words, "Dear Mary seems embodied in every tree and hid behind every hill. What a veil and curtain this world of sense is! beautiful, but still a veil."[12]

Dante, too, when faced with the mystery of death experienced his own spiritual exile and felt the loss of Beatrice as a kind of "near death experience" for himself. Such radical losses and afflictions in life are like "dying in installments," as Karl Rahner expressed it. But they bring believers into a deeper realization of what their faith is and where it takes them. The believer before the mystery of death instinctively knows that *sola fides sufficit* — only faith suffices — as St. Thomas Aquinas sang before the mystery of Christ present in the Eucharist.

As Dante reflected on the death of Beatrice he sought the meaning of it and of death itself and found it through his faith in God's mysterious plan for His creatures which He wrote for us in the inspired pages of His book. Dante knew that he could read and see God's face (and faces) on those pages. In a marvelous passage of *Purgatory* (Canto III, 124-135) he reprimands a bishop and pope for not having read the face of the merciful, loving God on the pages of the Bible. They had read only one page (or face): the justice of God. The same Italian word *faccia* means either a human face or a page of a book. They had failed to read the other "face": God's merciful love. Dante denounced their decision to deny Christian burial to a controversial figure whom Dante considered a real believer who had repented at the last moment. In so doing Dante the layman was asserting his *sensus fidelium,* that instinctive faith which believers cling to even when the hierarchy seems to contradict it.

Such strong assertiveness on Dante's part may appear to us as inappropriate arrogance from a layman, although such honest, righteous indignation and criticism from the laity have become so commonplace in today's Church. But in Dante's time when inquisitions were omnipresent and heretic hunts were so frequent, it was a rare, courageous layman who voiced dissent from papal or episcopal decisions and policy. In many other passages of his works Dante criticized the way clerics, especially preachers, either neglected or abused the Scriptures. Typical of Dante's excoriations is the following passage:

> The Gospel and the Fathers of the Church
> lie gathering dust, and Canon Law alone
> is studied, as the margins testify.
> The Pope and Cardinals heed nothing else;

their thoughts do not go out to Nazareth
where Gabriel once opened wide his wings.
(*Par.* IX, 133-138)

An even more acerbic passage can be cited in which Dante places
in Beatrice's mouth words of unmitigated rage against the preachers
who grew fat and rich from their preaching. Beatrice calls them liars,
rationalists, entertainers, and identifies their real motives as greed,
self-aggrandizement and lust. They are compared to fat pigs who by
their preaching support even fatter pigs: their concubines and illegiti-
mate children. This long passage is worth quoting since it expresses
Dante's righteous indignation at preachers who exploit the Word to feed
their own greed and lust. Clear parallels with contemporary scandals
involving popular television evangelists come immediately to mind:

You mortals do not keep to one true path
philosophizing: so carried away
you are by putting on a show of wits!
Yet even this provokes the wrath of Heaven
far less than when the Holy Word of God
is set aside or misconstrued by you.
Men do not care what blood it cost to sow
the Word throughout the land, nor how pleasing
he is who humbly takes Scripture to heart.
To make a good impression they contrive
their own unfounded truths which then are furbished
by preachers — of the Gospel not a word!
Some say that during Christ's passion the moon
reversed its course intruding on the sun
whose light, then, could not reach as far as earth —
such preachers lie! For that light hid itself,
and men in Spain as well as India
shared this eclipse the same time as the Jew.
Fables like these are shouted right and left,
pouring from pulpits — more in just one year
than all the Lapi and Bindi found in Florence!
So the poor sheep, who know no better, come

> from pasture fed on air — the fact that they
> are ignorant does not excuse their guilt.
> Christ did not say to his first company:
> 'Go forth and preach garbage unto the world,'
> but gave them, rather, truth to build upon.
> With only His word sounding on their lips
> they went to war to keep the faith aflame;
> the Gospel was their only sword and shield.
> Now men go forth to preach wisecracks and jokes,
> and just so long as they can get a laugh
> to puff their cowls with pride — that's all they want;
> But if the crowd could see the bird that nestles
> in tips of hoods like these, they soon would see
> what kind of pardons they are trusting in.
> What folly in mankind's credulity:
> no need of proof or testimonials,
> men rush at any promise just the same!
> On this Saint Anthony fattens his pig,
> and bigger pigs than his get fatter too,
> paying their bills with forged indulgences.
> (*Par.* XXIX, 85-126)

Noteworthy is Dante's criticism of those preachers who deny the miraculous aspect of the darkening of the sun at Christ's death. Many Christians today are rightly disturbed by preachers who give rationalistic explanations to what the Scripture writers describe as supernatural phenomena. Such displays of "enlightened" and "sophisticated" exegesis from the pulpit were obviously common in Dante's time, just as they are today.

Another aspect of this passage worth noticing is Dante's dark humor in discussing the subject of indulgences and "pardons." This passage might be compared with Chaucer's "Prologue to the Pardoner's Tale" in *The Canterbury Tales*. There we read sharp criticisms from another medieval layman who exposes the friars' crafty greed and the laity's naive ignorance as regards the preaching, selling and buying of indulgences and relics. Chesterton in his incisive and charming *Chaucer* has pointed out many similarities between Dante and Chaucer.

On many topics Chaucer shows the influence of Dante, whom he deeply admired and in some ways imitated. He certainly shared with Dante a contempt for preachers who, like "hustling advertising agents dragged religion in the mire; but they got the money."[13]

Besides the friars' exploitation of the Word for self-interest and the clergy's neglect of the Bible, the distortion of Scripture by heretics was another target of Dante's fury. In the following passage Dante not only denounces the intellectual pride and folly of heretics but also warns everyone of the danger of abandoning the clear truth taught by God's Word in favor of following one's private judgments and opinions:

> Opinions formed in haste will oftentimes
> lead in a wrong direction, and man's pride
> then intervenes to bind his intellect.
> Worse than useless it is to leave the shore
> to fish for truth unless you have the skill;
> you will return worse off than when you left.
>
> . . .
>
> So did Sabellius and Arius
> and all those fools who were to Holy Scripture
> swordblades distorting images of truth.
> Nor should one be too quick to trust his judgment;
> be not like him who walks his field and counts
> the ears of corn before the time is ripe,
> for I have seen brier all winter long
> showing its tough and prickly stem, and then
> eventually produce a lovely rose,
> and I have seen a ship sail straight and swift
> over the sea through all its course, and then,
> about to enter in the harbor, sink.
> (*Par.* XIII, 118-138)

Such strident tirades against the neglect and abuse of Sacred Scripture disclose Dante's unshakeable conviction that God's truth as revealed in the Bible infinitely surpasses human wisdom, so often the fruit of erroneous speculation and merely personal opinions. Some clergy and friars in Dante's time dispensed this drivel to the laity, who deserved to hear the pure, nourishing Word of God. Feeding the faithful with such a counterfeit of the true Bread of Angels was not only a betrayal of their sacred mission within the Church but, even worse, it had become a means for personal profit which fed their pride, lust and greed.

Dante knew by experience how insidious the pursuit of human wisdom could be. His own relentless search for universal truth had driven him down many paths which proved to be only *culs de sac*. His intellectual adventures, like Icarus' flight to the sun and Ulysses' voyage beyond the limits of the earth, had turned out to be flights of folly which left him in a dismal, meaningless no-man's land, lost and bewildered until Divine Wisdom in the person of Beatrice came to rescue him.

This infinite abyss between divine and human wisdom is perhaps nowhere in Dante's works more dramatically and personally expressed than in the climactic episode on the summit of Purgatory in the earthly Paradise where Beatrice encounters Dante, requires a confession of sin, and commissions him to communicate to the world a prophetic message. The complex episode on top of the mountain unfolds through a succession of scenes which, for the sake of simplicity, might be summarized as four acts of a drama which not only narrates Dante's own spiritual story but places it within the broad context of universal history and God's salvific plan for the human race. This drama places the microcosmic history of an individual's entire life with its adventures, failures, conversion and future destiny within the vast macrocosmic framework of the divine plan revealed in the history of the Church and the Empire. Dante narrates this complex personal and universal history in the space of six cantos (*Purg.* XXVIII - XXXIII) — a dense, compact, unified vision which is one of the most interesting, fascinating and important passages in his entire work. Some critics would say that it is the central event of the *Comedy*.

We will focus on the first two acts of the drama — the solemn procession and Dante's confession — in this chapter which deals mainly with the Bible's role in Dante's life and works. Then in the next chapter we will examine the last two acts which reveal Dante's role as prophet.

The opening scene of the first act is the "divine" forest, presented in striking contrast with the "dark" forest, the opening scene of the entire *Comedy* (cf. *Inf.* I), where Dante had described the utterly confused state of his soul midway in life's journey. There he had experienced the terrifying loneliness of his own spiritual chaos, describing it as a "nowhere" or a desert inhabited only by the ferocious beasts of sinful desires or as a tempestuous sea in which he was desperately foundering. But now after his descent into Hell and his ascent of the purgatorial mountain he has reached another forest, the primeval garden of Eden which God had created for human happiness.

The dark forest of meaningless existence haunted by sin, fear and guilt was the man-made counterpart of the divinely created paradise. But here Dante discovers, or rediscovers, the pristine world of nature as a beautiful garden of delights which inebriates the innocent human soul, represented by the solitary lady, Matelda. She is so filled with joy and love that she bursts into song. The lyrics of her song are from Psalm 91: "You have delighted me, Lord, by your work and I will rejoice in the works of your hands. How praiseworthy are your works, O Lord!"

These words express the human delight experienced in the contemplation and enjoyment of pure nature; but more importantly they express the human recognition, praise and love of the God who created the beautiful work of nature. This pure nature before human sin has perfect qualities which we might describe as somewhat "supernatural" or "preternatural," to use rather loosely two technical terms from Scholastic theology. The conditions of nature are in perfect harmony and peace. All blends together — the purity and movement of the air and waters, the variety of plants, flowers and animals — to produce a symphony of sounds, colors and scents which completely delight Dante and Matelda, who correspond in many ways to Adam and Eve before the fall. Matelda at this point alludes to the dreams and visions of the ancient pagan poets who had sung of this place as the "Age of Gold" and the "Eternal Spring." (cf. *Purg.* XXVIII, 139-144)

John Ruskin, truly one of the great nineteenth-century critics of art, architecture and literature (in spite of his sometimes fanciful, romantic and hyperbolic digressions — and his unabashed medieval chauvinism), has offered some appropriate, insightful comments on this passage. Although not a professional Dante scholar or theologian,

Ruskin possessed a remarkable poetic and moral sensibility as well as a deep knowledge and appreciation of Dante's *Comedy*. He considered Dante "the central man of all the world, as representing in perfect balance the imaginative, moral and intellectual faculties, all at their highest." Ruskin described this particular canto (*Purg.* XXVIII) as "the sweetest passage of wood description which exists in literature." Some of his further comments on this passage are worthy of our attention:

> Now, therefore, we see that Dante, as the great prophetic exponent of the heart of the Middle Ages, has, by the lips of the spirit of Matelda, declared the mediaeval faith, — that all perfect active life was the expression of man's delight in God's work. . . .
>
> I called this passage the most important, for our present purposes, in the whole circle of poetry. For it contains the first great confession of the discovery by the human race (I mean as a matter of experience, not of revelation) that their happiness was not in themselves, and that their labour was not to have their own service as its chief end. It embodies in a few syllables the sealing difference between the Greek and the mediaeval, in that the former sought the flower and herb for his own uses, the latter for God's honour; the former, primarily and on principle, contemplated his own beauty and the workings of his own mind, and the latter, primarily and on principle, contemplated Christ's beauty and the workings of the mind of Christ. [14]

Noteworthy is Ruskin's observation that Greek culture was man-centered, whereas medieval culture was God-centered. The theocentric worldview embodied in Dante's works and in medieval culture soon yielded to a revival of the classical Greek mentality in the Renaissance. Later the Enlightenment and the Industrial Revolution carried this mentality into our modern age. These sweeping movements dethroned God, religion and theology as the centers of man's adoration, activity and study and enthroned man, his reason and his progress. Contemporary "secular humanism" with its idolatries of science, art, communication, sexuality, etc., seems to be the direct heir of these movements which followed the dissolution of the medieval *Weltanschauung*. These remarks, simplistic and general as they are, contain, I believe, a profound truth: that Western culture after the high Middle Ages to a great extent slipped into a decadence and decline by abandoning gradually its God-centered vision and values.

The medieval period was certainly not an ideal "age of faith." It was tainted by many serious shortcomings, blind spots and evils, many of which Dante vehemently exposed and denounced, but Western civilization in its post-medieval ages has undergone a profound transformation and suffered a tremendous loss in the process. Thomas Merton has expressed this loss very succinctly:

> Man has lost Dante's vision of that "love which moves the sun and other stars," and in so doing he has lost the power to find meaning in his world. Not that he has not been able to understand the physical world better. The disappearance of the simple medieval cosmogony upon which Dante built his structure of hell, purgatory, and heaven has enabled man to break out of the limitations imposed upon his science by that ancient conception. And now he is prepared to fly out into those depths of space which terrified Pascal — and which continue to terrify anyone who is still human. Yet, though man has acquired the power to do almost anything, he has at the same time lost the ability to orient his life toward a spiritual goal by the things that he does. He has lost all conviction that he knows where he is going and what he is doing, unless he can manage to plunge into some collective delusion which promises happiness (sometime in the future) to those who will have learned to use the implements he has discovered. [15]

Mortimer Adler has expressed this same tragic loss of the medieval vision in these words:

> The central problem of mediaeval culture was the relation of faith and reason, religion and philosophy, supernatural and natural knowledge. The so-called mediaeval synthesis, the

> cultural harmony and unity of the mediaeval world, de-
> pended on the solution of that problem. . . . When, after
> such preparation, the time was ripe, two men solved the
> problem by sheer intellectual mastery of every relevant
> truth: Moses Maimonides solved it for the Jewish commu-
> nity, and St. Thomas Aquinas for the Christian world. That
> later Jews and Christians did not sustain the solution, or
> even repudiated it, was part of the cultural tragedy which
> the modern era went through at its birth. [16]

Dante expressed St. Thomas' God-centered synthesis and vision
of reality in all his works, but his description of the earthly Paradise in
the final cantos of *Purgatory* is exceptional for its comprehensive view
of history and Dante's personal involvement in that history. There in
the earthly Paradise Dante describes Matelda who, having shared her
joy in God's work of nature, now announces to Dante that something
entirely new was making its appearance. She tells him: "My brother,
look and listen." (*Purg.* XXIX, 15)

What appears is indeed new and different. It is a sudden burst of
brilliant light, a flash of lightning that floods the forest with an unearthly
radiance. Dante is amazed by its suddenness, its brightness and the
beautiful melody that accompanies it. He describes the atmosphere in
terms such as "ineffable delights," "blissful trance," and "first fruits of
eternal joy." We are definitely in the presence of something wonderfully
new and truly supernatural. This "something" outstrips the wondrous
beauty of nature.

Dante tantalizes our already aroused curiosity at this point — the
strategy of a progressive revelation — by describing seven approaching
lights as "seven trees of gold." He identifies the forms as candlesticks
and the words of the chant as "Hosanna." What eventually comes into
full view is an extraordinarily dazzling triumphal procession, a heavenly
or divine pageant, which completely stuns Dante's imagination.

The various details of the procession and the sources from which
Dante drew his inspiration have been the object of much research by
Dante scholars. Ultimately the main source is the Bible, particularly
Ezekiel's famous vision of the divine chariot-throne (cf. Ezk 1), a
passage which holds a central place in Jewish mysticism. Ezekiel's

vision is echoed in St. John's visions of heaven in the Book of Revelation, whose images are for the most part derived from Ezekiel. Dante acknowledges his indebtedness to these two sources in the course of his description of the scene before him. He also blends into the scene many elements from Roman history, Greek mythology, ancient Eastern religions and especially Christian art and liturgy. The whole scenario is typical of Dante's eclectic art.

We have noted in earlier chapters that the ecclesiastical art in Dante's Italy left a deep impression on him. The magnificent mosaics of Byzantine inspiration in the basilicas of Rome, Ravenna and Venice were no doubt seen and admired by Dante. In particular, the great triumphal arches in the Roman churches (Saint Mary Major and Saint Praxede come to mind) and the majestic processions portrayed in the nave of *Sant' Apollinare Nuovo* in Ravenna were undoubtedly inspired by St. John's visions of the heavenly liturgy. [17]

In John's visions (cf. Rv 1:4) there are flashes of lightning and seven lighted torches, which are identified as the seven Spirits of God. John had already noted that God's Spirit had taken control of him to enable him to see this vision of heaven. The activity of the Holy Spirit and His sevenfold presence dominate John's vision; the same is true in Dante's description of the beginning of the sacred procession. The seven flames (not carried by human figures, it should be noted) move along slowly and solemnly. They are the source of this new light — a blazing fire — which transforms the air of the forest into the color of flame. Dante is obviously suggesting the presence of God's Spirit: divine love or charity. The procession will be no ordinary procession; it is led by the supernatural activity of the Holy Spirit.

In a remarkable passage of his *Convivio* Dante had identified the gifts of the Holy Spirit as a divine seed sown in the human soul by God, the sower, who out of love bestows His goodness and power on humanity. In this passage Dante carefully distinguished two ways by which God shares His goodness and nobility with His human creatures: the natural way and the divine or spiritual way. The "natural way" is the production of the human soul, which for Dante is a direct creation of God, who sows his "divine seed" in the individual soul, thus constituting its natural nobility and goodness as well as its potential for receiving ulterior "sowings" from the Divine Sower.

Dante supports his theory of the soul's origin with many citations from the philosophical works known to him, especially the writings of Cicero, who was influenced by the Stoic ideas on the soul. It is beyond our scope here to investigate the many philosophical theories on the soul's origin and nature which influenced Dante. Suffice it to mention that for Dante the human soul, which by creation receives the divine seed, is already constituted by this divine gift or grace as an individual capable of developing the divine potentiality bestowed on it. He goes so far as to state that the human soul which receives such an excellent share of divine goodness is "as it were, another god incarnate, and this is, as it were, all that can be said of the natural way." He then goes on to write:

> By way of theology one could say that the highest deity, that is, God, sees His creature prepared to receive His benefi- cence in such a large measure according to its preparation to receive it. And since these gifts come from His unspeak- able love (charity) and the divine love is the specific characteristic of the Holy Spirit, it follows that they are called gifts of the Holy Spirit. As Isaiah the prophet distin- guishes them, they are seven: wisdom, understanding, counsel, fortitude, knowledge, piety and fear of God. What a good crop, what a good and admirable seed! What an admirable and benign Sower, who expects only that human nature prepare the soil for sowing them.
>
> And blessed are those who cultivate such seed, as is fitting. Let it be known that the first and most noble off- spring that buds from this seed, which is intended to be fruitful, is the appetite of the spirit, which in Greek is called *hormen* (zeal, impulse); and if this is not well cultivated and maintained and directed by good habits, the seed would have little value and it would be better if it were not sown. Thus Augustine and also Aristotle in his second book of *Ethics* want man to habituate himself to restrain his pas- sions so that this plant may grow hardy and strong by good habits and righteousness and thus bear fruit. From its fruit will come the sweetness of human happiness.
>
> (*Conv.* IV, XXI, 11-14)

This passage is taken from among many in which Dante distinguishes "nature" and "grace," even though he considered pure nature
itself as a grace or gracious gift of God. It seems particularly appropriate
to cite this passage in the context of the garden of pure nature (already a
divine creation) which receives now a further outpouring, sowing or
planting of divine love: the gifts of the Holy Spirit. The seven flames of
the Spirit leading the procession are described by Dante as an artist's
brush strokes that paint the seven colors of the rainbow across the sky,
producing a new light and a beautifully new heaven. One recalls the
rainbow around the heavenly throne in the visions of Ezekiel and John.
This new sky forms a kind of canopy over the entire procession. The
scene unfolding before Dante's eyes is thus a supernatural event: an
activity of the Spirit similar to the Spirit's moving over the waters of
creation and the activity of God's Spirit in the creation of man and the
garden (cf. Gn 1:2; 2:7-8).

The garden of Eden, the natural "nest of mankind," is thus an
image of the human soul created as a pure garden, a field sown with
divine seeds of nobility and goodness and further potential for greater
gifts and seeds. Later when the mystical procession comes to a halt,
Dante will be interrogated on how he cultivated his own garden. But let
us now return to the beginning of the procession.

Following the leadership of the seven flames are twenty-four
elders in garments "supernaturally white." They are wearing crowns of
lilies. In Dante's allegory these figures represent the books of the Old
Testament, according to St. Jerome's division of the *Vulgate*. Following
them are the famous four living creatures (from Ezekiel's and John's
visions), wearing crowns of forest greens. These figures, which represent the four Gospels, are at the four corners of the splendid triumphal
chariot, which is drawn by a griffin, a half-eagle, half-lion animal.
Flanking the wheels on one side are three dancing ladies in red, green
and white; on the other side are four dancing ladies dressed in purple.
The three ladies represent the theological virtues (faith, hope, charity)
and the other four the cardinal virtues (prudence, justice, fortitude and
temperance).

Behind the chariot are seven other figures which represent the
remaining books of the New Testament. The author of the Acts of the
Apostles, Luke, walks with the figure representing all the Pauline

letters. This figure carries a bright, sharp sword — the usual portrayal of Paul in Christian iconography. The last figure — the author of the Book of Revelation — walks alone. He is described as an old man with an inspired face, walking as though in a dream. Dante specifies that these figures too are clad in white, but they are crowned not with lilies but with roses 'and other red flowers, like flames encircling their heads. Then a thunder clap is heard.

Dante's description of the procession reveals his genius for expressing poetically and visually a most profound and complex doctrinal truth: the divine activity through the Bible in the course of salvation history. He envisions all the inspired writers led by the same Spirit, under the Spirit's new canopy-sky of flaming rainbow colors. They either precede, accompany or follow the griffin and chariot, whose meanings eventually unfold as Christ and His Church. The figure in the chariot will be Beatrice representing Divine Wisdom or Revelation, always present in the Church.

One could summarize this scene as the apotheosis of the Scriptures: the Spirit's gift of divine revelation which led the world to Christ, the Servant of God, who according to Isaiah's prophecies (cf. Is 11:2-3; 42:1) will bear the seven gifts of the Spirit to the world. The position of the various figures in the procession and their colors are all signs pointing to theological and mystical realities. Noteworthy is the color of the representatives of the sacred books: they are all dressed in dazzling white, a detail which points to the unity and continuity of the two covenants. The colors of their crowns, however, show their difference: the Old Testament was the time of faith (white generally symbolized faith), which looked forward to the coming of Christ. The central biblical figures — the four evangelists — are crowned with green to represent the fulfillment of hope in the arrival of Christ, our Hope. The other sacred writers wear flaming red crowns to signify divine love brought by Christ to the world.

As the procession comes to a halt, the figures representing the Old Testament books turn to the chariot "as to their source of peace." One of them sings *"Veni, Sponsa de Libano"* (Come, Bride, from Lebanon) three times and all the other voices join his. This familiar verse from the Song of Songs (4:8) is significant here since it announces the arrival of someone or something of extraordinary importance. That someone turns out to be Beatrice and the something that she represents is Divine Wisdom or Revelation.

The Old Testament figure who sings the verse is probably, in Dante's mind, Solomon, the reputed author of that well-known book in the Middle Ages, the Song of Songs. In medieval biblical scholarship four books of the Old Testament were attributed to Solomon: Proverbs, Ecclesiastes, the Song of Songs, and Wisdom. The influence of these last two books on the theology, mysticism and art of the twelfth and thirteenth centuries can hardly be exaggerated. Solomon was a familiar "figure" or "type" of Christ, since he was the son of David and thus the human ancestor of Christ. As king of Israel he was also a type of Christ, and as the initiator in the building of the Temple he was considered a type of the Church. Because he had requested and received the supreme gift of God's wisdom he was also considered an inspired prophet.

The importance of Solomon in Dante's theology was enormous and is often neglected by the commentators. Dante quotes extensively from Solomon's books, as we noticed in his *Convivio,* but the position he gives Solomon in Paradise reveals best Dante's high esteem for him. Solomon is placed in the heaven of the sun in the company of the great luminaries of patristic and medieval theology, such as Dionysius the Areopagite, Albert the Great and Thomas Aquinas. Solomon, the only non-Christian there, is introduced to Dante by Thomas Aquinas as:

> The fifth light, the most beautiful of all,
> breathes from a love so passionate
> that men still hunger down on earth to know his fate;
> his flame contains that lofty mind instilled
> with wisdom so profound — if truth speak truth —
> there never rose a second with such vision.
> (*Par.* X, 109-114)

For Dante Solomon was the wise man *par excellence,* the light that exceeded all the great Christian theologians. Dante even calls him the "fifth light," thus identifying him with the sun itself, symbolized by the number five in medieval astrology. Besides, the sun in Dante's works was the natural symbol of God and of His Incarnate Wisdom, Christ.

Dante in the passage cited above makes an allusion to the medieval controversy over the eternal salvation of Solomon. Many medieval theologians followed St. Augustine's opinion that Solomon was damned because of the sinful conduct of his old age: his many marriages with pagan women (700!), his numerous concubines (300!), and above all his construction of shrines for the worship of foreign gods. The Bible records that Solomon himself turned from the true God and worshipped false gods (cf. 1 Kings 11:1-13). Since there was no biblical account of his repentance, Augustine's view of his eternal fate was generally held.

Dante, however, was an independent, courageous thinker and in many respects, especially on the topic of the salvation of non-Christians, an original theologian. Perhaps his exaltation of Solomon can be explained by his theological-political views which contradicted the papal claims that God had ordained one supreme luminary for the world — the Pope, symbolized by the sun. According to these papal theories the papacy and the empire were symbolized respectively by the sun and the moon. The emperor (the moon) derived his light and power from the sun and was thus subordinate to that supreme light. Dante by exalting Solomon, the worldly king, as the brightest light and the "fifth light" — the sun itself — was thus asserting his own political theology which he had elaborated in his *De Monarchia,* a major work which we will consider in more detail in the next chapter.

Another factor which might explain Dante's choice of Solomon as the most brilliant light is of a more personal nature. In his famous dedicatory letter to his patron Can Grande della Scala, Dante gives a defense of his audacity in claiming to have had a supernatural vision of Paradise. He cites examples, from biblical history, of sinners who received the grace of extraordinary revelations, among whom that very embodiment of evil in the Old Testament, Nebuchadnezzar. He concludes that God "sometimes in compassion for their conversion, sometimes in wrath for their chastisement . . . manifests His glory to evil-doers, be they ever so evil."

With these words Dante justifies his apparently presumptuous claim to have had a mystical foretaste of heavenly glory. He was quite conscious of his unworthiness and sinfulness, but was also aware that God's grace is not a reward for human merit. God's absolute freedom and liberality in bestowing grace was an undisputed first principle in

Dante's theology. Therefore the medieval debate over the salvation of Solomon, the great sinner, was an open question for Dante. He thus challenged the awesome authority of Augustine and others. I think this theological boldness of Dante makes him a sympathetic voice to our modern sensibilities. Perhaps Dante, conscious of his own carnal sins, felt a certain affinity to Solomon. Boccaccio in his biography alluded to this possible resemblance between Solomon and Dante. In any case, we can feel a certain closeness to Dante, the sinner§theologian, who writes, so to speak, "a theology for sinners." It is, however, a theology that lifts us to a communion with the God who receives the repentant sinner into His glory. I have not found so far any passage where Dante rebuts the charge that Solomon died unrepentant, but Dante was never at a loss for inventing such stories where history was silent about the final hour of one of his heroes.

From the many passages of Dante's works where he quotes Solomon one has particular relevance for the meaning of the sacred procession in the earthly paradise. It is a passage from his *Convivio*, quoted in chapter three, which described theology, the divine science, as the unique Dove and the Bride in the Song of Songs. It was also called "the peace of Christ," given to His Church. That passage sheds light on the scene before our eyes of the elder, Solomon, greeting the chariot with the song "Come, O Bride." Solomon as spokesman for the entire Old Testament is looking toward the griffin, the chariot and Beatrice — allegorically, Christ, the Church and Divine Wisdom. The three are linked together since Christ brings the Church, which is His vehicle of divine revelation. Just as Christ is inseparable from His Church, so His revelation is found in that vessel. The Bride therefore is both the Church and Divine Wisdom. Commentators on this passage have been divided for centuries over what symbolizes what. The solution seems to lie in Dante's own intention of giving fluid, interpenetrating and multi-dimensional meanings to his allegorical figures.

This approach to interpreting Dante seems to be supported by the next words heard in the scene. A multitude of angels rises from the chariot singing "alleluia" in response "to the voice of so great an elder," (i.e., Solomon). They all sing *"Benedictus qui venis"* — Blessed are you (masculine form) who come. This biblical verse recalls Christ's triumphal entry into Jerusalem on the donkey, the animal Jesus purposely chose to indicate his peaceful Kingship, in contrast with the horses of warrior kings.

The theme of peace dominates this scene of triumph and heavenly glory, which is also in Dante's mind an anticipation of Christ's final coming. Dante had noted that the elders look to the chariot as to their peace. We might recall here a popular medieval etymology which interpreted the name Solomon as *pacificus,* i.e., "the peaceful one" or "peace maker." It is perhaps no accident that in the passage quoted earlier from the *Convivio* Dante had described theology as the peace which Christ gives us, the peace in which our souls find their rest. Dante was also aware of the Pauline text describing Christ as "our peace" (cf. Ep 1:11-18).

Thus the great jubilation that Dante witnesses on the summit of Purgatory is the arrival of Christ, the bearer of peace, wisdom and revelation — all represented by Beatrice. It is thus the advent of Christ and of His Spouse, the Church, also represented by Beatrice. The figures which symbolize the various books of the Bible are also an integral part of this theophany or apotheosis of Wisdom. They all form a compact unity together with the other gifts of the Spirit, the theological and cardinal virtues, and so manifest the divine presence in this world — divine grace in communion with human nature.

This wonderful scene describes with so many images Dante's rich concept of what divine revelation, Bible and theology are in relationship to the Church and to the world. They all express the sacramental presence of God, intelligible only in terms of the Incarnation. We mentioned briefly in chapter two the sacrament of the Eucharist in connection with Beatrice as a Christ figure. Here in this scene her symbolism as Eucharist, the central sacrament of the Church, is much more pronounced. Dorothy Sayers, among others, has noticed this important aspect of Beatrice and compares the symbolic pageant in the garden to a Corpus Christi procession and to the celebration of the Mass. [18]

All of these divine gifts — Bible, Sacrament, Church — are an incarnate presence of the transcendent God in our world of nature. It seems that in some quarters we have come a long way in our modern (or post-modern, as some would say) age from this medieval awe for the Scriptures, divine revelation and the sacraments. Dante in this pageant celebrating divine revelation articulated the typical medieval *stupor* at the divine presence in the Word and the Sacrament. Such awe for the primacy of the Word of God was expressed in the Vatican II document on divine revelation:

> Sacred theology rests on the written word of God, together with sacred tradition, as its primary and perpetual foundation. By scrutinizing in the light of faith all truth stored up in the mystery of Christ, theology is most powerfully strengthened and constantly rejuvenated by that word. For the Sacred Scriptures contain the word of God and, since they are inspired, really are the word of God; and so the study of the sacred page is, as it were, the soul of sacred theology.
>
> (*Dogmatic Constitution on Divine Revelation,* VI, 24)

Dante, the layman, by his assiduous study of the Scriptures had anticipated by many centuries Vatican II's strong exhortation to the faithful to pursue the study of the Bible:

> This sacred synod earnestly and specifically urges all the Christian faithful, too, especially religious, to learn by frequent reading of the divine Scriptures the "excelling knowledge of Jesus Christ" (Ph 3:8). "For ignorance of the Scriptures is ignorance of Christ." Therefore, they should gladly put themselves in touch with the sacred text itself, whether it be through the liturgy, rich in the divine word, or through devotional reading, or through instructions. . . .
>
> In this way, therefore, through the reading and study of the sacred books, let the Word of the Lord run and be glorified and let the treasure of revelation entrusted to the Church increasingly fill the hearts of men. Just as the life of the Church grows through persistent participation in the Eucharistic mystery, so we may hope for a new surge of spiritual vitality from intensified veneration for God's word, which "lasts forever." (*Ibid.,* 25-26)

The Council, besides exhorting all the faithful to read and study the Bible, also gave its unabashed endorsement to the scholars' modern historical-critical methods of biblical research. With profound respect and admiration for the biblical scholars and theologians of our age, whose rigorous scholarship has led us to a deeper understanding of the sacred page, we should note that the popular impression often (and unfortunately) given by their efforts and progress is that the Bible is merely a work of human production and that theology is only a matter of personal opinions. Perhaps the superficial over-simplifications which the mass media communicate are partly responsible for this impression of the scholars' serious work. Progress in the last two centuries in literary criticism, psychology and in other social sciences — welcome, needed and praiseworthy as it is — sometimes obscures the quality of revelation as a unique, objective gift of God which transcends, challenges and judges human wisdom and scientific progress. This contemporary obfuscation of the nature of revelation and theology can be detected in the way that theology has lost ground in the last thirty years, especially in American Catholic institutions of higher education. Catholic theology in many of these colleges and universities has often been drastically reduced as a requirement or absorbed into a Religious Studies department as one among many religious traditions. Or even worse — a trend in many "Catholic" colleges — Catholic theology has been classified as one of the humanities, a totally absurd (one might say blasphemous) reduction of the "unique and perfect Dove" of God's Wisdom to the level of merely human literature.

Recently Allan Bloom in his provocative *The Closing of the American Mind,* a book which infuriated many academicians perhaps because of the exposition of unpleasant truths about grave deficiencies in American higher education, wrote concerning the teaching of the Bible:

> To include it in the humanities is already a blasphemy, a denial of its own claims. There it is almost inevitably treated in one of two ways: It is subjected to modern "scientific" analysis, called the Higher Criticism, where it is dismantled, to show how "sacred" books are put together, and that they are not what they claim to be. It is useful as a mosaic in which one finds the footprints of many dead

civilizations. Or else the Bible is used in courses in comparative religion as one expression of the need for the "sacred" and as a contribution to the very modern, very scientific study of the structure of "myths." (Here one can join up with the anthropologists and really be alive.)

A teacher who treated the Bible naively, taking it at its word, or Word, would be accused of scientific incompetence and lack of sophistication. Moreover he might rock the boat and start the religious wars all over again, as well as a quarrel within the university between reason and revelation, which would upset comfortable arrangements and wind up by being humiliating to the humanities. Here one sees the traces of the Enlightenment's political project, which wanted precisely to render the Bible, and other old books, *"undangerous."* This project is one of the underlying causes of the impotence of the humanities. The best that can be done, it appears, is to teach "The Bible as Literature," as opposed to "as Revelation," which it claims to be. [19]

Allan Bloom addressed these comments to the teaching of the Bible in secular universities. Perhaps he could not even imagine that the situation is very similar in many Catholic colleges and universities. John Henry Newman more than a hundred years ago foresaw this "development" when he addressed the tendency of liberal education to view revealed religion as something to be tamed and domesticated, something to be made "undangerous," as Bloom put it. Newman exposed this inherent tendency of human knowledge with these words:

Knowledge, viewed as Knowledge, exerts a subtle influence in throwing us back on ourselves, and making us our own centre, and our minds the measure of all things. This then is the tendency of that Liberal Education, of which a University is the school, viz., to view Revealed Religion from an aspect of its own — to fuse and recast it — to tune it, as it were, to a different key, and to rest its harmonies —

to circumscribe it by a circle which unwarrantably amputates here, and unduly develops there; and all under the notion, conscious or unconscious, that the human intellect, self-educated and self-supported, is more true and perfect in its ideas and judgments than that of Prophets and Apostles, to whom the sights and sounds of Heaven were immediately conveyed. A sense of propriety, order, consistency, and completeness gives birth to a rebellious stirring against miracle and mystery, against the severe and the terrible.

This intellectualism first and chiefly comes into collision with precept, then with doctrine, then with the very principle of dogmatism; — a perception of the Beautiful becomes the substitute for faith. . . . Catholicism, as it has come down to us from the first, seems to be mean and illiberal . . . it must be treated with discrimination and delicacy, corrected, softened, improved, if it is to satisfy an enlightened generation. It must be stereotyped as the patron of arts, or the pupil of speculation, or the protege of science; it must play the literary academician, or the empirical philanthropist, or the political partisan; it must keep up with the age; some or other expedient it must devise, in order to explain away, or to hide, tenets under which the intellect labours and of which it is ashamed — its doctrine, for instance, of grace, its mystery of the Godhead, its preaching of the Cross, its devotion to the Queen of Saints, or its loyalty to the Apostolic See. [20]

We have observed Dante's unambiguous reverence and awe for Divine Revelation, expressed through the solemn procession in the first act of the drama in the garden. Let us now turn to the second act in which this Divine Wisdom confronts Dante and speaks to him personally. Up until this point he has been a spectator, but now he finds himself on center stage. Beatrice, the object of his youthful love, is now the glorious Lady, transformed and appearing to Dante as the stern judge and spurned lover. This encounter — or rather, confrontation — is truly the dramatic center of the *Comedy*, charged with emotional pain, spiritual soul-searching, and tears of shame and repentance. Beatrice ruthlessly exposes Dante's sins: his betrayal of her, his aberrations and his infidelities. Dante is shaken and shattered as his life and motives are laid bare and condemned with such severity.

Although the setting and the style of this scene is allegorical, nonetheless this confrontation is deeply personal and has all the pathos of classical Greek drama, of Shakespearean plays and of modern masterpieces of dramatic art. Perhaps Dante's psychological insights are at their keenest here as he describes the story of his own soul: his vulnerability, his broken spirit, his shame and guilt over the tragedy of his infidelity and- ill-spent life. Beatrice demands this catharsis and requires a verbal confession because she loves Dante and desires his total conversion and salvation — Dante's ultimate good. And Dante, the author, knows this.

This utterly painful encounter with Beatrice reveals Dante's profound concept of sin and his understanding of God's compassion, forgiveness and salvific will. Beatrice, representing God's Wisdom, acts not only as a dispassionate judge but also as a compassionate healer and lover who rehabilitates Dante and even entrusts him with a prophetic mission for the Church and the world. Dante, from being a broken, helpless sinner, emerges forgiven, renewed and empowered with a new purpose in life — a truly miraculous event!

But when and where did this spiritual event actually take place in Dante's life? It is difficult to say. In the previous chapter we explored Dante's personal crises and his periods of *traviamento*. When he was writing these concluding cantos of *Purgatory* Dante was probably in his late forties. There is still a great divergence of opinions among Dante scholars over exactly when and where he composed the *Comedy*. Although these facts are most important for an understanding of the genesis of the work and its relationship to the life and spirituality of Dante, there is little consensus among the scholars; this area of Dante studies will doubtless remain an arena of learned debate for many generations to come.

However, there is substantial evidence that Dante composed the *Purgatory* between the years 1308 and 1315. As we know, these were years of exile, fraught with the hardships of uprootedness and poverty and two of the most shaking disappointments in Dante's life: the failure of the papacy (the Avignon period began in 1309) and the dashing of his hopes for the empire (Henry VII died in 1313). Although passionately involved during these years in promoting the reform of the papacy and the restoration of the empire, Dante no doubt occasionally found some peaceful interludes of retreat where he could reflect upon the world, the Church and himself in the light of divine revelation.

Dante probably found the places for his contemplation in the quiet hills of the upper valley of the Arno known as the Casentino. We noted in the preceding chapter that the exiled Dante found shelter there in the castles of the powerful Ghibelline family, the Guidi. We also noticed that Dante was familiar with the monastic foundations of St. Romuald in this same region. The most famous in Dante's time was at Camaldoli, not far from the Guidi castles. These foundations were designed by Romuald for hermits who would devote themselves to contemplation within the framework of the Benedictine tradition. These *eremi* (literally, deserts) were scattered in the woods and valleys in Dante's time and it is likely that Dante knew them by his own experience.

He mentions in his works (cf. *Par.* XXI, 109-111) another famous foundation of St. Romuald: Fonte Avellana. There is a strong tradition, mentioned in the previous chapter, that Dante spent some time there where St. Peter Damian had been prior in the eleventh century. In any ·case, Dante gives ample evidence that he was familiar with these places of contemplation. We can, therefore, reasonably conclude that he found solitude in these "deserts" where he was able to enter deeply into the "I - Thou" relationship with the Lord.

It is significant in this encounter with Beatrice that Dante turns to his constant companion, guide and mentor, Virgil, and finds that Virgil is no longer with him :

> I turned to the left — with all the confidence
> that makes a child run to its mother's arms,
> when he is frightened or needs comforting —
>
> .   .   .
>
> But Virgil was not there. We found ourselves
> without Virgil, sweet father, Virgil to whom
> for my salvation I gave up my soul.
> (*Purg.* XXX, 43-51)

No doubt the repetition of "Virgil" three times suggests a sacred invocation, similar to the verse "Come, O Bride from Lebanon," which had just been sung three times by Solomon to herald the arrival of Divine Wisdom. Repetition three times of the divine name or attributes (e.g. the *trisagion)* was a familiar liturgical practice in Dante's time. It seems that by these words Dante has already unwittingly confessed the sin of placing his salvation in human wisdom, since Virgil in the *Comedy* generally represents human wisdom and the light of reason. But Virgil is no longer with him.

Dante alone must now face Beatrice, Divine Wisdom and the light of faith. This solitude before the light of divine revelation is at first terrifying for Dante since he had sought and found comfort and even "the salvation of his soul" in the human resources of philosophy and reason. The role of Virgil had indeed been salvific for Dante (Virgil had received his mission at the request of Beatrice), and there was something truly sacred in it. Perhaps nowhere in Dante's works is the contrast — and complementarity — of nature and grace better expressed. Human nature and human wisdom are indeed sacred gifts — graces, in the general sense of communications of God's gratuitous love — but they are nonetheless quite inadequate for attaining complete salvation. They await their completion and perfection by supernatural grace and Divine Wisdom, given initially in the gift of faith. The well-known Scholastic axiom, "Grace builds on nature," comes to mind as we see Dante ingeniously translating those abstract terms into poetic and personal images that tell the drama of his own spiritual story.

The profoundly personal aspect of this passage is highlighted by one word, which may not strike us modern readers as anything unusual. It is the personal name *Dante,* which appears only once in the entire *Comedy.* It is Beatrice who uses it to address him at this point:

> Dante, though Virgil leaves you, do not weep,
> not yet, that is, for you shall have to weep
> from yet another wound. Do not weep yet.
> (*Purg.* XXX, 55-57)

Dante a few verses later defends this mention of his name by stating, "hearing my name called out, which of necessity I here record. . . . " According to the canons of "high poetry," which prevailed in Dante's time, a poet should avoid writing about himself except when a serious necessity arose. We know from Dante's *Convivio* of two occasions when a writer could properly do so:

> Speaking of oneself is allowed for necessary reasons, and among several necessary reasons two are more obvious. One would be when great disgrace or danger could not be avoided if a man did not speak of himself. It is then conceded for the reason that choosing the lesser evil of two paths is almost like choosing the good one. This necessity moved Boethius to speak of himself so that under the pretext of consoling himself he might apologize for the perpetual infamy of his exile and demonstrate that this was unjust, seeing that no one else was defending him.
>
> The other necessity arises when speaking about oneself produces a great advantage for others by way of teaching; this reason moved Augustine in his *Confessions* to speak of himself because through the process of his life, which was from bad to good and from good to better, and from better to best, he gave us an example and a teaching which could not be received by any testimony so true as this.
>
> (*Conv.* I, II, 12-14)

Both these necessities are present in Dante's *Comedy*. His self-consolation and self-defense, in the manner of Boethius, are very obvious at times, especially in his encounter with Cacciaguida (*Par.* XI) and in his examinations by Peter, James and John (*Par.* XXV - XXVII). However, the second necessity prevails in the Comedy. In his letter to Can Grande he explicitly stated that his purpose in writing the *Comedy* was "to remove people from misery to happiness." With these and other words of that letter Dante clearly defined the scope of his major work as a moral teaching and example for his fellow Christians. He thus presents his own conversion story as an example for the salvation of others.

Like Augustine in his *Confessions* Dante tells his own conversion and his ascent to mystical union with God. There are many similarities between Augustine's *Confessions* and Dante's *Comedy*, as we have already noticed. Many scholars have studied these likenesses in detail, some concluding that the very structure of Augustine's work served as a model for Dante's.[21] Without attempting a detailed comparison of these two masterpieces of Christian autobiography, we can notice at least that for Dante, as for Augustine, the spiritual journey was an intimately personal conversion after radical intellectual, moral and psychological crises which led to a discovery of God's love. In these "searchers," philosophy and theology played major roles, and in both men erotic love and its purification were major factors in the process. Both shared the fruit of their lived experience of theology (their "spiritualities") with their fellow Christians as an example, teaching and concrete testimony. We today enjoy the advantage of these two monumental and moving witnesses to the Christian experience.

Let us now turn our attention to Beatrice, who is described initially in masculine terms as an admiral supervising his ship (cf. *Purg.* XXX, 58). There is a regal sternness in her face and the tone of her voice is sharp and authoritative. She commands Dante to look at her, and then addresses her reprimands to the on-looking, compassionate angels as she describes Dante in the third person:

> Not only through the working of the spheres,
> which brings each seed to its appropriate end
> according as the stars keep company,
> but also through the bounty of God's grace,
> raining from vapors born so high above
> they cannot be discerned by human sight,
> was this man so endowed, potentially,
> in early youth — had he allowed his gifts
> to bloom, he would have reaped abundantly.
> But the more vigorous and rich the soil,
> the wilder and the weedier it grows
> when left untilled, its bad seeds flourishing.
> (*Purg.* XXX, 109-120)

We recognize in these verses the content of the passage from the *Convivio* in which Dante had described the human soul as a "divine

seed" or a field sown with divine seeds — the gifts of nature and grace
which flourish into an abundant harvest, if the human will worked at
eliminating the weeds and cultivating the good plants sown by God. In
Beatrice's reprimand Dante is made painfully aware of his abuse of the
gifts and talents that had been given him. It should be noted that
Beatrice does not accuse Dante of any of the "capital sins," but rather of
a neglect of gifts given him — the neglect and degradation of a person
who did not develop his natural and supernatural potentials.

Strong and incisive as these words of Beatrice are, the more
caustic accusations are yet to come:

> There was a time my countenance sufficed,
> as I let him look into my young eyes
> for guidance on the straight path to his goal;
> but when I passed into my second age
> and changed my life for Life, that man you see
> strayed after others and abandoned me;
> when I had risen from the flesh to spirit,
> become more beautiful, more virtuous,
> he found less pleasure in me, loved me less,
> and wandered from the path that leads to truth,
> pursuing simulacra of the good,
> which promise more than they can ever give.
> I prayed that inspiration come to him
> through dreams and other means: in vain I tried
> to call him back, so little did he care.
> To such depths did he sink that, finally,
> there was no other way to save his soul
> except to have him see the Damned in Hell.
> That this might be, I visited the Dead,
> and offered my petition and my tears
> to him who until now has been his guide.
> (*Purg.* XXX, 118-141)

In this passage Beatrice reminds Dante how her presence on earth
— her beautiful eyes and face — had kept him in youth on the "straight
path to his goal." But then, after her death when she had passed into her

"second age" and had changed her earthly life for "Life itself," Dante had abandoned her and strayed after others. Her second beauty, which transcended her earthly beauty, was not an object of Dante's intense love. He wandered from the path that leads to truth and pursued "idols of the good, which promise more than they can give." Beatrice mentions that she had visited him in dreams and, by other means, had tried in vain to save him. But he did not respond. Dante had sunk to such depths that only the vision of the damned in Hell could move him. So as a last resort Beatrice had visited that land of the dead and tearfully petitioned Virgil to help Dante.

This dramatic passage is no mere reprimand for a man's neglect of his talents. It is the outpouring of a jealous lover's heart. Such an outburst reminds us of wrenching passages in the Hebrew prophets — Hosea and Jeremiah come to mind — in which God as an outraged lover rebukes Israel for her infidelities and love affairs with pagan gods. Beatrice, the jealous lover — image of the Divine Hound of Heaven — had gone to all lengths to "hunt down" and save Dante. Later in the *Comedy* Dante will address these words of recognition, praise and petition to her:

> O lady in whom all my hope takes strength,
> and who for my salvation did endure
> to leave her footprints on the floor of Hell,
> through your own power, through your own excellence
> I recognize the grace and the effect
> of all those things I have seen with my eyes.
> From bondage into freedom you led me
> by all those paths, by using all those means
> which were within the limits of your power.
> Preserve in me your great munificence,
> so that my soul which you have healed may be
> pleasing to you when it slips from the flesh.
> (*Par.* XXXI, 79-90)

Beatrice's descent into Hell for Dante's salvation is similar to Christ's descent into Hell for humanity's salvation (cf. *Inf.* IV, 52-63). The divine condescension for human salvation is expressed in Christ's death and descent to hell, and thus reveals the pattern of divine grace as a descending love which undergoes suffering and humiliation for the sake of the beloved. Beatrice, the lady who stoops to conquer, secures Dante's salvation in a way analogous to the *Christus Victor,* who conquered death and won human salvation by his descent into death and Hell.

Beatrice's harsh rebukes so overwhelm Dante with shame and guilt that he becomes paralyzed and speechless. But Beatrice continues to make her grave charges. She accuses him of forsaking the journey "of love for that Good beyond which nothing exists to which a man's heart may aspire." She wants Dante to confess what pitfalls and chains forced him to abandon the journey. Dante finally confesses, as he weeps: "Those things with their false joys, offered me by the world, led me astray when I no longer saw your countenance." Beatrice comments on his confession with these words:

> You never saw in Nature or in Art
> a beauty like the beauty of my form,
> which clothed me once and now is turned to dust;
> and if that perfect beauty disappeared
> when I departed from the world, how could
> another mortal object lure your love?
> (*Purg.* XXXI, 49-54)

Beatrice then becomes sarcastic, comparing Dante to a full-fledged bird that should know by experience the dangers of the nets, traps and arrows used by hunters to ensnare and kill young birds:

> No pretty girl or any other brief
> attraction should have weighed down your wings,
> and left you waiting for another blow.
> The fledgling waits a second time, a third,
> but not the full-fledged bird: before his eyes
> in vain the net is spread, the arrow shot.
> (*Purg.* XXXI, 58-63)

Her sarcasm is relentless as she commands Dante, now bending his head like a scolded child, to lift his "beard," rather than his head or chin. She thus calls attention to Dante's mature age, which should have made him aware of dangers to his spiritual welfare.

We have quoted many passages from this moving dialogue in the garden because they seem to be the key which opens the heart of Dante. They reveal the essential story of his inner life from his youth to his old age. Although we have already in previous chapters gleaned many elements of Dante's interior life from his earlier works, here in this scene we witness a dramatic summary of his spiritual life up to this point. Dante essentially tells his story here in terms of a love affair with Beatrice, the central theme of his *Vita Nuova* and an important theme of the *Convivio,* as we noticed in the previous chapter.

Here on the summit of Purgatory Dante expresses the very essence of sin in the traditional terms found in the Hebrew prophets, the Christian Gospel and the great saints and mystics. Even though Dante was influenced by Greek philosophical concepts of sin as ignorance or error — an offense against nature, self or others — he perceives here in the encounter with Beatrice the profoundly personalistic dimension of sin as a free, willful betrayal of the love given by God to His children: a violation of the great Covenant of Love.

In this poignant allegorical scene on the mountain Beatrice is not a conventional, lifeless personification of some abstract idea or quality (the "allegory of the poets," known to Dante through his classical studies). Dante employs here the "allegory of the theologians" and biblical authors, who wrote of real persons and events in history. The historical Beatrice is speaking, accusing and forgiving, just as the Divine Lover once spoke through His prophets and ultimately through His Son, the Word made flesh.

In the sacred history recorded in the Bible God's call of a prophet is often accompanied with a purification rite which follows a confession of sin. A classical description of a prophet's call is found in the sixth chapter of Isaiah. There Isaiah describes his call in the context of a vision of the divine glory which he received in the temple of Jerusalem. The awe-inspiring aspect of divine holiness and glory fills him with a profound sense of his personal sin and the sins of his people. He feels hopeless and doomed as he confesses his sinfulness. This confession is a prelude to the purification rite administered by a heavenly creature (a *seraph*) who cleanses the prophet's lips with a burning coal. By this action the prophet receives forgiveness of his sins and is then sent on his mission.

After Dante's confession of sin to Beatrice he was immersed in the purifying stream of the river Lethe in the earthly paradise (cf. *Purg.* XXXI, 94-105). The waters destroy all memory of sin and prepare Dante for the further graces and visions which will be given for his mission as a prophet. His baptism in water evokes many biblical passages in which salvation and rebirth take place through water: the passage of Moses and the Israelites through the Red Sea, the crossing of the Jordan, and many healing miracles recorded in the Old Testament. In the New Testament there are many passages in which water and ritual purifications function as sacraments and preparations for a prophetic mission. Christ's baptism in the Jordan is certainly a paradigmatic event, prefigured in so many events, such as the crossings of the Red Sea and the Jordan. At His baptism Jesus is designated by God as His Son and Prophet and is given the mission to enlighten the nations by His saving words and deeds. The Acts of the Apostles described Paul's call to be a prophet: the heavenly voice and light sends him on a sacred mission which begins only after his baptism in water.

These biblical antecedents were undoubtedly in Dante's mind as he describes his baptism in the earthly paradise and his commission to be a prophet which occurs toward the end of the four-act drama in the garden. Beatrice will bestow on him the prophetic mission of communicating to the world the vision she gives him. The content of that vision, which concerns the salvation of the Church and of the world, will be the subject of the next chapter.

Chapter Five

PROPHET OF HOPE

In the last chapter we explored the influence of the Bible on Dante's life and writings mainly by focusing on a particular passage of his *Comedy* which articulates that influence so clearly. That passage, which we partially explicated, is, as we noted, a drama in four acts. So far we considered only its first two acts: the solemn procession and Dante's confession before Beatrice. In this chapter we will resume the drama, which leads to Beatrice's bestowal on Dante of a prophetic mission. The subjects of Dante as *prophet* and his prophetic message will then be the main topics of this chapter.

The last two acts of the drama in the earthly Paradise are just as complex and dense with meanings as were the first two acts. They correspond to and complement the first two acts in this way: the first act was a formal, allegorical pageant in which impersonal figures represented the books of the Bible and other divine gifts; then the very personal encounter between Dante and Beatrice takes place in act two. In the third act the personal dimension continues as Beatrice unveils the beauty of her eyes and smile to Dante — a revelation in which Dante sees the splendor of Christ and His love, which blind him temporarily. Then the last act is somewhat similar to the first: allegorical figures will reenact the drama of salvation history beginning with Christ's sacrifice on the cross in reparation for Adam's sin, His resurrection, ascension and finally the history of the Church down to Dante's time. At the end of this complex vision the degradation and corruption of the Church — the violation of God's salvific plan for humanity — will be the sad message that Beatrice will commission Dante to convey to the world. Like the

messages of the Hebrew prophets before him, Dante's message will be
a word of gloom, a severe warning and a call to conversion. But above all
it will be a word of hope for future salvation.

The third act of the drama in which Beatrice reveals her beauty to
Dante could be best described as a quasi-mystical experience in which
Dante momentarily sees the brilliant beauty of Christ, reflected in
Beatrice's eyes and smile. We will comment further on this Christocentric experience in the next chapter where we will also reflect more
deeply on the allegorical figure of the griffin, which represents Christ in
this scene. At present we could summarize the scene in this way: the
griffin who draws the chariot (the Church) in which Beatrice (Divine
Wisdom) is enthroned comes to the tree (Divine Justice) in the garden.
He attaches the wooden pole (the Cross) to it, causing the tree, which
had been defoliated by Adam's sin, to burst into new life. The allegorical
meaning of the scene is obviously the redemptive work of Christ, the
new Adam, who restores man's original justice with God. The griffin
then ascends into heaven, leaving on earth the chariot and Beatrice: His
Church and His abiding presence in Word and Sacrament.

Beatrice then invites Dante to witness the final act of the drama:
the history of Christ's Church, which suffered from persecutions, the
acquisition of wealth and power, heresies, schisms and then finally
reached her catastrophic nadir in the sinful alliance of the papacy with
the French monarchy in Dante's time. Beatrice introduces this final act,
composed of seven tableaux, with these words to Dante:

> A short time you shall dwell outside the walls;
> then you, with me, shall live eternally,
> citizen of that Rome where Christ is Roman.
> Now, for the good of sinners in your world,
> observe the chariot well, and what you see,
> put into writing, when you have returned.
> (*Purg.* XXXII, 100-105)

Dante then observes the history of the Church, expressed through
allegorical figures, beginning with the persecutions from the Roman
Emperors (the eagle), then the donation of Constantine (the eagle
again) which, though well-intentioned conferred on the Church the

burdens of corrupting wealth and temporal rule, then the heresies and schisms (the fox and dragon) which ravaged for centuries the already damaged chariot. Finally the chariot is transformed into a hideous monster on which is seated an "ungirt whore," exchanging kisses with a lustful giant, who beats her and drags the monster off into the woods. The whore and the giant represent respectively the papacy and the French monarchy.

The details of this last tableau, which depicts the horrible metamorphosis of the Church, are taken from John's visions in the Apocalypse. Dante uses them to describe the horrendous state of the Church at the time he was writing this passage — the early fourteenth century, when the papacy in the persons of Boniface VIII and Clement V had entered an "adulterous" alliance with the French kings, particularly Philip the Fair. The beating no doubt refers to Philip's assault through his agents and army on Boniface at Anagni; the removal to the woods symbolizes the transferal of the papacy with the cooperation of Clement V to Avignon in southern France. Mutual greed for power and money — portrayed as erotic lust — issued in violence and disaster for the Church.

Beatrice then explains the meaning of the scenes that Dante has just witnessed and confers on him this prophetic mission:

> Know that the vessel which the serpent broke
> was, and is not. Let him who bears the blame
> learn that God's vengeance has no fear of sops.
>   The eagle that shed feathers on the car
> that would become a monster, then a prey,
> will not remain forever without heirs;
>   I tell you this because I clearly see
> those stars, already near, that will bring in
> a time — its advent nothing can prevent —
> in which five hundred, ten, and five shall be
>   God's emissary, born to kill the giant
> and the usurping whore with whom he sins.
> Perhaps my prophecy with its dark words,

> obscure as those of Themis or the Sphinx,
> has not convinced you but confused your mind;
>
> .   .   .
>
> Note well my words: what I have said to you,
> you will repeat, as you teach those who live
> that life which is merely a race to death.
> And when you write, be sure that you describe
> the sad condition of the tree you saw
> despoiled, not once but twice, here on this spot.
> Whoever robs this tree or breaks its limbs
> sins against God, blasphemes in deeds, for He
> created it to serve His Holy Self.
> Because God's first soul tasted of this tree,
> more than five thousand years in pain he yearned
> for Him Who paid the penalty Himself.
>
> .   .   .
>
> it is my wish you carry back with you
> if not my words themselves, at least some trace,
> as pilgrims bring their staves back wreathed with palm.
> (*Purg.* XXXIII, 34-78)

The identification of the mysterious figure, called the "five hundred, ten and five," has baffled and intrigued readers and scholars for centuries. No precise solution or agreement has yet been reached, and most likely Dante was purposely being vague here. It is probably a code in the manner of the Jewish Cabala, which was popular in Dante's time. The Roman numbers, when rearranged, correspond to the letters DUX, a Latin word meaning "leader." The leader here is obviously a savior, and perhaps can be identified with another cryptic savior figure: the hound, endowed with the divine qualities of "wisdom, love and power," announced by Virgil (cf. *Inf.* I). Many interpreters think that Dante is alluding here to Henry VII, whom he hailed as the true Roman emperor who would restore peace to Italy and to Christendom in general. As we shall see later, Henry will be described in terms of a savior and Christ figure, but even after Henry's failure and death Dante still looked forward to a savior. In any case, this is a prophecy of hope in the coming of "God's emissary," who will destroy the evils which unworthy popes and secular powers have perpetrated on the sacred vessel, Christ's Church.

This passage clearly shows that Dante was acutely aware and convinced of his urgent prophetic mission to the Church. Divine Revelation in the person of Beatrice has willed it. Beatrice's direct command to put into writing what he has seen recalls the Book of Revelation (cf. 1:11) where John the prophet and visionary is told by the angel to "write down what he has seen." The Book of Revelation, the record of an apocalyptic vision which came to John through the mediation of an angel, is an important source for understanding Dante's vision in the garden and his mission as prophet. Dante obviously saw himself as another John, communicating a divine message to the troubled Church of his time. Dante was most likely also influenced by the famous interpretation of the Book of Revelation (or the Apocalypse) by Joachim of Fiore, whom Dante believed to be endowed with the true "prophetic spirit." Joachim's apocalyptic prophecies about the imminent reform and renewal of the Church were enthusiastically invoked by the Spiritual Franciscans in Dante's time, especially by Pier Giovanni Olivi and Ubertino da Casale, two fiery preachers whose sermons and writings were known to Dante. Although Dante shared their zeal for Church reform, he differed from them in many other respects. [1]

We might pause here to examine Dante's concept of the Church and her role in human salvation, since Dante perceives his mission in life now as a prophet in the service of the Church and ultimately of Divine Providence, identified as God's justice or will. Dante has not left us a specific treatise on ecclesiology. St. Thomas himself did not compose a *De Ecclesia* treatise. But we can find scattered throughout Dante's works many descriptions of the Church, which, gathered together, present a profoundly rich ecclesiology. We could thus conclude that Dante arrived at an original and bold synthesis of ecclesiology based on the biblical data, the theological reflections of his time and from his own lived experience. [2]

In his famous treatise on political philosophy, the *De Monarchia*, Dante presents many insights on the nature and purpose of the Church, especially on her relationship to the Empire. Although the *De Monarchia* is not his final word on the Church, Dante never repudiated the opinions expressed in it. In his later years while composing the final cantos of *Purgatory* and the *Paradise* Dante saw the Church's role in human salvation as more and more important and crucial vis-à-vis the role of the Empire. It is impossible to trace the exact evolution of Dante's thought on the Church, since we cannot date with precision the writing of the *De Monarchia* or specific parts of the *Commedia;* nonetheless we do notice an increasing conviction on Dante's part that the Church's, and not the Empire's, mission is more significant for human happiness and salvation. No doubt the failure and death of Henry VII in 1313 was a determining factor in Dante's loss of confidence in the Empire's capacity to bring about peace and unity in the world.

In his *De Monarchia* (henceforth abbreviated as *DM*) he enunciates his basic understanding of the Church in these simple words:

> The form of the Church is none other than the life of Christ, which includes both His words and His deeds. For His life was the model and exemplar of the Church militant, especially for its shepherds and above all for its chief shepherd whose office it is to feed the lambs and the sheep.
>
> (*DM* III, XIV, 3)

This succinct description of the nature of the Church goes right to the heart of the matter, presenting as the primary "model of the Church" the very mystery of Christ. It reminds us of the opening lines of the Vatican II document on the Church, *Lumen Gentium.* For Dante the mystery of the Church can be understood only in terms of Christ and His life. Christ's life — His poverty, humility and above all His charity — is *the* exemplar for all Christians, especially for the leaders of the flock.

Even though Dante was strongly influenced by the philosophy of Aristotle, which recognized the real worth of nature and of man's natural capacities for attaining wisdom and moral virtue, he nonetheless saw the Church's office as necessary and absolutely different from nature's. The Church had been given "goods" which nature cannot give. Her office was to administer these gifts given only to her by God Himself. They were gifts freely given to Her, constituting Her as the voice of God Himself, as a Light to illuminate man's daily struggles in life. For Dante, "The Church is not caused by nature, but is the work of

God, Who says, 'On this rock I will build my Church' (Mt 16:18) and 'I have finished the work You gave me to do' (Jn 17:4)."[3]

In Dante's ecclesiology the Church, as God's work in the world, has the office of meeting and helping man so that he may not feel like a boat adrift in a stormy sea. The Church has the authoritative mission to reveal truths which are outside the possibility of human reason's capacity to comprehend. Her task is to teach the truth, administer the sacraments, and practice charity. She is not a political guide, a legislator or a punisher; her office is to be a messenger of truth and a light of perfect love. She may only administer temporal goods, not possess them.

Dante was boldly radical on this last point and opposed many of the theologians, canon lawyers, curialists and popes of his time on this issue. His uncompromising audacity is clearly stated in this famous passage:

> But the Church is in no sense properly disposed to receive temporal things, on account of the express prohibition recorded by Matthew: 'Possess no gold or silver, no money in your belts, no purse for your journey.' (Mt 10:9) . . . Even though we assume that Constantine on his side could make the donation, the act itself was impossible because the receiver did not have the proper disposition. It is clear, therefore, that the Church was no more able to accept it as a possession than the Emperor could grant the Church guardianship over one part or other of his patrimony so long as it was without prejudice to his supreme ownership, which is a unity admitting no division.
>
> Similarly the vicar of Christ may accept a grant, not as proprietor, but as administrator of the fruits for the benefit of the Church and the poor of Christ — as the Apostles are known to have done. *(DM* III, X, 14-17)

The "poor of Christ" is a recurrent theme in Dante's works and reminds us of the Church's "preferential option for the poor," a grave concern expressed repeatedly by recent popes, bishops, and exponents of liberation theology in our times. Dante often excoriated the

canon lawyers of his day and age — the "Decretalists" — whose
concern was ecclesiastical benefices, which amounted to money and
prestige for themselves and their families. He comments on these
"presumptuous jurists" with these contemptuous words:

> These same people have no pity on Christ's poor, whom
> they rob not only by taking Church revenues but by daily
> plundering the very patrimony of the Church. The Church is
> impoverished while they make a pretence of justice as a
> means of excluding the very dispenser of justice. Nor can
> the element of divine judgment be excluded from such
> impoverishment, since the Church's riches are used neither
> to help the poor — who may claim them as their patrimony
> — nor administered with gratitude toward the Emperor
> who provided them. . . .
>
> What does it matter to them that the Church's sub-
> stance is being wasted so long as it swells the estates of
> their own relatives? But perhaps it is better to continue with
> our argument, meanwhile in pious silence awaiting the help
> of Our Savior.   (*DM* II, X, 1-3)

A smile naturally comes to our lips as we read those last words of
Dante: when did Dante ever keep a "pious silence"? We have observed
earlier some of Dante's vehement invectives against the ecclesiastical
exploiters of Christ's poor and we will observe later some even more
virulent outbursts. Dante always put his trust and hope in Our Savior's
help, but while he waited he never remained silent for very long. Here
in the *DM* Dante employs subtle arguments from reason and divine
revelation, systematically organized and written in Latin after the
fashion of the Scholastics. Later he will express in his native tongue
with bursts of passionate indignation his deepest feelings and convic-
tions in several passages of his *Paradise* — of all places!

Before we examine those passages we might enumerate some of
Dante's favorite images of the Church. The one that recurs most often
is the Church as the Spouse or Bride of Christ — *la bella sposa* — whom
Christ acquired for Himself by His blood shed on the cross. Another
favorite image is the vineyard or garden, often laid waste by earthly

rulers or ecclesiastical leaders who have become ravaging wolves. The Church as most faithful mother (*mater piissima*) is also a recurrent theme. These are all biblical images which Dante found in the Old and New Testaments, revealing once again Dante's profound biblical faith. The earthly Church as militant, i.e., as an army on the march toward her purification in Purgatory and her ultimate triumph in Paradise as the heavenly White Rose, is also a familiar concept in Dante's writings. He perceives the Church in these three stages as the total mystical Body of Christ: militant, suffering and triumphant. He perceived himself in military terms as a knight-errant and champion of the militant Church when he has Beatrice introduce him to St. James in Paradise with these words: "There is no son of the Church Militant with greater hope than his . . . and this is why he is allowed to come from Egypt to behold Jerusalem before his fighting days on earth are done." (*Par.* XXV, 51-57)

This brief self-description focuses on Dante's virtue of hope; it also sums up his role as a Christian pilgrim who has experienced a foretaste of his final goal, the heavenly Jerusalem. The Church as pilgrim was a dominant theme in Dante's ecclesiology, as it was in the documents of Vatican II.

Dante was always a loyal Catholic layman, not a disgruntled, angry rebel against the Church, as some historians and literary critics have portrayed him. His "militant" temperament was expressed verbally in defense of the Church and the Gospel. His aims were those of an apostle and prophet; his love for Christ's vineyard echoed the Hebrew prophets' love for Israel, God's chosen vineyard. There is perhaps no stronger or more eloquent expression of his love, outside the *Comedy,* than in his letter to the Italian Cardinals, written probably in 1314, when the Cardinals were assembled in conclave after the death of Clement V. The conclave, which took place near Avignon, numbered only twenty-four Cardinals, six of whom were Italian, the rest French. The French monarchy had enticed Clement to reside in France and the French Cardinals were also puppets of the monarch in the fierce power struggle between the French kings and the papacy at that time. Dante is addressing this pathetic situation in his letter.

He begins by quoting Jeremiah's lament over the fallen Jerusalem, "solitary and widowed." He then compares Jerusalem to Rome, the sacred fold chosen by Christ, the shepherd. Rome, once bathed in the blood of Peter and Paul, is now abandoned and widowed. Dante's prophetic role, similar to Jeremiah's, is quite obvious here. He castigates the cardinals for their irresponsibility, their greed and their neglect of the Church's welfare:

> But you, who are, as it were, the centurions of the first rank of the Church militant, neglecting to guide the chariot of the Spouse of the Crucified along the track which lay before you, have gone astray from the track, just as the false charioteer Phaethon did. And you, whose duty it was to enlighten the flock that follows you through the forest on its pilgrimage here below, have brought it along with yourselves to the verge of the precipice. . . .
>
> You who sell doves in the Temple, where what is priceless is made merchandise to the detriment of those who come and go there. . . . Do not make light of the patience of Him who awaits your repentance. . . . How else can I enlighten you except by comparing you to Demetrius who consented to Alcimus?   (*Epistula* VIII, 4)

This passage contains several forceful comparisons. One of the most fascinating is the comparison of the cardinals to Phaethon, a mythological character who often appears in Dante's works. Dante's version of the myth follows closely Ovid's rendition in his *Metamorphoses*. According to the fable Phaethon was the son of Phoebus (Apollo, the sun god). When Phaethon's divine origins were questioned, his father, to demonstrate his affection, solemnly promised him whatever he wished. Phaethon made the request to drive the chariot of the sun for an entire day. Phoebus tried in vain to dissuade him from such a dangerous and mad enterprise, but Phaethon insisted. Once in the sky Phaethon became terrified, and the horses, accustomed to the experienced hands of his father, began a wild course, upsetting the cosmic order and the heavenly constellations. The mountains and woods were set on fire, the rivers dried up, and entire cities destroyed. The burning Earth invoked the intervention of Jove, who put an end to the disaster with a lightning bolt and the body of Phaethon fell into the Po river.

Dante alluded to this myth in the final cantos of *Purgatory,* where he described the Church as a chariot more beautiful "than the chariot of the sun which strayed and was destroyed at the devout petition of the Earth, when Jove in his mysterious way was just." Here in the letter to the Italian cardinals Dante sees himself as "the devout earth" — as a spokesman for all Christendom — praying for the justice of God to intervene, as the cardinals lead the chariot of the Church on a destructive course. We have to admire Dante's poetic imagination here and, even more, his extraordinary courage. It is interesting to note that Newman in his *Apologia* used the same classical example of Phaethon to describe the assault of Liberalism upon the Church of England of his day. [4]

Another poignant example in this passage is Dante's comparison of Clement V to Alcimus and the cardinals to Demetrius. This biblical allusion comes from the First Book of Maccabees (7:9). Alcimus was the wicked high-priest appointed by Demetrius, the Syrian king, in opposition to the truly religious leader, Judas Maccabaeus. The cardinals, who had cooperated with Philip the Fair in the election of Clement were like the pagan king who chose the ungodly Alcimus over the real man of God.

Dante anticipates the objection that he was arrogantly posing as a protector of the Church and did not fear the punishment of Uzzah (cf. 2 S 6:6), who was struck dead for his irreverence toward the Ark of the Covenant. He responds to this accusation by stating:

> Truly I am one of the least of the sheep of the pasture of Jesus Christ; truly I abuse no pastoral authority, seeing that I possess no riches. By the grace, therefore, not of riches, but of God, I am what I am (1 Cor 15:10), and the zeal of His house has consumed me (Ps 8:3). For even from the mouth of babes and sucklings has been heard the truth well pleasing to God (Ps 63:10); and the man born blind confessed the truth, which the Pharisees not only concealed, but in their malice even tried to pervert. These are the justifications of my boldness. . . . Nor does Uzzah's presumption infect me,

> for he gave heed to the Ark, I to the unruly oxen that are
> dragging it away into the wilderness. May He who opened
> his eyes to bring salvation to the sinking boat (cf. Mt 8:26)
> give aid to the Ark!   (*Epistula* VIII, 5)

Dante continues in his diatribe against the cardinals, accusing them of usurping the office of shepherds and of leaving the sheep untended. He feels so alone in his protest as he cries out: "Only one voice, one alone of filial piety and that of a private individual, is heard at the funeral, as it were, of Mother Church!"

He also accuses the Italian prelates of neglecting the works of the great Fathers of the Church, such as Gregory the Great, Ambrose, Augustine, Dionysius, John Damascene and Bede. Instead, they study the works of the canon lawyers: "The Fathers sought after God as their end and highest good; these others get for themselves riches and benefices."

Dante reminds the cardinals that everyone is murmuring, muttering or thinking about what he is shouting out, but they do not testify to what they have seen. Some are even lost in sheer amazement at it all. Dante is astonished that the same Lord who moved the tongue of Balaam's donkey to speak does not move the brutes of his time to speak out and bear witness to their Maker.

At the end of the letter Dante ardently implores the cardinals to "fight together manfully for the Spouse of Christ, for the seat of the Spouse, which is Rome, for our Italy and, to speak more widely, for the whole City now in pilgrimage on earth . . . so that by offering yourselves in the contest with glory you may be able to hear 'Glory in the highest.'"

These outpourings from Dante reveal the soul of a sincere layman who, conscious of being only "one of the least sheep of the flock," is not content to remain dumb and timid at the sight of the Church's ruin. For him the role of the laity was not merely to "pay, pray and obey," as the pre-Vatican II adage put it. (Dante certainly prayed and obeyed, but was too poor to pay!) However, he was convinced of the duty and right of every Christian to speak out when it seemed necessary for the common good of the Church. He anticipated in this respect the clear teaching of Vatican II:

> An individual layman, by reason of the knowledge, com-
> petence or outstanding ability which he may enjoy, is
> permitted and sometimes even obliged to express his opi-
> nion on things which concern the good of the Church. . . .
> Let it always be done in truth, in courage, and in prudence
> with reverence and charity toward those who by reason of
> their sacred office represent the person of Christ.
>
> *(Lumen Gentium,* IV, 37)

It might be objected that Dante lacked prudence and reverence in this letter, but a careful reading of it will show that he addressed the cardinals reverently as "my Fathers" and repeatedly expressed respect for their sacred office as well as a child-like love for the Church, "most loving Mother and Spouse of Christ."

Dante's filial love for the Church, articulated through his bold exercise of the prophetic office within the Church, pervades this remarkable letter to the cardinals. The prophetic office of the laity was a most unpopular theme in the ecclesiastical circles of the early fourteenth century. It was fraught with justified suspicions of heresy. In fact, heresies abounded in that era, especially among reform movements initiated by the laity who saw the blatant corruption of the clergy and the need for a return to evangelical poverty and simplicity.

Distorted understandings of the priesthood of the laity and of the prophetical office of the laity were the main sources of almost all the heretical movements in the thirteenth and fourteenth centuries. Many of the heretics not only attacked the decadent lives of the clerics and religious, but they also sought to undermine the clerical office itself, which, in their opinion, claimed a monopoly on sacred charisms. They aimed at destroying the very distinction between clergy and laity. Dante had no sympathy for this heterodox aspect of the reformers, even though he joined in their ruthless condemnations of clerical corruption. He was always orthodox in his defense of the ordained priesthood and the unique charisms entrusted to the legitimate authorities in the Church. But he was also convinced of the legitimacy of the prophetic role of the laity in the Church, as his writings so clearly and so often demonstrate.

The role of the laity in the Church received little attention from the orthodox theologians of Dante's time. Historically this can be explained because of the countless heresies of lay origin which erupted in the Middle Ages, followed by even more serious divisions in the Church in the fifteenth and sixteenth centuries. It was not until the latter half of the nineteenth century that another courageous voice was heard in the midst of the Church that proclaimed in an orthodox way the prophetical office of the laity. It was the voice of John Henry Newman, often called a pioneer for the layman and an exponent of the "infallibility" of the laity.

Newman expressed his views on the laity's voice within the prophetical tradition in a series of lectures, collected in his *Via Media,* a work he composed while still an Anglican. This work proved to be a turning point in his intellectual and spiritual journey toward the Catholic Church. His views on this topic would reach their final form later when he wrote as a Catholic his famous article, "On Consulting the Faithful in Matters of Doctrine." Here are two paragraphs from his "Prophetical Office" lectures, which seem to summarize his position at that time:

> The humblest and meanest among Christians may defend the Faith against the whole Church, if the need arise. He has as much at stake in it and as much right to it, as Bishop or Archbishop, and has nothing to limit him in his protest, but his intellectual capacity for making it. The greater his attainments the more serviceably of course and the more suitably will he enter into the dispute; but all that learning has to do for him is to ascertain the fact, what is the meaning of the Creed in particular points, since matter of opinion it is not, any more than the history of the rise and spread of Christianity itself.
>
> There is what may be called Prophetical Tradition. Almighty God placed in His Church first Apostles, or Bishops, secondarily Prophets. Apostles rule and preach, Prophets expound. Prophets or Doctors are the interpreters of the revelation; they unfold and define its mysteries, they illuminate its documents, they harmonize its contents, they apply its promises. Their teaching is a vast system, not to be comprised in a few sentences, not to be embodied in

one code or treatise, but consisting of a certain body of Truth, pervading the Church like an atmosphere, irregular in its shape from its very profusion and exuberance; at times separable only in idea from Episcopal Tradition, yet at times melting away into legend and fable; partly written, partly unwritten, partly the interpretation, partly the supplement of Scripture, partly preserved in intellectual expressions, partly latent in the spirit and temper of Christians; poured to and fro in closets and upon the housetops, in liturgies, in controversial works, in obscure fragments, in sermons, in popular prejudices, in local customs. This I call Prophetical Tradition, existing primarily in the bosom of the Church itself, and recorded in such measure as Providence has determined in the writings of eminent men. This is obviously of a very different kind from the Episcopal Tradition, yet in its first origin it is equally Apostolic, and, viewed as a whole, equally claims our zealous maintenance.[5]

Newman saw that the authority-obedience relationship between hierarchy and laity needed completion by a special emphasis on the wholeness of the Church in which the laity could exercise its authentic freedom, creativity and responsibility. He saw the command-obedience model in the Church as being true, but not the whole truth; as being good, but not good enough for the needs of the Church at certain times. In this respect he was an adventurous forerunner of the Second Vatican Council and of our present post-conciliar age. Shared responsibility and collaboration between clergy and laity were aspects of Newman's vision, which he enunciated more clearly in his famous formula "consulting the faithful" — a phrase which was to cause so much trouble and suffering in Newman's life as a Roman Catholic. In fact most of his life as a Catholic was under a cloud of suspicion in the circles of the English Catholic hierarchy and the authorities in Rome. Although an orthodox theologian, he was considered an outsider, even in spite of the belated honor of the cardinalate, conferred on him by Pope Leo XIII in 1879. Because of his "novel" theological opinions, especially on the laity's office in the Church, Newman was like a prophet without honor in his own country and home; he lived a sort of spiritual exile within the bosom of the Catholic Church. In this respect Dante and Newman were kindred spirits.

Newman's article "On Consulting the Faithful in Matters of Doctrine," published in the Catholic periodical *The Rambler* in 1859, sent shock waves through the upper echelons of the Catholic clergy in England, resulting in accusations of heresy and his eventual recall to Rome to explain his bold statements. It would be beyond our scope here to present an analysis of that ground-breaking article. In it and in many of his works Newman was seeking to remedy some of the deficiencies in the Catholic Church, among which was the denial to the laity of their rightful place in the Church. He sought the truth, bore witness to it; but was often thwarted and suffered acutely for it. [6]

Some of the salient points of Newman's theology of the laity might be summarized by the following brief observations. He perceived the laity and the hierarchy as two distinct, but not separate, functions in the Church. The teaching Church (the *magisterium* invested in the pope and bishops) and the Church taught (the laity) both exercised an infallibility. Divine tradition resided in the whole Church and, while the teaching Church alone is endowed with the divine authority and power of defining revealed truth, it also at times needs various "instruments of .tradition." Among these instruments are the liturgy, the Fathers, and the *"consensus fidelium"* — the general agreement of the laity on a doctrine of faith. Their testimony to the truth, their "sense" of what is the true tradition, was considered by Newman to be an additional instrumental aid, together with Scripture, liturgy and the Fathers in defining the authentic faith of the Church. The *sensus fidelium* was certainly not in Newman's mind a substitute for the *magisterium* or for Scripture, but rather a living testimony of what the faithful actually believed. Newman claimed that the faithful should be "consulted" in this way: as witnesses to an already existing state of belief. Naturally, the word "consult" seemed heterodox at that time and Newman had to defend this ambiguous term in order to clear himself of charges of heresy.

Perhaps one excerpt from Newman's defense will help to elucidate his ideas on the laity's function:

In most cases when a definition is contemplated, the laity will have a testimony to give; but if ever there be an instance when they ought to be consulted, it is in the case of doctrines which bear directly upon devotional sentiments. Such is the Immaculate Conception, of which the *Rambler* was speaking in the sentence which has occasioned these remarks. The faithful people have ever a special function in regard to those doctrinal truths which relate to the objects of worship. Hence it is, that while the Councils of the fourth century were traitors to Our Lord's divinity, the laity vehemently protested against its impugners. Hence it is, that in a later age, when the learned Benedictines of Germany and France were perplexed in their enunciation of the Real Presence, Paschasius was supported by the faithful in his maintenance of it. The saints, again, are the object of religious cultus; and therefore it was the faithful, again, who urged on the Holy See, in the time of John XXII, to declare their beatitude in heaven, though so many Fathers spoke variously. And the blessed Virgin is pre-eminently an object of devotion; and therefore it is, I repeat, that though Bishops had already spoken in favour of her absolute sinlessness, the Pope was not content without knowing the feelings of the faithful. [7]

One of the examples that Newman gives of the laity's witness to a doctrinal truth that was not clearly defined by the *magisterium* is the belief in the beatific vision, a disputed question at the time of Pope John XXII. This was exactly the time when Dante was writing his *Paradise*. In fact the entire *Comedy* was a most eloquent witness to the belief which he, a layman, held together with most of the laity of his time that souls after Purgatory were admitted to the beatific vision in Paradise even before the final resurrection of the body. That particular belief was publicly and repeatedly denied by Pope John XXII throughout most of his pontificate. He retracted his position only toward the end of his life.

A brief excursus into this pope's life and teaching will be very illuminating and interesting at this point, since it will illustrate so clearly what Newman said in his article about the witness of the faithful to a doctrinal truth. John XXII was an elderly French bishop who was elected pope after the death of Clement V, several unsuccessful conclaves, and many disputes and strife. The Italian cardinals, to whom Dante wrote his famous letter, were threatened by the French and barely escaped with their lives from the first conclave which met in 1314 to elect a successor to Clement V.

The newly elected pope proved to be the most political of all the popes who lived in Dante's time. He even outdid Boniface VIII in his "sin of clericalism" and pompous imperialism. Boniface had already alienated the laity in his bull *Clericis Laicos* (1296), in which he stated "That the laity are hostile to the clergy is proved abundantly by antiquity, and is clearly taught by the experiences of the present." It was no great surprise that Boniface was arrested and abused by Catholic laymen, such as the Italian Sciarra Colonna and the Frenchman Nogaret at Anagni in 1303.

But John XXII widened the chasm between laity and clergy by using even more tyrannical and high-handed measures than Boniface used. He launched an "all out" heretic hunt with all the machinery of canonical Inquisition processes and varying degrees of penalties. He imposed interdicts on numerous cities and on entire territories. He also conducted a genuine crusade — troops included — against his political enemies in northern Italy. This crusade was intended to strengthen papal finances and extend French domination over the Ghibelline rebels there.

In theological matters he was the prototype of the Decretalist mentality. He interpreted everything in terms of legal, financial or political interests; he imposed ecclesiastical censures on purely political grounds and identified his politics with the Church itself. Hierarchy for him was equated with religion. His sermons were punctuated with political views, unambiguous remarks against the Immaculate Conception of Mary, and repeated denials that souls separated from the body enjoy the beatific vision before the final bodily resurrection.

On this last doctrinal matter he was opposing the commonly held belief of the faithful and many theologians. After much pressure from the laity and a commission of cardinals and theologians he was finally forced to retract his teaching and to recognize the "common doctrine" and belief of the Church on this point. [8] His retraction came after Dante's death. Perhaps that retraction together with his canonization of Thomas Aquinas in 1323 (two years after Dante's death) might have helped Dante see some saving graces in this man whom he vigorously condemned in *Paradise* XVIII.

However, it is difficult, even for the most dispassionate historian, to appreciate any redeeming qualities in John XXII. He caused untold harm in the Church of his day by ruthlessly using his sacred office as a weapon against his political enemies. His cruel, inhuman (not to say unchristian) treatment of the Spiritual Franciscans during the poverty dispute, which raged during his pontificate, is one of the darkest pages of Church history. He declared "heresy" their belief that Christ and the Apostles possessed nothing as individuals or as a group. Many Spiritual Franciscans (the *fraticelli*) were burned as heretics after "trials" before an inquisition. The Franciscan minister-general himself declared the pope a heretic. John XXII in turn excommunicated him. The Franciscan order, deeply involved in these ecclesiastical and political struggles, became the champion of the lay power against the Avignon papacy.[9] All of this turmoil is reflected in the popular novel (and later motion picture) *The Name of the Rose* by Umberto Eco — a strange best-seller in our age!

Dante in one of his most ecstatic visions in Paradise — the spectacular revelation of Divine Justice in the heaven of Mars — was moved to think about its antithesis on earth: Pope John XXII's injustice and avarice, which were ruining the Church. He bursts into this prayer for divine retribution:

> Therefore, I pray the Mind — for there begins
> your movement and your power — to examine
> the place whence comes the smoke that dims your rays,
> so that its wrath descend upon, once more,
> all those who buy and sell within the temple
> whose walls were built with miracles and martyrs.
> O Heaven's army to whom my mind returns,
> pray for those souls on earth who are misled
> by bad example and have gone astray.
> It used to be that wars were waged with swords,

> but now one fights withholding here and there
> the bread our Father's love denies to none.
> And you who write only to nullify,
> remember that Peter and Paul, who died
> to save the vineyard you despoil, still live.
> But you will answer: "I, who have my heart
> so set on him who chose to live alone
> and for a martyr's crown was danced away,
> know nothing of your Fisherman or Paul."
> (*Par.* XVIII, 118-136)

This searing apostrophe to the reigning John XXII is one of the most cynical passages of the *Comedy*. Dante describes John as having his heart set only "on the one who chose to live alone and was danced away for a martyr's crown." This is a reference to St. John the Baptist, whose image was engraved on the gold *florin* of Florence. Thus the pope's heart was where his treasure lay: in money. He had no memory or concern for Saints Peter and Paul who died in Rome to save the Church, the vineyard of Christ which he was devastating by his greed.

One of the most glaring sins of the pope condemned by Dante was his waging war by denying the sacraments, particularly "The Bread which Our Father's love denies to no one." This is a clear allusion to John XXII's frequent issuance of excommunications and interdicts, by which the innocent faithful (God's beloved children) were denied the Eucharistic Bread of Life. Some commentators think that Dante may have had in mind here the pope's excommunication in 1317 of his friend and patron, Can Grande della Scala, one of the Ghibelline lords in northern Italy who resisted the aggressive Avignon papacy.

The memory of John XXII in the fourteenth century calls to mind his antithesis in the twentieth century: Pope John XXIII, who opened the Second Vatican Council with the words: "The Church has seen the emergence of a laity which has become ever more conscious of its responsibilities within the bosom of the Church and in a special way of its duty to collaborate with the Church hierarchy . . . thus, though the world may appear profoundly changed, the Christian community is also in great part transformed and renewed . . . It has been interiorly purified and is thus ready for trial."

The trial of which Pope John XXIII spoke is no doubt that same struggle and ongoing reform which Dante called for and which Newman also indicated in his teaching on the pain of growth and development, the chief characteristics of any truly living body. In Newman's famous words: "Here below to live is to change and to be perfect is to have changed often." The Second Vatican Council gave impetus to this change and reform. This same impetus Dante and Newman gave to the Church of their times. Newman has often been called "the absent father at the Second Vatican Council." Dante might be called a very distant lay consultant of the Council — a prophet who, like Newman, fearlessly exposed deficiencies in the Church while always remaining a loyal believer and committed to the "obedience of faith."

Dante's "obedience of faith" was a virtue which he maintained throughout his life, even while he was contradicting in his writings certain policies and teachings of the popes, such as John XXII's doctrine on the beatific vision or Boniface VIII's teaching on the pope's absolute authority in temporal matters. He was true to the *sensus fidelium* even when bishops (the *Ecclesia docens*) were "unfaithful to their commission" or their functions were in a state of "temporary suspense" — phrases used by Newman in his infamous article which caused such an uproar from the hierarchy. Newman responded to the objections against such phrases by citing the sad, but true, history of the Arian controversy.

Newman carefully documented this period of Church history after the Council of Nicea when there was a temporary confusion, darkness and "suspense." During this period the majority of bishops were actually in communion with the Arians. He also noted that, like gleams of sun on a cloudy day, the testimony of a bishop like St. Athanasius was enough to guide the people in the correct faith. Newman in his earlier work, *Arians of the Fourth Century,* had cited St. Hilary of Poitiers (another orthodox gleam of light in the dark night of Arian confusion), who maintained that the piety of the laity subjected to Arian teaching enabled them to interpret expressions *religiously* which were originally invented as evasions of the orthodox doctrine. [10]

It is interesting to note that Saints Athanasius and Hilary, two ecclesiastical mavericks, suffered long periods of exile for their fidelity to the true faith. Many other examples from Church history could be given of clerics and laymen, such as Boethius, who suffered banishment for their orthodox beliefs. Dante, too, belongs in that company. To quote Newman again: "The individual loses, but his cause (if good and he powerful-minded) gains. This is the way of things: we promote truth by a self-sacrifice."[11] Although it may be objected that Dante was merely a victim of local political vicissitudes in Florence, it was basically his objection to Boniface's interference in temporal affairs that was the real issue: an erroneous religious teaching and practice, which Dante opposed.

Dante was a brash, outspoken exponent of truth, even when the majority opinion and the powers that ruled the earth — such as Boniface and John XXII in collusion with the French monarchy — were against him. He did not hesitate to liken himself to Daniel the prophet in the lions' den, a defender of the truth who was protected by divine power.

Dante opens the third book of his *DM* with a quotation from the book of Daniel: "He shut the mouths of the lions and they did not harm me, for I was found just in His sight" (Dn 6:22). He then gives us in a magnificent passage his self-justification for contradicting the papal teaching on the relations between the two luminaries, the Roman pope and the Roman prince:

> Since the truth about it can scarcely be brought to light without putting certain people to shame, it may give rise to anger against me. But since truth from its immutable throne requires it . . . I take courage from the words of Daniel quoted above, assuring us that defenders of the truth are shielded by divine power; and, in accordance with the exhortation of St. Paul, I put on the breastplate of faith (1 Th 5:8), and on fire with the burning coal which one of the Seraphim took from the altar of heaven to touch Isaiah's lips with (Is 6:7), I will now enter this arena, and in the strength of Him who liberated us from the powers of darkness by His very blood, and before the gaze of the whole world I shall fling the impious and the liar out of the arena. And why should I fear, when the Spirit, who is coeternal with the

Father and the Son, promised through the mouth of David:
'The just shall be held in everlasting remembrance and shall
have nothing to fear from evil report'? (Ps 3:7)

(DM III, I)

Dante then enumerates three classes of people who resist the
truth on the issue of papal authority in temporal matters:

The first class includes the Supreme Pontiff, Vicar of Our
Lord Jesus Christ and successor to Peter, to whom we
should render not what is due to Christ but what is due to
Peter, and certain pastors of the Christian flock. Perhaps it
is through his zeal for the keys that the former opposes the
truth I am to demonstrate and I well believe that the latter
are motivated solely by zeal for Mother Church . . . but
there is a second class whose obstinate greed has extinguished the light of reason; though they profess themselves
to be sons of the Church (Dante is referring here to
temporal rulers), they have the devil for their father. . . .
Then there is a third class, known as the Decretalists, who
are totally ignorant of both theology and philosophy. . .

(DM III, III)

To be noted here is Dante's respect for the popes and bishops and
his attribution to them of good intentions, even though they were in
Dante's opinion misguided by unenlightened zeal for the Church. Later
in the same paragraph Dante gives a summary of his understanding of
the relationships between Christ, the Scriptures, Church Councils and
traditions. It is a brilliant résumé which reveals Dante's theological
acumen and his firm grasp on the basics of Catholic faith:

We must point out that some Scriptures are found previous
to the Church, some at the Church's birth and some subsequent to it. Previous to the Church are the Old and New
Testaments, which are 'established for eternity' (Ps
110:8), as the prophet says; for this is what the Church
says in speaking to the Bridegroom: 'Draw me after Thee'
(Cant. 1:3). Contemporaneous with the Church are those

venerated principal Councils at which no one doubts Christ to have been present, because we have it upon the testimony of Matthew that He himself said to the disciples as He was about to ascend into heaven: 'Behold, I am with you always, even to the consummation of time.' (Mt 28:20)

In addition there are the writings of the Doctors, St. Augustine and others; and if anyone doubts that they were prompted by the Holy Spirit, either he has never seen the fruits of their work, or, if he has seen them, has not tasted them. Afterwards came the traditions known as Decretals. . . . There is no doubt that we must give them a lower place than the fundamental Scriptures, since Christ castigated the priests for doing the opposite: 'And why do you transgress God's command for the sake of your tradition?' (Mt 15:2); by which He clearly indicates the inferior status of tradition. Since it has been shown that the Church's traditions are subsequent to the Church, it follows that the Church does not derive its authority from the traditions but that the traditions derive their authority from the Church.

(DM III, III)

In this marvelous passage Dante points out with such theological equilibrium the primacy of Christ the Bridegroom, whom the Church follows, the fundamental importance of the Scriptures in the Church's faith, the abiding presence of Christ in the Councils and the Holy Spirit's inspiration of the approved Doctors of the Church. Other "traditions" are given an inferior place in this hierarchy of truth. Dante's understanding of the interrelationships of Christ, Scripture, Church and traditions is practically identical with the teaching of the Vatican II document on Divine Revelation (cf. *Dei Verbum,* ch. I, 9-10).

We might mention here that Dante's *DM* was placed on the *Index of Forbidden Books* in 1554 at the time of the Council of Trent, when the Church was protecting herself against the Protestants' assertion of the primacy of the Bible over the authority of the Church. Dante's statement about the beginning of the Church after the books of the New Testament was therefore highly suspect and capable of heretical interpretation at the time of Trent, although Dante was never labeled a heretic by the Church. We might recall Newman's wry comment when he obediently gave up the *Rambler* because "if you do the right thing at the wrong time, you become a heretic."[12]

It is a strange coincidence in history that Pope Leo XIII, who lifted the cloud of suspicion from Newman and vindicated him against those who had labeled him as unsound doctrinally and as "only half a Catholic" was the same pope who removed Dante's *De Monarchia* from the *Index*. This was a rather late apology and rehabilitation of Dante's reputation, one might say; but then again Galileo had to wait until the late twentieth century for ecclesiastical apologies.

Dante's "dangerous" statements about the relationship between Bible and Church authority were, of course, understood anachronistically at the time of Trent, when the Church was forced to assert her tradition and teaching authority over against the Protestants' *sola scriptura* principle. At Vatican II the Church balanced her Tridentine emphasis on her own authority by stressing the primacy of the Word. The truths taught by both Trent and Vatican II are both aspects of the mysteries of faith, which receive true, but only incomplete, articulations in the course of history.

In fact there are numerous teachings in Vatican II documents which confirm officially what Dante had been doing and proclaiming seven centuries before. Dante's exercise of the prophetic office, for example, was clearly a distant anticipation of what the Council taught on the laity's participation in the prophetic role of Christ:

> Christ, the great prophet, who proclaimed the Kingdom of His Father by the testimony of His life and the power of His words, continually fulfills His prophetic office until His full glory is revealed. He does this not only through the hierarchy who teach in His name and with His authority, but also through the laity. For that very purpose He made them His witnesses and gave them understanding of the faith and the grace of speech, so that the power of the Gospel might shine forth in their daily social and family life.
>
> (*Lumen Gentium* IV, 35)

Dante, as we have seen in his writings, displayed eloquently and abundantly his "understanding of the faith" and his "grace of speech." He always attributed these gifts to the power of Christ within him. By his active participation in the prophetic office he anticipated in a remarkable way the ideas that Cardinal Newman was advancing a century before Vatican II. One of Newman's passionate goals during his life as a Catholic was to promote the education of the laity, a concern which Vatican II later expressed so strongly in its document on *The Apostolate of the Laity*. Newman in his writings, especially *The Idea of a University*, and in his work as founder and rector of the Catholic University in Dublin relentlessly promoted the scientific, philosophical and theological training of the laity; but he was continuously thwarted in his efforts by the higher clergy. The frustrations and failures in Ireland he attributed not to the Irish but to the clergy there: "It was not Ireland that was unkind to me. The same thing would have happened in England or France. It was the clergy, moved as they are in automaton fashion by the *camarilla* (clique) at Rome."[13]

We might expect to find in Newman's works, especially in *The Idea of a University*, words of high praise for Dante, but instead we find quite the opposite. Of the only two references to Dante in that work, the more lengthy one is a negative judgment. In the context of a chapter on English Catholic literature he reviews the literatures of the French, Italians and Germans, finding them deficient as Catholic literature and downright skeptical, indecent and secular to the point of being anti-Catholic. On Dante he writes: "Dante certainly does not scruple to place in his *Inferno* a Pope, whom the Church has since canonized and his work on *Monarchia* is on the *Index*."[14]

In spite of Newman's vast knowledge of literature, his acquaintance with Dante seems to have been very limited. Although there was a great revival of interest in Dante as a poet in nineteenth-century England, promoted mainly by Coleridge, Cary, Ruskin, Shelley, Byron and many others, an interpretation of Dante as an anti-papal revolutionary, precursor of the Protestant revolt, and hero of the Italian *Risorgimento* was also prevalent. These latter ideas were advanced by several authors, among whom was Dante Gabriele Rossetti, a political exile from Italy who often projected into his interpretations of Dante his own political and religious prejudices. It is very likely that Newman was influenced by these distorted impressions of Dante that were common in nineteenth-century England.

It was only after Newman's death that the great critical studies of Dante flourished in England, beginning with Edward Moore, who made Oxford University the center of some of the best Dante research in the late nineteenth and early twentieth centuries. The English ever since have been among the leading Dante scholars in the world. But this happened only after Newman's sojourn at Oxford and after his earthly sojourn itself. Had Newman known Dante more profoundly, I think he would have appreciated more his role as a Catholic layman and prophet, but it seems instead that he was influenced by certain biased interpretations of Dante popularized by Rossetti and others. Thomas Carlyle's narrow and sometimes anti-Catholic interpretation of Dante may also have influenced Newman's appraisal of Dante. Carlyle's appreciation of Dante was based mainly on his reading of one work, the *Inferno*.

As to the matter of Dante's placing in *Inferno* a pope later canonized by the Church, there is great divergence today among Dante scholars as to the identity of the unnamed figure in *Inferno* III, 60: "The coward who made the great refusal." In Newman's time it was generally believed to be Pope Celestine V who abdicated the papacy in 1294 and was canonized in 1313 as St. Peter Celestine. It is not at all certain that Dante had him in mind. And besides, the publication and circulation of news of canonizations sometimes took many years. Dante, who died in 1321, may not have known of his canonization.

In spite of Newman's apparent limited knowledge and appreciation of Dante, he does share Dante's deep religious faith and often writes on the very subjects so dear to Dante. Louis Bouyer describes Newman's beautiful poem *The Dream of Gerontius* as "something of a *Divine Comedy* of the soul."[15] Newman and Dante also share similar ideas on an issue that was at the center of lively controversy during the lives of both men: the role of the papacy in temporal affairs. This is a topic too vast for any simplistic summary, let alone a résumé of the thought of either man on that subject or a comparison of their views. Let it suffice to observe that Newman looked upon many of the "powers that be" which existed in his time, such as the temporal power of the Pope, as relics of a barbarous past which should go the way of all flesh.

In his refusal to defend that exercise of power he followed his conscience and waited for a solution of difficulties in the future; but his Catholic "piety" and respect for papal authority kept him from heterodoxy and revolutionary politics. To comment any further on Newman's ideas of papal authority in temporal matters would require the expertise of a Newman scholar and of an historian knowledgeable of the complex political movements of nineteenth-century Europe, especially the famous question of the papal states in Italy.

Dante's opposition to papal usurpation of temporal power was one of the issues which preoccupied him for much of his life. His *De Monarchia* is an eloquent and sophisticated refutation of the papal claim to possess that authority directly from God. In his *DM*, with cogent reasons derived from philosophy and divine revelation, Dante proves that God in His providence has ordained two great luminaries to guide humanity to its two goals, its earthly happiness and its heavenly happiness. These two guides are the Emperor and the Pope. On this score he flatly contradicted the papal teachings, especially Boniface's *Unam Sanctam,* a document well known in Dante's time. With intricate Scholastic terminology and arguments he refutes the papalists' doctrine in Book III of *DM.* Dante expresses poetically this same basic teaching in the famous speech given by Mark the Lombard in Purgatory. Mark identifies the reasons why the world is in such a chaotic state:

> You are free subjects of a greater power,
> a nobler nature that creates your mind,
> and over this the spheres have no control.
> So, if the world today has gone astray,
> the cause lies in yourselves and only there!
> Now I shall carefully explain that cause.
> From the fond hands of God, Who loves her even
> before He gives her being, there issues forth
> just like a child, all smiles and tears at play,
> the simple soul, pure in its ignorance,
> which, having sprung from her Creator's joy,
> will turn to anything it likes. At first
> she is attracted to a trivial toy,
> and though beguiled, she will run after it,

if guide or curb do not divert her love.
Men, therefore, needed the restraint of laws,
needed a ruler able to at least
discern the towers of the True city. True,
the laws there are, but who enforces them?
No one. The shepherd who is leading you
can chew the cud but lacks the cloven hoof.
And so the flock, that see their shepherd's greed
for the same worldly goods that they have craved,
are quite content to feed on what he feeds.
As you can see, bad leadership has caused
the present state of evil in the world,
not Nature that has grown corrupt in you.
On Rome, that brought the world to know the good,
once shone two suns that lighted up two ways:
the road of this world and the road of God.
The one sun has put out the other's light;
the sword is now one with the crook — and fused
together thus, must bring about misrule,
since joined, now neither fears the other one.
If you still doubt, think of the grain when ripe —
each plant is judged according to its seed.
(*Purg.* XVI, 79-114)

Dante, by comparing the Pope and Emperor to "two suns" con-tradicts the papalists' doctrine that the authority of the Emperor (symbolized by the moon, a lesser luminary) was derived from the Pope (the *only* sun, the greater luminary). In his *DM* he ridiculed these popular metaphors which expressed the relationship of the Church and Empire; but here in the *Comedy* he abolishes that imagery altogether by introducing a peculiar and original metaphor: two suns, i.e., two coordi-nate and equal powers with different tasks which no longer reflect a major and minor light. For Dante the human race has two distinct goals ordained by Divine Providence. His image of "two suns" was bold and innovative, since thereby he affirmed the independence and autonomy of the Empire vis-à-vis the Church.

This seemingly strange and irrational metaphor of Rome's two suns is not just a flash of poetic inventiveness, but rather a strong reinstatement of the emperor in his old rights. This basic concept was not original to Dante, since it was the traditional Catholic position, established as far back as Pope Gelasius I in the fifth century. The doctrine of the two powers which developed in the time of Gelasius was still accepted by Pope Innocent III in the early thirteenth century. According to this theory the ecclesiastical and secular powers are mutually independent, but related to each other; the spiritual power is nobler, but it is not possessed of superior authority. The claims of Boniface VIII, Clement V and John XXII in Dante's time were thus anti-traditional, excessive and also historically obsolete. They reflected a clericalism that was out of step with the awakening of an educated, responsible laity, the growth of cities, and a vast resurgence of intellectual, artistic and religious forces. All of these processes that developed in the thirteenth century were reflected in the individual person of Dante who understood his place as both a believer and a citizen. [16]

So the arrogant pretensions of political popes like Boniface, Clement and John were really "modern" and anti-traditional policies that were supported and justified by their curialists and canon lawyers. Their learned opinions plus the popes' "clout" were enough to impose a "hierocracy" which did not brook any dissent. Dante's dissenting voice was followed by many educated laymen in the fourteenth century who challenged papal political claims. We can understand why Dante's *De Monarchia* was publicly burned by the Roman Curia in 1329, after the poet's death. It was not burned because it contained errors in Catholic dogma, but because its political teaching contradicted the prevailing wind in the papal court.

Dante's teaching on the relationship between Church and Empire is a vast topic which would require volumes to explicate. There is a certain evolution in his thought from his *Convivio* to his *De Monarchia* and then to the *Commedia*; there is also a complex interaction of philosophy, theology and political circumstances which would need to be analyzed. Gilson's analysis of these interrelationships is perhaps one of the finest available in English. [17] He clearly shows how Dante differs substantially from St. Thomas on these issues: for Thomas there is only one final end, or goal, of man — the eternal, beatific vision. For Dante there are two final goals: an earthly and a heavenly, the one not subordinated to the other as the means to an end, as Thomas taught. For that reason there is a real autonomy and independence of the Empire from the Church, and consequently the offices of the Emperor and the Pope are quite distinct.

Dante's Pope has absolutely no control of temporal power. Thomas' Pope is the Vicar of Christ, "to whom all the kings of the Christian people owe submission as to Our Lord Jesus Christ himself." Dante's Pope is "the Vicar of Our Lord Jesus Christ and Peter's successor, to whom we owe what is the due, not of Christ, but of Peter." The two concepts of the pope are thus worlds apart! According to Dante, Christ as God possessed all sovereignty, including the temporal which he did not use and which returned to heaven with him. The popes have *not* inherited it. [18] In a few words, this is the sum and substance of Dante's philosophical and theological teaching on the subject.

Thus in Dante's conception of authority there is a pyramid with God at the summit directly bestowing authority in temporal affairs on the monarch (the Empire) and directly bestowing authority in spiritual matters on the pope (the Church). Both powers come directly from God; the emperor's power does not come indirectly through the pope's authority.

That is the meaning of the two suns in Rome which had extinguished one another, as Dante stated in Mark's speech. Dante's concept of Rome can be found in many of his works; it is developed in great length in Book I of *DM* where he describes God's Providence which predisposed Rome and a certain period of her history as the "fullness of time" when His Son became incarnate. The world until that time had wandered down sinful paths, restless and without peace. It was only under the rule of the Roman monarch, *divus Augustus,* that the human race was blessed with the "tranquility of universal peace." St. Luke, "the scribe of Christ's gentleness" was the witness to this. This "fullness of time" meant that "no ministry to our happiness was then vacant of its minister."[19]

Dante describes this "Rome that made the world good" in a

lengthy passage of his *Convivio* which is profuse in theological and historical details:

> When the immeasurable Divine Goodness willed to recon-form to itself the human creature who was separated from God by the sin of disobedience of the first man, it was appoihted in the most lofty and united divine consistory of the Trinity that the Son of God should descend to earth to effect this harmony. And since at His coming into the world it was fitting that not only heaven but earth should be in its best disposition, and the best disposition of earth is when it is a monarchy . . . Rome was ordained by the Divine Providence. And since the abode wherein the heavenly king must enter ought to be most clean and pure, there was likewise ordained a most holy family from which should be born a woman supremely good from among all the rest, who should be the chamber of the Son of God.
>
> This family was David's and the triumph and honor of the human race: Mary. . . . And it was at the same point of time that David was born and Rome was born, i.e., Aeneas came into Italy from Troy. . . . The divine election of the Roman Empire is thus manifest enough. . . . Nor was the world ever so perfectly disposed, nor shall be again, as then when it was guided by the voice of one prince and comman-der of the Roman people, as Luke the evangelist testifies. Thus there was universal peace, which never was before nor shall be, and the ship of human fellowship was speeding straight to the due port in tranquil voyage.
>
> (*Conv.* IV, V, 3-8)

The mention of Aeneas as founder of Rome is significant here, since it evokes an ancient tradition about the name of Rome which Dante may have known. [20] According to this tradition the common name of Rome was derived from its legendary founder Romulus, an origin that Dante practically ignores. The "secret name," however, of *Roma* (the Latin original for Rome) was *Amor* (the Latin word for love). Note that the letters of *Roma,* reversed, spell *amor.* The secret name *Amor* came from its true founder, Aeneas, the son of Venus, the goddess of *amor*. Dante always traced Rome's origin to Aeneas whose divine mission it was to found it.

This derivation may seem somewhat esoteric, but it has deep significance if we look at the central cantos of the *Comedy*: cantos XVI, XVII and XVIII of *Purgatory*. There Mark the Lombard's famous speech occurs as well as Virgil's magnificent discourse on love. Both speeches focus on the most important themes of the *Comedy*: love, free will, Rome and her two suns, reason and faith, nature and grace. It would be impossible to summarize all these dense themes in a few sentences, but a few comments might suffice which would illuminate the topics under discussion, namely, the earthly goal of man and the role of the Empire.

Mark had described the human soul as a simple little child created by a loving God who instilled in her a love for whatever is good. But the human creature, besides being endowed with a natural desire for what is good, is also given free will. Since the innocent soul erred in the use of her freedom and committed sin, God in his same loving goodness ordained two guides that help her to direct her love to the proper objects and also to curb the unruly drives that lead her astray from her two goals of earthly and heavenly happiness. These are the two suns in Rome: the Church and the Empire, God's gifts of love to a fallen humanity. But when the two guides abandon their respective missions, humanity is left shipwrecked and in total darkness. Hence the state of chaos in Dante's time.

Virgil, spokesman for reason and nature, discourses in cantos XVII and XVIII on love. He endorses and expands on Mark's speech by describing love as the natural tendency toward good, which is sometimes diverted from its proper goals or fails by excessive or deficient desire. Virgil also stresses the necessity of the light of faith and divine grace, and points to the future arrival of Beatrice, who will lead Dante to the vision of God, the Love who moves all.

In the very center of the *Comedy* these two discourses focus on the two "ends" of humanity. Dante never loses sight of man's ultimate goal in God, but he also never diminishes or abandons the natural goal of earthly happiness, whose conditions are peace and justice — the divine task given to the Empire.

Both the Empire and the Church, then, have distinct missions from God. At the conclusion of the *DM* Dante expresses how the two guides, the emperor and the pope, are related to one another:

> Yet the truth of this last issue (i.e., that the monarchy's authority derives directly from God) is not to be narrowly interpreted as excluding the Roman Prince from all subordination to the Roman Pontiff, since in a certain fashion our temporal happiness is subordinate to our eternal happiness. Caesar, therefore, is obliged to observe that reverence towards Peter which a first-born son owes to his father, so that when he is enlightened by the light of paternal grace he may the more powerfully enlighten the world, at the head of which he has been placed by the One who alone is ruler of all things spiritual and temporal.   *(DM, III, XVI)*

In the paragraphs which precede these words just quoted Dante had described his ideal emperor. He should be the "protector of the world" who would devote all his energies toward providing freedom, peace, justice and temporal happiness for the entire world. But Dante, the idealist and theorist, was also a very practical man who sought an incarnation of his ideals in real history. He found that "fleshing out" of his theory in the historical person of Justinian I, the Byzantine Emperor in the sixth century. Justinian occupies an exceptional place in the *Comedy*: he is the only person in the *Comedy* whose speech fills an entire canto *(Par.* VI). As a servant of Divine Justice, codifier of Roman Law, reformer of the Empire, disciple of the Bishop of Rome in matters of faith, defender of the Church and Catholic faith, he exemplifies all the virtues of the ideal emperor described theoretically in the *DM*.

Dante purposely does not choose Constantine, the first Christian Roman Emperor. He had carried the Roman eagle to the East (the transferal of the seat of government from Rome to Byzantium) and, worse yet, he had bestowed on the Pope and the Church temporal powers — that disastrous act which unleashed so many evils. Even though Dante places Constantine in Paradise, since his intentions were good, he elects Justinian to be the great spokesman who recites the history of Rome, her glories and her failures. Justinian is actually a mouthpiece for Dante's own conception of Rome and the emperor's mission.

Justinian's extensive speech, which is too long to quote here, includes an allusion to his conversion from the Monophysite heresy to orthodox faith through the instrumentality of Pope Agapetus:

> Caesar I was, Justinian I remain
> who, by the will of the First Love I feel,
> purged all the laws of excess and of shame.
> Before I had assumed this task I thought
> that Christ had but one nature and no more,
> and I was satisfied with this belief;
> but blessed Agapetus, he who was
> supreme shepherd of God, directed me
> with his enlightened words to the true faith;
> I trusted him, and what he knew by faith
> I now see clear, as clear as you can see
> all contradictions are both true and false.
> And once I was in step with Holy Church,
> God in his grace inspired me to assume
> that task to which I gave all of myself:
> *(Par.* VI, 10-24)

That task was the reform of Roman Law and the restoration of the Roman Empire. The reconquest of Italy, devastated by the barbarians' invasions, was one of his priorities, although the gains were small and ephemeral. The establishment of an imperial outpost at Ravenna — the residence of the Byzantine governors for about two hundred years — was only a minor triumph in the grandiose plan of Justinian. Ravenna, with its many remains of that glorious period still intact, speaks to us today of Dante's ideal of Church and Empire united. No doubt Dante worshiped at the Byzantine basilicas there under the luminous mosaics so remarkably preserved to this day. In the basilica of San Vitale we can see the mosaics depicting Justinian and his astute wife, the Empress Theodora, presenting the Eucharistic gifts. These mosaics express in art Dante's political and religious ideals. It seems fitting that Dante spent his last years in Ravenna, surrounded by these memories of Justinian and the Empire.

It is most interesting to notice that Justinian closed his speech in *Paradise* VI by introducing another radiant light in that same sphere. It is the humble Romeo whom we mentioned in the context of Dante's exile. Romeo is described as a poor pilgrim, whose "great and beautiful work" went unrewarded. This humble, just man was a victim of human injustice who wandered in his old age, begging his bread from door to door. Justinian predicts that "though praised today he would be praised still more" in the future. Romeo is obviously a portrait of Dante himself. It might seem to us that Dante is indulging here in some sinful pride, but we should note that the souls in this sphere are those "whose zealous deeds on earth were prompted by desire for lasting fame." They all had deviated for a time from "true love" while on earth, but they eventually changed and found the "sweetness of True Justice," which cannot turn to bitterness. This reveals Dante's humility: that marvelous aspect of hope which preserved him from the pitfalls of presumption and despair. Justinian, the great and glorious emperor and champion of Divine Justice, thus has a "little" companion in glory — the poor, humble pilgrim who also loved Justice, suffered for it, and later tasted its sweetness in Paradise.

Dante's hunger and thirst for Justice, however, was never satisfied by simply recalling examples from the past. He was not just a nostalgic *laudator temporis acti.* He was a man actively engaged in the present struggle to bring about that Justice. In his lifetime he poured all his energy and literary skills into promoting the cause of the Empire, especially the legitimate claim of Henry VII of Luxembourg to be the Holy Roman Emperor. He wrote numerous letters in support of Henry, two of which we have today, as well as a letter to Henry himself. The letters abound in biblical language and images used by the Hebrew prophets. They reveal admirably Dante's self-consciousness as a prophet who fearlessly exhorts his fellow Italians and Florentines to welcome Henry as God's appointed instrument of peace and justice.

In his letter to the Italian rulers and people (*Epistula* V) he refers to Henry as "the sun of peace" who will dawn and bring justice and joy to a world which had become a night in the wilderness. He gives Henry many messianic titles borrowed from the biblical writers of both

Testaments: "the lion of Judah," another Moses, the Bridegroom, the consolation of the world, and "the glory of your people."

Dante argues in this letter that this enterprise and this hope may seem "beyond the range of human efforts," but in the past God has worked similar effects through men, just as He can create new heavens. Dante asserts that "we are from time to time the instruments of God" and "the human will in its inherent natural freedom is directly acted upon by the divine will, and so often unconsciously subserves it." What wonderful optimism in Dante — a true prophet! He supports his argument by citing the time of Caesar Augustus when the world enjoyed twelve years of peace — an accomplished fact — which revealed the face of the Son of God who was made man at that time to reveal the Spirit, preach the Gospel, and divide the whole world between Himself and Caesar, thus establishing the two kingdoms.

Dante pleads with his fellow Italians to believe that "the Lord Himself has appointed a king for us. This is he whom Peter, the Vicar of Christ, admonishes us to honor, whom Clement, the present successor of Peter, irradiates with the light of apostolic blessing." Dante is alluding to Clement V's encyclical letter of 1310 that supported Henry. Clement at the time was playing "power politics" with the French king. He eventually yielded to threats from the French ruler and withdrew his support from Henry. This wretched pope, who had moved the papacy to Avignon and had betrayed Henry, was also a greedy simoniac who even practiced witchcraft, according to the contemporary chronicles. Dante, without mentioning his name, had assigned him to a place among the simoniacal popes in Hell.

Dante's letter to the Florentines (*Epistula* VI) is perhaps his most vitriolic outpouring of righteous anger against his fellow citizens. The Florentines had opposed Henry as emperor, and Dante in this letter accuses them of opposing God's will and warns them of divine vengeance if they should not repent. Nowhere is Dante's prophetic rage so caustic. He hurls at the Florentines such insults as "the most empty-headed of all the Tuscans, crazy by nature and by corruption," and "pathetic offshoot of Fiesole, barbarians now due for a second chastisement." In the letter Dante repeats his usual philosophical and scriptural arguments in support of the Emperor, whom he calls "King of the world and servant (*minister*) of God." The Florentines who abandon God's holy emperor are also compared to the builders of a second tower of Babel.

In this letter Dante refers to his own prophetic soul, which is not deceived but rather has a message given him "by unmistakable omens and by incontrovertible arguments." He exhorts the Florentines to repent and welcome Henry, "who carries the burden of the Roman Commonwealth, thirsting not for his own personal interests, but for the general good of the world." Dante claims that Isaiah's prophecy of the suffering servant who "bore our griefs and carried our sorrows" applies not only to Christ but also secondarily to Henry.

In his letter to Henry (*Epistula* VII) Dante begins by recalling God's immeasurable love which wills our inheritance of peace, even in the midst of hardships during the present state of the Church militant on her way to "our eternal home, the Church triumphant." He compares the absence of an emperor to the condition of the ancient Jews weeping by the rivers of Babylon (cf. Ps 136). But now, as Henry enters Italy, a new hope has dawned and Italy can now sing with joy the song of Virgil (cf. his famous fourth Eclogue) that prophesied the return of the Golden Age and of Justice. Henry is addressed as "our sun," as a "second Joshua" and as the one whom John the Baptist announced as "the Lamb of God who takes away the sins of the world." Henry is also hailed as "the minister of God, the son of the Church and promoter of Rome's glory." Dante reminds Henry that his fiercest enemy is Florence, the center of corruption, but he assures Henry of a victory like David's over Goliath and the Philistines. He concludes the letter with these words: "Then our inheritance (peace) whose loss we lament without cease, shall be restored to us in full; and as we now groan in our exile at Babylon when we remember the holy city of Jerusalem, we shall then be citizens again and draw breath in peace and look back in joy at the sorrowful waters of confusion."

Henry met with some success in Italy, especially in the Ghibelline cities of Lombardy, but his victories were short-lived. Although he was crowned emperor without ceremony in Rome's cathedral, St. John Lateran, in 1312, he lost papal support, fell ill and died near Siena in 1313. Florence and the Guelph cities rejoiced; Dante was crushed. In the white rose of Paradise Beatrice will point out to Dante the empty imperial throne awaiting Henry, the only living person at the time of his writing that Dante places in Paradise. But in spite of all his disappointments from Henry's failure and from the betrayals of the Pope, the Florentines and the Italians in general, Dante, a true prophet, continued to believe and hope that God in His mysterious providence would in some way save the Church and humanity.

Dante understood his mission as prophet essentially in biblical terms, i.e., as a spokesman for God and for His Justice. He was not, as some commentators have presented him, merely a proponent of partisan politics and defender of his own idea of the Empire. Gilson has summarized Dante's chief inspiration in this way:

> Being the work of a poet, the *Divine Comedy* is infinitely mightier and more splendid than the political passions of its author. Taken as a whole, it is an exaltation of all divine rights: that of the Emperor, most certainly, but equally those of the Philosopher and the Pope, since all rights are interdependent as being expressions of the living justice of God. The *Divine Comedy* accordingly appears as the projection, on the artistic plane, of the vision of that ideal world which Dante dreamed of — a world in which majesty would always be honored according to its rank and every act of treason chastised as it deserved. In short, it is the final judgment passed on the mediaeval world by a God Who will consult Dante before making His abjudications. [21]

Thus in Paradise we see the divine right of the Emperor exalted in the persons of Henry VII, Justinian, Constantine and even the pagan Roman Emperor Trajan. The divine right of the Pope is repeatedly exalted in the person of St. Peter and many of his good successors. But what about the divine right of the Philosopher?

Gilson and many other interpreters see the autonomy and the majesty of pure philosophy and reason exalted in the person of Siger of Brabant, a very controversial figure in his time, opposed by St. Thomas and highly suspect in the eyes of the Roman Curia, which kept him under "house arrest" for many years until his mysterious death in 1284. It would be impossible to discuss here all the opinions surrounding this

controversial philosopher at the University of Paris whom Dante places
in Paradise. Rivers of ink have flowed down through the centuries on
the reason why Dante has St. Thomas eulogize his earthly adversary
Siger. The much-debated passage is this encomium given by Thomas:

> This light from which your eyes return to me
> shines from a soul once given to grave thoughts,
> who mourned that death should be so slow to come:
> this is the endless radiance of Siger,
> who lectured on the Street of Straw, exposing
> invidiously logical beliefs.
> (*Par.* X, 133-138)

What seems to be the most convincing reason is the one given by
Gilson, namely, that Dante saw in Siger the "martyr of pure
philosophy." Siger suffered for the cause of truth. He is thus exalted in
the heavenly circle of the wise men which includes Solomon, Albert the
Great, Thomas Aquinas, Boethius and others. It is certainly a surprise
to find Thomas praising a philosopher whom he had opposed on earth
and whose teachings had been condemned by the Church. Siger had
defended his beliefs before the Roman Curia by maintaining the mutual
independence of reason and faith, and thus also of the temporal and
spiritual orders. It is probably for this reason that Dante places him in
Paradise and has Thomas praise him, even though Thomas as well as
Dante held that there is no contradiction between philosophy and
theology, between reason and faith.

Dante wanted to point out that human philosophy, represented by
Siger, who might be called "the vicar of Aristotle," can confer a *temporal*
happiness on humans, just as temporal happiness can be given through
the Empire. Basically what is at stake for Dante is the legitimate and
divinely ordained autonomy and independence of the natural, human,
temporal order — one of the two "ends" or goals of human existence.
Although Thomas paid tribute to this by his boldly innovative use of
Aristotle — and was himself suspect on this score by ecclesiastical
authorities in Paris — he nonetheless on several issues opposed Siger,
who suffered more than Thomas for the sake of pure philosophy. Siger

represented an extreme, but a truth that Thomas, according to Dante, had to recognize and praise. Thomas, so Dante thought, had left some unfinished business on earth — a clear delineation of two autonomous "ends" of man. [22]

Another extreme — but a truth just as important — is represented by another controversial figure placed by Dante in Paradise. It is Joachim of Fiore, a Cistercian abbot and visionary who founded his own order of reformed monks. Dante places him in Paradise in another circle, actually the outer circle which circumscribed the circle of the wise men already mentioned. The inner circle, which included Thomas, the Dominicans and many of the more "intellectual" wise men, is surrounded by this outer circle, headed by St. Bonaventure, the Franciscan theologian who represents the "affective" or "mystical" aspect of wisdom. Bonaventure points out to Dante the last light in that circle: "And here at my side shines the Calabrian Abbot Joachim who had received the gift of prophecy." (*Par.* XII, 140) Joachim occupies the same place in the outer circle as Siger has in the inner circle.

Both men were controversial figures whose teachings had been condemned by Church authorities. Even though Joachim had to his dying day professed perfect obedience and submission to the Church's *magisterium,* after his death some of his doctrines were condemned at the Fourth Lateran Council in 1215. His apocalyptic writings, which envisioned a new age — the age of the Holy Spirit — and proclaimed a radical reform of the Church, were extremely popular in Dante's time. Some of his fanatical followers had published works which they attributed to him. As a result the so-called Joachimists were condemned in 1255 as a heretical movement. The Spiritual Franciscans, so enthusiastic for Church reform, held Joachim in such high esteem that Bonaventure, as Minister General of the Franciscans and also as a Cardinal of the Church, in an effort to bring peace and equilibrium to the shattered order, had to oppose some of Joachim's teachings. Many of Joachim's prophecies had been interpreted in the heretical sense that only a "spiritual" Church will survive after the reform and annihilation of the visible, "carnal" Church.

But Bonaventure, like Thomas in the case of Siger, praises in heaven Joachim, whom he had opposed on earth, because the truth which Bonaventure as a representative of the institutional Church highlights is that the spirit of prophecy — the purely "spiritual" aspect of the Church — is also autonomous and independent: an expression of divine providence which must be acknowledged and respected. Joachim's controversial spirit of prophecy is thus vindicated by Bonaventure. Joachim had been a herald of a third human era — an era of charity and freedom in which the clerical order of the visible Church would be absorbed into the spiritual Church. Dante apparently appreciated this complete "detemporalization" of the Church, even though he always defended, as Thomas and Bonaventure had, the divinely ordained visible aspect of the institutional Church on earth. But according to Dante the institutional Church must always listen to her prophets through whom the Spirit, Who blows where He wills, speaks and acts.

Dante's adventurous beatification of these two ambiguous figures, Siger and Joachim, might seem to contradict all his theses and beliefs and place him in a dangerously suspect position as a loyal Catholic layman; but on the contrary, it is a courageous statement which expresses his prophetic mission as a spokesman for the divine right of the Empire (the temporal order) and the divine right of the Church (the spiritual order). It is certainly an original position. Von Balthasar has called it a "conversion to the laity":

> For Dante, conversion to the laity means turning away from the Scholastic study of essences to reflection on the reality and the conditions of the possibility of an authentic Christian experience; indeed — and this is in contrast to the mendicant orders and the mysticism of the day — of an ethico-political existence in the world. From Dante to our own times this has been the route taken by every theology that has made its mark on history. [23]

Dante did not endorse any of the Joachimists' heterodox ideas (whether they were Joachim's or his followers' is often difficult to decipher since many works were attributed to him but not actually written by him); nor did Dante share what may be called the extreme Aristotelianism (often called the Averroism) of Siger. Dante's vision sprang from his loving zeal as a Catholic layman for the spiritual riches of Christ found in the institutional Church, for the ethical freedom and human justice found in the rightful rule of the Empire, and for the nobility of the intellect found in philosophy. All three — the Church, the Empire and Philosophy — are independent but in many ways also interrelated and interdependent expressions of the *one* Divine Justice. Dante was the intrepid prophet of the autonomy of all three, and thereby the prophet of God's supreme gifts to humanity: His Spirit, first of all, and then human freedom and intelligence.

Dante's prophetic vision of what the world should be according to God's will was truly a catholic one. Unlike the Joachimists of his time, whose interests were limited to the reform of the Church and her spiritualization, Dante also embraced the secular world and the restoration of the Empire which was responsible, according to the divine plan, for peace and justice. Dante was a man of the Church, but also a man of the world who considered the attainment of its specific goal a priority in his life just as important as the Church's goal. For him the world was a vast community, a fellowship and brotherhood based on friendship and "the bond of love that nature makes."

The world should be under the guidance of God's servant, the Emperor, whose temporal "ownership" of all things would be the safeguard against human greed, the root of all sins and disruptions of peace. His authority and his just administration of all goods were the guarantors of universal peace and happiness. Under his just rule states would not war against other states over land, nor would cities fight against cities, nor would neighborhoods or families be in strife, since complete possession of all things would be his. His justice would bring about a peace in which all would be able to satisfy their needs. This peace would be the condition in which cities, neighborhoods, families and individuals "could love one another and attain joy, which is the end for which man was born."[24]

Although this prophetic message of Dante seems so utopian and totally unrealistic to us today, his vision remains valid. We may need to search for other means in order to realize the end, but the goal is the same. It was basically the same prophetic message of twentieth-century popes such as Pius XII, who promoted peace as the fruit of justice. It was echoed recently by John Paul II's paraphrase, peace as the fruit of solidarity, in his marvelous encyclical *On Social Concern*. And then there are the monumental and prophetic encyclicals of John XXIII and Paul VI voicing the same message. We should also mention the many brave heroes and heroines of peace and justice in recent times: Gandhi, · Martin Luther King, Dorothy Day, Daniel Berrigan, Jean Donovan, Oscar Romero and so many others who are prophetic witnesses to the same vision.

The Second Vatican Council endorsed with vigorous, forceful language Dante's concern for this world and its autonomy. The Council's wording is actually similar to Dante's formulations:

> If by the autonomy of earthly affairs we mean that created things and societies themselves enjoy their own laws and values which must be . . . regulated by men, then it is entirely right to demand that autonomy. Such is not merely required by modern man, but harmonizes also with the will of the Creator. For by the very circumstance of their having been created, all things are endowed with their own stability, truth, goodness, proper laws and order. . . . For earthly matters and the concerns of faith derive from the same God.   (*The Church in the Modern World* III, 36)

Another clear statement of the Council's insistence on the intrinsic value of the temporal order and of man's earthly goal is found here:

> God's plan for the world is that men should work together to restore the temporal sphere of things and to develop it unceasingly. Many elements make up the temporal order . . . political institutions, international relations. . . . All of these not only aid in the attainment of man's ultimate goal, but also possess their own intrinsic value. This value has been implanted in them by God, whether they are considered in themselves or as parts of the whole temporal order. . . . This destination (i.e., their fulfillment in Christ),

however, not only does not deprive the temporal order of its independence, its proper goals, laws, resources and significance for human welfare, but rather perfects the temporal order in its own intrinsic strength and excellence and raises it to the level of man's total vocation upon earth.

(*Decree on the Apostolate of the Laity* II, 7)

The Council further proclaims that "the laity must take on the renewal of the temporal order as their own special obligation. Led by the light of the gospel and the mind of the Church, and motivated by Christian love, let them act directly and definitively in the temporal sphere. . . . Everywhere and in all things they must seek the justice characteristic of God's Kingdom" (*ibid.*).

We began this chapter with Beatrice's bestowal on Dante of his prophetic mission in the earthly paradise. Later in the heavenly paradise Dante confesses to his ancestor, Cacciaguida, that he is "a timid friend of truth." Cacciaguida then predicts that people in high places on earth will react hostilely to Dante's message, but he comforts his descendant with these words:

> The conscience that is dark
> with shame for his own deeds or for another's,
> may well, indeed, feel harshness in your words;
> nevertheless, do not resort to lies,
> let what you write reveal all you have seen,
> and let those men who itch scratch where it hurts.
> Though when your words are taken in at first
> they may taste bitter, but once well-digested
> they will become a vital nutriment.
> Your cry of words will do as does the wind
> striking the hardest at the highest peaks,
> and this will be for honor no small grounds;
> (*Par.* XVII, 124-135)

Later in the journey through the heavenly spheres Dante will meet
St. Peter who flares up in wrath as he looks down at the condition of the
Church. He compares the popes of Dante's time to rapacious wolves
who have brought the holy beginning of the Church to such a foul
ending. He gives, however, a message of hope to Dante and commands
him to carry it back to earth:

> But that high Providence which saved for Rome
> the glory of the world through Scipio's hand,
> will once again, and soon, lend aid, I know;
> and you, my son, whose mortal weight must bring
> you back to earth again, open your mouth down there
> and do not hide what I hide not from you!
> (*Par.* XXVII, 61-66)

Dante thus receives a confirmation of his prophetic mission from
St. Peter; Beatrice then joins in Peter's indignation as well as in his hope
for a savior in the near future:

> My words should not surprise you when you think
> there is no one on earth to govern you
> and so the human family goes astray.
> Before all January is unwintered —
> because of every hundred years' odd day
> which men neglect — these lofty spheres shall shine
> a light that brings the long-awaited storm
> to whirl the fleet about from prow to stern,
> and set it sailing a straight course again.
> Then from the blossom shall good fruit come forth.
> (*Par.* XXVII, 139-148)

Peter had spoken about the papacy being vacant and Beatrice had
referred to the absence of a temporal ruler. For this reason the whole
human family is off course like a fleet of ships in a storm. But Beatrice
predicts that soon a light sent from heaven will set the world on the

straight course again. Dante the prophet must never lose hope in the eventual coming of divine intervention for human salvation. He never did. Nor should we, when we are tempted to indifference, helplessness and despair as we look at the evils and injustices which reign in our world: hunger, homelessness, denial of human rights, abortions and the rampant violence and wars, not to mention the dreadful possibility of holocaust by nuclear weapons and bombs.

Chapter Six

CHRIST-CENTERED MYSTIC

Since the middle of our twentieth century there have been some dramatic shifts and significant changes in the way Catholic theologians have approached the subject of Christ. The many Christologies produced since the fifties are the fruit of Catholic theologians' appropriation of modern biblical criticism, a new historical consciousness, evolutionary theories, and a number of other influences, such as personalism, anthropology, political and social concerns. The many changes in human society, its philosophies, psychologies and scientific progress have profoundly altered the way modern theologians perceive Christ.[1]

Medieval Christology, especially the synthesis of St. Thomas Aquinas, had dominated the theological schools and the catechetics of the Catholic Church from the thirteenth century until the middle of our own. Over those centuries there had been many noteworthy enrichments of that medieval Scholastic tradition in the form of popular religious movements such as Franciscanism in the thirteenth and fourteenth centuries and the widespread devotion to the Sacred Heart of Jesus, which developed from medieval mystics and continued well into the twentieth century. The many Christ-centered spiritualities that developed from the Middle Ages until the present are witness to a continuous tradition of a lived Christology, or, one might say, a Christ-centered spirituality.

The academic Christology, however, which prevailed in the textbooks and schools from the Middle Ages down to a few decades ago was in many ways incomplete and remained for the most part stagnant and undeveloped until recent times. The Christological syntheses of the great medieval Summas were indeed monuments of erudition and speculation which brought together centuries of Patristic and Scholastic reflection on the mystery of Christ, but no one period of theological reflection can ever exhaust the mystery.

The Second Vatican Council accepted the concept of the "development of dogma," a subject which preoccupied John Henry Newman and many other Catholic theologians since his time. The Council's document on Divine Revelation (*Dei Verbum*), which mentioned this topic, was, after much heated debate, a compromise between "traditional" and "progressive" elements; but it did endorse "a much more dynamic and developmental sense of tradition."[2] This particular paragraph from the Council document confirms this appraisal:

> This tradition which comes from the apostles develops in the Church with the help of the Holy Spirit. For there is a growth in the understanding of the realities and the words which have been handed down. This happens through the contemplation and study made by believers, who treasure these things in their hearts (cf. Lk 2:19, 51), through the intimate understanding of spiritual things they experience, and through the preaching of those who have received through episcopal succession the sure gift of truth. For, as the centuries succeed one another, the Church constantly moves forward toward the fullness of divine truth until the words of God reach their complete fulfillment in her.
>
> (*Dogmatic Constitution on Divine Revelation* II, 8)

What is most interesting in this conciliar statement is its assertion that the first medium of this development is the role of the faithful in their "contemplation and study," their "intimate understanding" and their "experience" of divine revelation. Later on the document deals with the contributions of the "Holy Fathers" and the theologians. We might recall here the stress that Newman placed on the "sense of the faithful" in matters of Christian dogma. We may also recall that Dante considered himself "one of the least of the sheep of the pasture of Jesus Christ." He claimed that, even though he had no pastoral authority, even the "babes" and "the man born blind," as the Scriptures attest, are capable of proclaiming the truth.

Dante, whose fidelity to the official teaching authority of the Church invested in her shepherds cannot be questioned, was acutely aware of the charism of truth which he shared with all the other "sheep" of Christ's fold. He was also aware that he was not a professional theologian, and compared himself to one who gathered the crumbs that fell from the table where these experts, the theologians and philosophers, feasted on "the bread of angels" — divine wisdom itself.

Of all the theologians from whom Dante gleaned his own theological synthesis St. Thomas Aquinas stands out as the principal authority and source. Thomas' theology, however, was by no means the only major influence on Dante. We have seen that Dante in theology as well as in philosophy and politics was original and individualistic — "a party unto himself," as his ancestor Cacciaguida described him in *Paradise* XV. Aquinas' Christology in the Scholastic tradition of the Middle Ages, placed great emphasis on questions concerning the relationship of divinity and humanity in Christ, i.e., on the ontological mystery of Christ, His essence — who and what He is "in Himself." Thomas also stressed Christ's knowledge and consciousness of Himself as God and man.

One of the modern criticisms of this medieval concern with the metaphysical or essential aspect of Christ is that the soteriological or "economical" aspect of Christ — what He is "for us" — was somewhat obscured and neglected. This important aspect of Christ, however, was certainly not absent in medieval theology: St. Anselm's monumental work on the redemptive purpose of the Incarnation (his *Cur Deus Homo*) is a sufficient witness to this soteriological dimension of Christology which focused on the redemptive value of Christ's life and death. Nor are these themes absent in St. Thomas.

Probably the passionate interest in metaphysics, generated by the Scholastics' fascination with the works of Aristotle in the thirteenth century, accounts for this stress on the ontological and psychological aspects of Christ in medieval theology. St. Thomas, in the wake of his master St. Albert the Great, incorporated into Catholic theology all that could be taken from Aristotle's metaphysics and psychology which accorded with orthodox faith. Thomas' intellectualism, however, did not blind him to the meaning of Christ "for us," nor did it obscure the value of Christ's earthly life and ministry. His systematic thought did not stifle the kerygmatic and functional Christology of the New Testament.

In his *Summa Theologiae* Thomas devotes fifty-nine "questions" to Christology. Although about twenty of these focus on Christ's "ontological makeup," twenty-seven deal specifically with Christ's earthly life, miracles, suffering, death, descent into Hell, resurrection and ascension. In these questions Thomas focuses on what Jesus was, and is, for us.

Unfortunately, later theologians and especially the manuals used in the schools emphasized only Thomas' metaphysical doctrine on Christ's natures, person and knowledge and neglected to a great extent his soteriological theology which stressed the redemptive acts of Christ's death and resurrection and the mysteries of Christ's life.[3] This soteriological and kerygmatic theology was the main concern of the New Testament writers and to a great extent of the Fathers and the Councils of the Church. True, the Christological controversies from the fourth to the seventh centuries dealt mainly with the ontological question of Jesus' two natures, a topic which preoccupied the theologians, bishops and the laity — in brief, the entire Church. But those ontological questions were intimately related to the pastoral concern for human salvation: only God (i.e., divinity) could save us, and what is not assumed by God (i.e., humanity) is not saved. This was a patristic principle which dominated the debates.

One of the great milestones in the Church's reflection on Christ was the Council of Chalcedon in 451. It may be regarded as a synthesis of centuries of theological discussion on the two natures of Christ. His divinity and humanity were expressed in the clearest metaphysical terms of the time. The dogmatic formulations of Chalcedon have remained the "litmus test" of Christian orthodoxy down to our own times. On the occasion of the fifteen-hundredth anniversary of that Council Karl Rahner wrote an influential article entitled "Chalcedon — End or Beginning?" In it Rahner argued that the truth proclaimed by the Council should not mark the end of Christological reflection but rather should be the beginning of re-thinking and further development. Truth should yield further truth, he insisted; every conciliar definition is both an end of a controversy and the beginning of a new phase of doctrinal discussion and growth.

What Rahner wrote almost forty years ago was, we might say, a kind of prophetic insight. Since then the interest in Christology has blossomed into a veritable harvest of Christological works which would require a lifetime to read and digest. One of the main characteristics of these new Christologies is its starting point: "from below." At the risk of oversimplifying, this term means that the Jesus of history, the human being like us in all things except sin, is the main focus and starting point of these Christologies. This would be a shift from the traditional focus, stressed in the Councils of Nicea and Chalcedon, which took as their departure point the theology of St. John's Gospel: Christology "from above" with its emphasis on the eternal, pre-existent Word of God who descends to earth to assume human flesh. This "high Christology" has remained the dominant theology of the Church. It stresses the divinity of Christ, the mystery of the Incarnation, and the Son of God's unique role in salvation history.

This "high Christology" certainly prevailed in the Middle Ages, as witnessed in the theological discussions and also in the plastic arts with their representations of Christ as the divine, universal judge enthroned in majesty and glory. On the other hand, the medieval mystics such as Bernard of Clairvaux, Francis of Assisi, Julian of Norwich, Mechtilde of Magdeburg, Marie d' Oignies, to mention only a few, developed a deep awareness of Jesus' humanity, tenderness and even "maternal" qualities. The vast mystical, Christ-centered literature which the Middle Ages produced was the fruit of the personal experiences and intense spiritual lives of so many women and men, some of whom were also "professional" theologians.[4] Thomas and Bonaventure, for example, were two outstanding speculative theologians; but they were also great mystics. Many laymen and laywomen, often members of the Third Orders of the Dominicans and Franciscans, such as Ramon Lull and Angela of Foligno, have left us remarkable testimonies of Christ-centered mysticism.[5]

Dante was an intellectual and spiritual heir of this "high Christology" of the theological schools and also of the mystical tradition which flowered within the Franciscan and Dominican movements. He assimilated the best of Scholasticism as well as the Christ-centered mysticism which flourished in the Middle Ages. We might ask ourselves if he contributed anything original to the academic Christology of his time and we may also ask if his "mystical" experience of Christ displayed any particularly original elements. The answer to the first question seems to be no, since Dante was not a theologian by profession, and the answer to the second will remain, it seems, a much disputed point among Dante scholars. Whether or not Dante was a genuine mystic (whatever that may mean!) has been, and continues to be, the focus of much Dante scholarship. We will attempt to explore that aspect of Dante in this chapter.

The subject of Dante as a mystic presents from the outset some almost insurmountable obstacles and problems. There is first of all the seemingly impossible task of defining mysticism, since a choice should be made from among the many good and acceptable definitions of it. Then there is the application of a definition to the case of Dante in order to qualify him or disqualify him for the exceptional label of "mystic."

Such a simplistic methodology may seem artificial and perhaps too scholastic in the sense of first defining terms and then making rigid applications of those terms to a particular case. This method apparently runs the risk of the proverbial Procrustean procedure of fitting a person into a pre-fabricated mold. That would be a disastrous mistake and would disqualify this brief study from being considered any kind of serious, unbiased appraisal of Dante as a mystic.

Perhaps the greatest difficulty in writing about anyone as a mystic is the sheer breadth of the term "mystic." It has been in use since pre-Christian times in the Western tradition and similar terms and concepts have been common to the religious traditions of the Near East, the Far East and many other ancient religious traditions. Besides, the explosion of information about mysticism and the increased and ever-increasing interest in mysticism and religious experience in the twentieth century could easily dazzle anyone's mind and even discourage or intimidate the scholar or layman who desires to make some small contribution to the field.

Faced with the overwhelming fund of information and the countless testimonies of extraordinary religious experiences that are available today, this writer will adopt and adapt Dante's own attitude of being a, "timid friend of truth" (cf. *Par.* XVII, 8). We saw that Dante described himself with these words in his conversation with his ancestor Cacciaguida, who prepared him to expect hostility and rejection on earth as a result of the harsh, prophetic message which he was about to communicate to the religious and civic leaders of his time.

In the hope of not doing violence to the context of Dante's self-description, I intend to be a "friend of truth" in the sense of being open to the vast literature on mysticism; but I cannot help being timid in the sense of recognizing the impossibility of digesting all the insights available today on this complex subject. A reverential awe fills me, but such wonder should not become what the three beasts became for Dante at the beginning of his journey (cf. *Inf.* I, 31-51). Those beasts so intimidated Dante that they blocked his way. May a certain reverential fear and wonder not cause me or the reader to retreat from such an endeavor as this. A wholesome fear of the sacred and a reverence for the subject of mystical experience can generate an appropriate humility and also perhaps lead to a certain boldness and a child-like trust that the mysterious Source of mystical experience will in some way aid this work and produce some good fruit and inspiration.

We might begin by letting Dante speak for himself on this subject. An excellent, perhaps the best, way of interpreting Dante is through Dante himself, by allowing his own writings to clarify the more difficult passages which puzzle us. What is usually considered his most difficult and challenging "mystical" work is the *Paradiso,* the third canticle of the *Commedia.* It has often been neglected as being too metaphysical and ethereal — in brief, too mystical. The more concrete and earthy atmosphere of the *Inferno* and the *Purgatorio* have been much more popular with readers. Oddly enough, the *Inferno* remains to this day the most read portion of all Dante's works. That is unfortunate, since the *Paradiso* is his real masterpiece, the fruit of his intellectual, emotional and spiritual maturity.

The entire *Paradiso* is about his "mystical experience" — from beginning to end. Dante — fully aware that his claim of having had what he describes at the very beginning of *Paradise* as a "transhumanizing" experience would raise some questions in the minds of his readers — gives an explanation and defense of this exceptional experience in his letter to Can Grande della Scala, the patron and friend to whom he dedicated this work. The questions which he anticipated in this letter were mainly of this nature: how could he, a layman whose human failures and sins were well known to the public, make such an outlandish claim? How could he, who appeared to be an enemy of Holy Church and her hierarchy, pretend to have received a special revelation, like the ones given to the Hebrew prophets, to St. Paul and to the recognized saints and mystics of the Church? Who does he think he is? His public image as a frivolous troubadour poet, as a disgraced statesman fallen from power, as a friend and ally of the powerful Ghibelline lords who opposed the papacy, as a parasite groveling for his bread at their courts — all of these public *personae* seemed to negate the possibility of his being a recipient of extraordinary graces and election for a sacred mission.

And yet in spite of all these negative impressions given to his public, he confidently offers them his extraordinary vision of Paradise, and — fortunately for us — left us the basic key for interpreting it in his letter to Can Grande, a letter which also justifies and defends his apparent arrogance and blasphemy in making such a claim to mystical experience. We have already examined in chapter three the famous passage of this letter in which he gives the fourfold interpretation of Scripture as the basic method for interpreting his own work — an almost blasphemous claim itself, since it practically places the *Comedy* on a level with the inspired Word of God in the Bible. In that passage the fundamental allegorical meaning given by Dante to his entire work is "our redemption through Christ," which indicates clearly the underlying Christ-centered meaning of the whole *Comedy*.

Later in the same letter Dante explains what he means by "Paradise" and what he means by his ascent and experience there. As to the "place" itself, Dante admits that he uses the word *Paradise* as a circumlocution for the highest of the ten heavens, according to the cosmological ideas of his time. He departs, however, from the commonly held Scholastic notion of a material heaven, and describes this highest heaven as totally immaterial and supernatural, beyond the movements of time and space. It is that heaven "which receives the glory of God, or His Light, in the most beautiful measure . . . and it is called the Empyrean, that is to say, the heaven glowing with fire or heat; not that there is material fire or heat therein, but spiritual, which is holy love, or charity."

This Empyrean, "which receives most of the light of God," is thus equated with the fire of divine love. It is the highest heaven since God, the first Cause of all things, perfection in its highest degree, is present there emanating his eternal love, which is the creative source of all things that exist. Dante goes on to quote St. Paul, who wrote of this heaven as the place to which Christ ascended: "He went up far above all the heavens so that He might fill the whole universe" (Ep 4:10). He also quotes Ezekiel who had referred to this heaven as "the delights of the Paradise of God" where Lucifer, "full of wisdom and beautiful in perfection" had once been (Ezk 28:12-13 in the Vulgate version).

Dante then comments on the opening words of his *Paradise* where he described himself as one who had ascended to that place where "he saw certain things which he who descends therefrom is powerless to relate." This powerlessness happens because "the intellect plunges itself to such depth in its very longing which is for God, that the memory cannot follow." The human intellect in this life, Dante notes, is so limited that after such an experience of this "height of exaltation" its memory cannot relate what it saw there. "It has transcended the range of its human faculty." He then gives several examples of this experience of transcendence:

> This is conveyed to us by the Apostle (Paul) where he says, addressing the Corinthians: 'I know a man (whether in the body or out of the body, I cannot tell, but God knows) who was caught up to the third heaven and heard unspeakable words, which it is not lawful for a man to utter' (2 Cor 12:2-4). Consider how the intellect once it has passed beyond the bounds of its human capacity in its exaltation cannot afterwards recall what took place outside of its range. This again is conveyed to us in Matthew, where we read that the three disciples fell on their faces and record nothing thereafter, as though memory had failed them (Mt 17:1-8). And in Ezekiel it is written: 'And when I saw it, I fell upon my face' (Ezk 1:28).
>
> And if these examples should not satisfy the envious, let them read Richard of St. Victor in his book *On Contemplation;* let them read Bernard in his book *On Considera-*

tion; let them read Augustine in his book *On the Capacity of the Soul;* and they will cease from their envying. But if on account of the sinfulness of the speaker (i.e., Dante), they should cry out against his claim to have reached such a height of exaltation, let them read Daniel where they will find that even Nebuchadnezzar by divine permission beheld certain things as a warning to sinners and immediately forgot them (Dn 2:3-5). For He 'who makes His sun shine on the good and on the evil and sends rain on the just and on the unjust' (Mt 5:45) sometimes out of mercy for their conversion, at other times out of severity for their chastisement, in greater or lesser measure, according to His will, manifests His glory even to evil-doers, be they ever so evil.

(*Epistula* X, 27)

This is a most important passage for our understanding and evaluation of Dante as a mystic. We might note first of all that he is ranking his experience with the prophet Ezekiel's vision of the divine glory, an important text of the Old Testament which provided the New Testament Apocalypse with so many images, which Dante had already employed so artistically in his description of the solemn procession in the earthly paradise. In the final verses of the final canto of *Paradiso* Dante will use again some of Ezekiel's images, such as the dazzling light, the rainbow, wings, wheels and the human figure in order to describe his vision of Christ and the Blessed Trinity.

It is significant that Dante cites Ezekiel in this context and gives Ezekiel's vision of the divine glory as an exemplar of his own. There were highly developed commentaries and studies of Ezekiel's visions in the Jewish mystical tradition which flourished in the Middle Ages, particularly in Spain and Italy. This esoteric tradition which focused on "the pattern of the throne of the chariot," generally known as Merkabah mysticism (from the Hebrew *merkavah,* meaning chariot), had its roots in pre-Christian Jewish circles such as the Qumran sect.[6] Whether or not Dante was directly influenced by this tradition is debatable, but we do know that he had Jewish acquaintances and contacts, especially in the person of Immanuel ben Zifroni, who wrote an imitation of Dante's *Comedy* in Hebrew.[7]

Besides alluding to Ezekiel's experience, Dante also refers to the experience of the three disciples, an evocation of the biblical narrative of the Transfiguration of Christ on the mountain where Peter, James and John enjoyed a momentary glimpse of His divine glory. This episode, often called the "Taboric experience" (from the traditional site of this event, Mount Tabor), had become a *locus classicus* in the patristic and medieval traditions for explaining ecstatic contemplation and the mystical experience of God in this life.

There are several other references to this episode in Dante's writings, which indicate the importance which Dante attached to this particular event. In his *Convivio* he cites it as an example of the third meaning of the Scriptures, the moral sense: "As in the Gospel when Christ ascended the Mount to be transfigured, we may be watchful of His taking with Himself the three Apostles out of the twelve; thereby morally it may be understood that for the most secret affairs we ought to have few companions" (*Conv.* II, I, 42-65). Dante also refers to this scene in his *De Monarchia,* citing Peter's words as an example of his misunderstanding of Christ's purposes (cf. *DM* III, IX).

But the most striking allusion to the Transfiguration is found in *Purgatorio* XXXII, 43-87, where the mystic procession in the garden on the summit of Mount Purgatory comes to a halt and the griffin, symbol of Christ, attaches the wooden pole of the chariot to the tree. The meaning of this action, as we noted before, is the death of Christ on the cross, the accomplishment of human salvation through His love-sacrifice, which reconciled the world to God by repairing the damage caused by Adam's sin, which was essentially a violation of the tree of Divine Justice.

When Dante witnesses this reenactment of the Redemption he sees the defoliated tree burst into bloom. This glorious scene of renewal and rebirth — compared to the outbreak of life and beauty in the blood-red blossoms of Spring — is accompanied by a joyous celestial hymn sung by all in the procession. This visual and auditory experience stuns Dante, who falls into an ecstasy — a sleep which is compared to the experience of the three disciples at the Transfiguration of Christ on Mount Tabor. He describes his experience in these words:

I did not recognize the hymn that group
began to sing — it is not sung on earth,
and then, I did not listen to the end.

* * *

So, I shall tell you only how I woke:
a splendor rent the veil of sleep, a voice
was calling me: "What are you doing? Rise!"
When they were led to see that apple tree
whose blossoms give the fruit that angels crave,
providing an eternal marriage-feast,
Peter and John and James were overpowered
by sleep, and then brought back to consciousness
by that same word that broke a deeper sleep;
they saw their company had been reduced,
for Moses and Elijah were not there;
they saw their Master's robe changed back again.
(*Purg.* XXXII, 61-81)

This exceptional passage, with its strong, sensuous references to
seeing, hearing and tasting and its evocation of the Bride of The Song of
Songs who speaks of her Beloved as the "apple tree" (cf. Songs 2:3), is
a clear reference to a mystical experience, which is an earthly foretaste
of the beatific vision in Paradise. Christ — and in particular his sacrificial
love — is the center and source of this ecstatic joy which provides the
nourishment and continuous joy of the angels in the celestial Paradise.
The three apostles caught a glimpse of the glory of divine love on the
mountain — a pause on their journey with Christ to Jerusalem where
the real act of love would take place on the cross. In order to prepare
His disciples for the scandal of the cross, Jesus revealed to them
beforehand the glory and triumph of the cross. Luke's version of the
scene describes the glorious Jesus speaking to Moses and Elijah about
His imminent "exodus," a significant word which links His death to the
ancient exodus, the event which liberated and led to the Promised
Land.

Christ, who revealed His glory on the mountain as an anticipation
of the glory of His love to be manifested on Mount Calvary, would

The cloister of Santa Maria Novella in Florence. Dante studied philosophy at this convent, although the cloister was built after his time.

The Baptistry of San Giovanni in Florence. Dante was baptized here in 1266.

The building of the important guild of the woolen workers in Florence.

The facade of the church of San Miniato al Monte in Florence.

The courtyard of the Bargello in Florence, originally called the building of the Captain of the People.

The cloister of the Franciscan basilica of Santa Croce in Florence. Dante continued his philosophical studies here.

Pope Boniface VIII. A portrait by Giotto (1267-1337) and his assistants in the church of St. John Lateran in Rome.

Pope Clement V. A fresco by Taddeo Gaddi in
the church of Santa Maria Novella in Florence.

The Holy Roman Emperor Henry VII on his deathbed. He died of malaria at Bonconvento near Siena in 1313.

A demon and a damned soul. A detail from a cycle of frescoes executed by Luca Signorelli between 1499 and 1503 for the chapel of San Brizio in the cathedral of Orvieto. They were inspired by the *Divine Comedy*.

Dante with Mount Purgatory in the background. A 15th-century fresco by Domenico di Michelino in the church of Santa Maria del Fiore in Florence.

Dante's meeting with Forese Donati in the *Purgatorio*. A 19th-century illustration by Gustave Dore.

A scene of Paradise painted by Fra Angelico in 1400 and now in
St. Mark's monastery in Florence.

Mary appearing to St. Bernard. A painting
by the Rinuccini Chapel Master which
calls to mind St. Bernard's prayer to Mary
in the final canto of the *Paradiso*.

A 19th-century representation of Beatrice.

Dante presenting Giotto to Guido Novello da Polenta, lord of Ravenna.
A painting by Mochi.

Moses being told by God to "take off your sandals, for the ground that you walk on is holy." (Ex 3:5) A 6th-century mosaic in the church of San Vitale in Ravenna.

Christ's Transfiguration portrayed as a vision of the Exaltation of the Cross. St. Apollinaris stands below. A 6th-century mosaic in the basilica of Sant' Apollinare in Classe, in Ravenna.

The Empress Theodora, wife of the Emperor Justinian. A 6th-century mosaic in the church of San Vitale in Ravenna.

Mary's Dormition and Assumption. A mosaic by Cavallini executed in 1291, in the church of Santa Maria in Trastevere, in Rome.

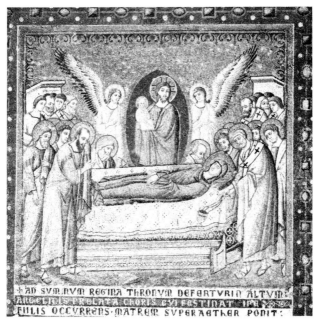

The kiss of Judas. A detail from a fresco by
Giotto in the Scrovegni chapel in Padua.

Pieta. A fresco by Giotto in the Scrovegni chapel in Padua.

A detail of Giotto's Pieta.

St. Francis receiving the stigmata. A fresco by Giotto in the church of Santa Croce in Florence.

Christ enthroned. A 6th-century mosaic in the church of
Sant' Apollinare Nuovo in Ravenna.

ascend to heaven where He would be an everlasting source of satisfaction and joy for the angels and saints in the eternal marriage feast of the lamb (cf. Rv 19:9).

The Transfiguration episode as a paradigm of mystical experience is found often in the Eastern and Western Fathers of the Church whose teachings flowed into the medieval mystical tradition known to Dante. Here is a passage from Richard of St. Victor's book *On Contemplation,* a work Dante cites in his letter to Can Grande. The work is known today as *Benjamin Major* or *The Mystical Ark* and shows the strong influence of the Eastern Christian tradition which Western Europe inherited by way of the mystical writings of Dionysius the areopagite, the chief vehicle for the Eastern mystical tradition developed particularly by Origen and St. Gregory of Nyssa:

> When Moses ascended the mountain he approached the Lord in the middle of a cloud. We can gather sufficiently from what has been said above how this can refer to the third stage or mode of contemplating. For what does it mean to go into a cloud on the occasion of the divine calling except to go into ecstasy of mind and to be darkened in the mind concerning the memory of nearby things by a cloud of forgetting, as it were? It concerns the same mode of contemplating that a luminous cloud overshadowed the disciples of Christ. One and the same cloud both overshadowed by shining and illumined by overshadowing, since it both illumined with respect to divine things and overclouded with respect to human things. And so every contemplation is accustomed to happen by these three modes: by enlarging of the mind, by raising up of the mind, by alienation of the mind. *(The Mystical Ark,* Book V, II)

St. Bonaventure, whose works Dante certainly knew, was also deeply influenced by the Dionysian tradition and makes several references to the Transfiguration as the culmination of the soul's six stages of ascent into God:

Just as God completed the whole world in six days and rested on the seventh, so the smaller world of man is led in a most orderly fashion by six successive stages of illumination to the quiet of contemplation. This is symbolized by the following . . . after six days the Lord called Moses from the midst of the cloud (Ex 24:16) and after six days, as is said in Matthew, Christ led his disciples up a mountain and was transfigured before them.

(The Soul's Journey into God, I, 5)

In his *Life of St. Francis* Bonaventure describes Francis' ascent to Mount La Verna in terms of the disciples' "being led apart by divine providence to a high place," a clear allusion to Mount Tabor and Christ's Transfiguration. It was on Mount La Verna that Francis — on the feast of the Exaltation of the Cross, Sept. 14, 1224 (Dante died on the same feast in 1321!) — was given the ecstatic vision of Christ crucified and the imprints (the stigmata) of Christ's passion in his own flesh:

When the true love of Christ had transformed his lover into his image and the forty days were over that he had planned to spend in solitude and the feast of St. Michael the Archangel (Sept. 29) had also arrived, the angelic man, Francis, came 'down from the mountain' (Mt 8:1) bearing with him the image of the Crucified, which was depicted not on tablets of stone . . . but engraved in the members of his body by the finger of the living God.

(The Life of St. Francis, 13, 1)

Thus Bonaventure sees in Francis the fulfillment of the soul's journey into God, an itinerary whose goal is found not by instruction, understanding or diligent reading but by grace, desire, and the groaning of prayer. To reach this goal one must "seek the Spouse, not the teacher, God not man, darkness not clarity, not light but the fire that totally inflames and carries us into God by ecstatic unctions and burning affections. This fire is God and His furnace is in Jerusalem and Christ enkindles it in the heat of His burning passion."[8]

The resemblances between these passages from Richard of St. Victor and Bonaventure and Dante's experience on the mountain of Purgatory are striking. Dante writes of his ecstatic joy upon contemplating Christ's supreme act of love on the cross and compares it to the three apostles' ecstasy on Mount Tabor. The theological connection between Christ's crucifixion and His transfiguration, that brief revelation of the glory of the cross, was well known to Dante through his study of the Fathers and medieval mystics. It was further confirmed, I believe, by his contemplation of the ecclesiastical art which surrounded him in his lifetime. Near Ravenna, where he spent his last years, he certainly beheld the splendid apse of the basilica of Saint Apollinaris in Classe which depicts in mosaics the Transfiguration of Christ as a glorious circle of golden stars against a blue background. Within the circle is a gold, jewel-laden cross in whose center is the face of Christ. Moses and Elijah are portrayed on either side of the circle, while below three sheep (symbols of the apostles) look up at the glorious circle. [9]

This resplendent mosaic may have had an influence on Dante's description of ecstasy in *Purgatorio* XXXII, and perhaps even more influence on a similar, and much more intense, experience recorded in *Paradiso* XIV — the ecstatic vision of Christ's triumphant cross, which we will discuss in the last chapter. In both episodes music and song dominate and in both places Dante is told to "arise," a word reminiscent of Christ's command to the three apostles on Mount Tabor.

The Transfiguration on Mount Tabor was often linked to Moses' vision of God on Mount Sinai, as we have observed in Richard and Bonaventure's commentaries on these parallel events. It is no accident that Dante enjoys a similar ecstatic experience on the summit of Mount Purgatory where he also confessed his sins and received his prophetic mission from Beatrice. The similarities between Mt. Sinai and Mt. Purgatory are numerous and have been the subject of many scholarly studies. [10] Since the fundamental pattern of Dante's *Comedy* follows the Exodus motif of the Old Testament, which is also the basis for understanding the liberating event of Christ's death and resurrection, revealed on Mt. Tabor, it is no surprise that Moses' experience on Mt. Sinai, the most significant phase of the Exodus event, should often be evoked as a figure and type of the soul's journey and pilgrimage to God.

The soul's pilgrimage to the vision of God was also the underlying spirituality of the medieval devotion of pilgrimage. In Dante's time the typical pilgrimage was planned and undertaken as a great circular movement beginning at Rome, proceeding to Egypt and then on to the Sinai desert, where the pilgrims climbed the mountain where Moses had seen God and received his divine revelation and mission. On Mount Sinai the medieval pilgrims made their confession and received Christ in Holy Communion under the splendor of a wonderful mosaic depicting the Transfiguration of Christ. It, too, like the mosaic in St. Apollinaris in Classe, had been commissioned by the Emperor Justinian and is still remarkably preserved today in the monastery of St. Catherine on Mt. Sinai, one of the few early Christian mosaics in the East which survived the tide of Islam. Dante's acquaintance with the pilgrims' circular route (from Rome via Egypt and the Sinai desert to Jerusalem and its return to Rome) has been studied in depth and richly documented by John G. Demaray in his illuminating volume, *The Invention of Dante's Commedia,* a rich storehouse of information about the "Great Circle Pilgrimage," explained and illustrated by abundant Biblical and Patristic commentaries, medieval maps and photographs of the sites today. A summary of his vast research can be found in this passage:

From the historical materials concerned with pilgrimage, from the analysis of Dante's writings and from the explanation of the poet's typological techniques, one should by now have a very cogent realization of how and why Dante's journey beyond life mirrors that of a Christian's in this world. And from the letter to Can Grande, one is given assistance in finding in the *Commedia* the primary and most immediate earthly events acted out by that Christian.

Now a believing man upon earth can walk in the Paschal Candle procession during Holy Week and so, Roman liturgy suggests, renew again the meaning of the Exodus; participation at Holy Mass joins the Christian spiritually to Christ's Death and Redemption; Christ Himself can be received through confession and communion. Prayer, fasting and long vigils before candlelit images of Christ and the

Apostles can spiritually relate the Christian to New Testament events and to the eternal glory of heaven.

And in Dante's poem such forms of figural imitation are variously shadowed, but most forcefully and tangibly reflected in the *Commedia* is a Christian on a long pilgrimage who confesses his sins on Mt. Sinai and in converting his soul on the Exodus journey, ascends to the place where Moses saw God. This Christian next receives Christ in Jerusalem, and there enjoys the fruits of the Redemption; and on a journey to the eternal city of Rome, this same Christian is spiritually exalted through the veneration of sacred images associated with Christ's Transfiguration. [11]

Dante's brief description of a certain foretaste of eternal glory on the summit of Mt. Purgatory, the earthly paradise, is thus only a stage, like the stages of the medieval pilgrims, in his journey toward the more luminous visions of Christ which he will describe in the heavenly Jerusalem, the eternal Rome, which is the Empyrean filled with the light and fire of God, Who is Love.

In his letter to Can Grande, besides citing the Transfiguration, Dante also refers to St. Paul's ascent to Paradise and his ecstatic vision there as another example of the mystical experience. This Pauline experience, together with Moses' vision on Mt. Sinai and the apostles' ecstasy on Mt. Tabor, were the most familiar "classical texts" in Patristic and Scholastic theology for describing spiritual ecstasy or rapture. Dante on numerous occasions throughout the *Comedy* alludes to Paul's experience and daringly compares his own journey through Hell, Purgatory and Paradise to Paul's journey to the underworld and to the highest heaven.

In Dante's time there was a popular apocryphal work, the *Visio Sancti Pauli,* which narrated Paul's journey through the realms of the dead. This work may have had some influence on Dante since he conceived his own journey through all these realms as an imitation of Paul's journey. At the very beginning of the *Comedy* when Virgil informs him of the journey they must take (cf. *Inf.* II, 25-36), Dante alludes to two famous journeys to the other world: Aeneas' and Paul's, the two journeys which led to the glory of Rome as both the seat of the Empire and the center of the Church. Dante confesses his unworthiness to be a successor of Aeneas and Paul, but in so doing he is really announcing his conviction that his spiritual journey is comparable to Aeneas' and to Paul's: a journey which is also a sacred mission ordained by God for the welfare of the world. Dante spoke to Virgil about these two journeys:

> This cannot seem, to thoughtful men, unfitting,
>   for in the highest heaven he was chosen
>   father of glorious Rome and of her empire,
>   and both the city and her lands, in truth,
>   were established as the place of holiness
>   where the successors of great Peter sit.
> And from this journey you celebrate in verse,
>   Aeneas learned those things that were to bring
>   victory for him, and for Rome, the Papal seat;
>   then later the Chosen Vessel, Paul, ascended
>   to bring back confirmation of that faith
>   which is the first step on salvation's road.
> But why am I to go? Who allows me to?
>   I am not Aeneas, I am not Paul,
>   neither I nor any man would think me worthy;
>   (*Inf.* II, 19-33)

Throughout the *Comedy* Dante will perceive himself as a second Paul, a "chosen vessel," called to communicate a divine message which will lead to the salvation of the Empire and the Church, both suffering grave crises and in dire need of reform. This vocation was the vocation of the prophet, a graced individual who had received a divine revelation for the common good of the Church and the world. In this respect the prophetic mission and the mystical experience are very closely related: the prophet communicates his mystical experience for the salvation of the community. In the theology of St. Thomas Aquinas, which Dante knew and followed on this topic, the prophet, the biblical writer and the mystic were all basically understood in this sense, i.e., as persons who had received graces "freely given" for the benefit and "edification" of the Church.

St. Thomas in his *Summa Theologiae* deals extensively with prophecy and follows closely the Pauline teaching on charisms outlined in his first letter to the Corinthians. Thus prophecy, like the other gifts and ministries from the Spirit, is intended for the "building up" of the Church, either by proposing what is to be believed by all (faith) or by manifesting the "higher mysteries" for the perfected ones (wisdom). Prophecy can also extend to the regulation of human acts and to the discernment of spirits. Also included by Thomas in his concept of prophecy is rapture, or ecstasy, which he calls a "certain degree" of prophecy. He gives Paul's mystical experience related in 2 Corinthians as well as Moses' vision on Mt. Sinai as the primary examples, even while he maintains that the "perfection of divine revelation will be in the eternal life of heaven — *in patria.*"

It is most interesting to notice in Thomas' theology of prophecy that the prophet himself need not be a person of good morals or a person in "the state of grace," that is, in charity. The gift of prophecy, Thomas insists, is a charism — *gratia gratis data* — a grace given regardless of the merits of the recipient, since it is given for the good of the community. Thomas clearly states that God does not always give this gift to the best persons *per se,* but to those whom He judges the best for the reception of that gift. [12]

In his comments on Paul's ecstasy Thomas maintains, following Augustine's interpretation of Scripture, that both Paul and Moses saw the essence of God in these visions. According to Thomas this is the highest degree of contemplation, which is not only the highest knowledge but also the highest "delight" enjoyed by the angels and saints in Paradise. He claims that for this reason Moses is aptly called "the first teacher of the Jews (*primus doctor Judaeorum*) and Paul the first teacher of the Gentiles (*primus doctor Gentium*)." [13]

It's apparent then that Dante was standing on solid theological ground when he claimed that even he, a sinner, could be given the extraordinary grace of divine revelation and rapture, not as a reward for virtue or as a gift for his personal delight, but rather for his own conversion and more importantly for the conversion of the Church and of humanity itself. It has often been pointed out that the "true test" of authentic Christian mysticism is its character as a charism in the service of the whole Church. The late Hans Urs von Balthasar brilliantly

brought out this aspect of authentic mysticism which he found in the life
and writings of Adrienne von Speyr:

> Adrienne von Speyr has brought mysticism back from the
> clandestine existence into which increasingly misunder-
> stood, indeed scorned, it had been exiled and silenced by
> official theology and proclamation, and returned it to the
> center of salvation history. This center is the exchange
> between the word of God in Christ and the hearing and
> responding to this word by the Bride-Church. . . .
>
> Who will hear it (i.e., the word of God) in the way it is
> said and intended, in the way it seeks to be understood and
> believed? Is it the people who only hear the Ten Command-
> ments . . . or is it Moses, who stands his ground before the
> consuming fire and listens to the end, so as, much later, to
> proclaim and then interpret to the people what he has
> received?. . . .
>
> What deserves to be called mysticism — not in the
> vague sense of the history and philosophy of religion, but
> rather in the Catholic, ecclesial sense — occurs when God's
> word is heard, not only with exegetical and theological
> understanding, but with the whole heart, the whole being,
> when one is steadfast before the self-disclosure of the heart
> of God despite fire and night. [14]

Von Balthasar often points out that the true Christian mystic
possesses an "ecclesial soul" — the *anima ecclesiastica* — an expression coined in the Middle Ages, but having its roots in Origen. Von
Balthasar states that "genuine Christian and ecclesial mysticism is in
essence a charism, which means a service to the whole Church assigned by God." He insists that genuine mysticism is a charism which
should not be considered simply as so many "private revelations, which
today's theologians sweep under the rug with a single stroke." Instead
it is a service to the Church's "central deepening and enlivening" of her
Christian faith. According to von Balthasar, "This begins as early as the
mysticism of St. Paul and continues uninterruptedly through the
centuries as we encounter such figures as Benedict, Gregory the

Great, Bernard, Tauler, Gertrude, Catherine of Siena, Therese of
Lisieux, Elizabeth of the Trinity, just to name a few at random. Such
charismatics were meant to set aglow the core of the faith in a new way
under the promptings of the Holy Spirit."[15]

Although von Balthasar in this passage does not mention Dante
among the charismatics, in his chapter on Dante in his monumental *The
Glory of the Lord* he often alludes to Dante's mystical experience of God
in connection with "his sense of mission which is without parallel in
Christian history inasmuch as it is not only lived out (as in the case of
many saints) but is energetically impressed upon men and is ratified by
the greatest poets of Antiquity as well as by the representatives of
Christianity."[16] On Dante's ecclesial soul he comments:

> Dante is devoted, in a childlike way, to the Church of Christ,
> to her Sacraments, to the Divine Word that she dispenses.
> And just as he hopes for a Savior-Emperor, so he longs for
> the purification of the Church. His anger over her defects
> . . . springs solely from the loving zeal of a Christian layman
> . . . who, on behalf of those who have been led astray,
> indeed on behalf of the Lord of the Church Himself, laments
> the dereliction of the holy city. [17]

Dante's prophetic mission, given in and through his mystical experience, was thus a charism which the Lord Himself through Beatrice
on the mountain in Purgatory and St. Peter in Paradise conferred on him
for the purification of His Bride, the Church. On numerous occasions,
as we have seen, Dante's prophetic mission and his Christ-centered
spirituality found expression in outbursts of rage over the tragic condition of Church and Empire. This passionate outrage, however, was
never isolated from a deep hope in Christ, who will not abandon His
Church and His world. What is considered by commentators to be the
strongest of his apostrophes to the entire world — the Church, Empire,
Italy and Florence — is an explosive interruption of a peaceful scene in
Purgatory. It begins with the words "O wretched Italy," and describes
in the most pathetic tones the shameful failures of Church leaders and
secular authorities to carry out God's will for peace and love in this

world. Right in the middle of this extraordinary passage is this passionate plea to Christ:

> O Jove Supreme, crucified here on earth
> for all mankind, have I the right to ask
> if Your just eyes no longer look on us?
> Or is this part of a great plan conceived
> in Your deep intellect, to some good end
> that we are powerless to understand?
> (*Purg.* VI, 118-123)

We see in this passage, as well as in so many others, that Dante's
prophetic mission and his spirituality are both Christ-centered and also
oriented toward the salvation of the world and of Christ's Church.
Dante's mission as a chosen vessel like St. Paul is also at the same time
a source of suffering and humiliation. Dante's journey through Hell is a
necessary stage in his mission. He *must* experience there the horror of
his own sin and then be purged on the mountain of Purgatory and
confess his sins before Beatrice. It is only after this humiliation and
conversion that he can receive the Word and experience the visions
which he must carry back for the conversion of Church and Empire.
Dante's visions of Hell, Purgatory and Paradise are thus all *necessary*
experiences which prepare him for his divinely ordained mission, which
then becomes a most terrible kind of moral exhortation to the whole of
Christendom.

Dante's mysticism, then, is not some sort of "spiritual high" or
"peak experience," given merely for consolation or delight: it is a painful
spiritual journey into a fearful confrontation with his own sin and need
for conversion as well as an encounter with God, Who, as purifying
Love and Justice, wills the purification and salvation of Dante and of His
beloved Church. It was fitting then that Dante chose to cast himself as
another Paul who, while journeying in darkness on the road to
Damascus, encountered the luminous Lord of the Church. Paul was
called to be a prophet, underwent a "conversion," and then experienced
in the desert of Arabia, and elsewhere perhaps, ecstatic visions of
Paradise which he transmitted to the Christian Church. In his many
missionary journeys he suffered untold hardships; and after his final

journey to Rome, the center of the Empire and the future center of the Church, he gave the ultimate prophetic witness to his faith and visions by a martyr's death in imitation of the Lord.

Dante, after citing the mystical experiences of Paul, the prophet Ezekiel, and the three disciples on Mt. Tabor, recommends in his letter to Can Grande that the "envious" readers of his *Paradiso* who object to his own claim to such experiences consult also the writings of Richard of St. Victor, St. Bernard and St. Augustine. We have considered already a passage from Richard; perhaps samples from Bernard and Augustine might clarify for us what Dante means by an extraordinary vision of Paradise which is possible to those still on earth.

Dante refers to only one work of Bernard from among the many works of Bernard which deal with mystical themes. It is the *De Consideratione,* written by Bernard toward the end of his life at perhaps the darkest time of his earthly pilgrimage. The conditions under which Bernard composed this work were strikingly similar to Dante's situation toward the end of his life. Bernard was suffering from the utter failure of the Second Crusade, which he had preached by word and pen and for which all Europe held him responsible. His *De Consideratione* is an impassioned defense of that failed enterprise and a final, peaceful abandonment to the mysterious abyss of God's judgments. We may recall that Dante's ancestor Cacciaguida was among those slain in that very crusade as a martyr who thereafter entered the peace of Paradise. In so many ways Bernard's work must have struck a sensitive chord within Dante's heart, since he had recently suffered the failure and death of Henry VII and the scandalous removal of the papacy to Avignon.

Bernard in this work, written toward the middle of the twelfth century and dedicated to Pope Eugenius III, shows himself as both the reforming prophet and the glowing mystic. Many of his strong exhortations to the pope remind us of Dante's harsh criticisms of popes over a hundred years later. Bernard sharply reprimands the pope for his worldly wealth and military pomp. His words ring out almost in Dantesque tones as he castigates the pope: "In these things you are the successor, not of Peter, but of Constantine." Bernard denounces the pope's use of temporal power with these incisive words: "Why do you strive once more to employ the sword, which you were once

commanded to put away into its sheath?" This is, of course a reference
to Christ's command to Peter (cf. Mt 26:52). Such passages are
remarkably similar to many passages in Dante's works. Bernard's ideal
picture of what the pope should be is almost identical to Dante's idea of
the papacy presented in his *De Monarchia*. Dante certainly found a
kindred spirit in Bernard, the reformer of a corrupt papacy.

But Bernard, although most actively involved in all the events of
European history in his day, was also the ardent mystic *par excellence*.
In this work, especially in its final book, he writes eloquently and
passionately on the stages of contemplation. He describes how the
earthly pilgrim and exile can ascend even now to a "consideration" of
the things above, that is, Paradise and God. He distinguishes three
stages in this ascent: opinion, faith and understanding. Dante may well
have taken these three stages to be the models for his three principal
guides in the *Comedy*: Virgil, Beatrice and Bernard himself. Dante
chooses Bernard as his final guide since Bernard, especially in this
work, shows himself to be the experienced master in contemplation,
the activity of the blessed in Paradise, which is best described as
contemplative love. Dante in the closing cantos of *Paradiso* will meet
Bernard and describe his face as radiating "the living charity of him who
in this world, by contemplation, tasted of that peace" (cf. *Par*. XXXI,
109-111).

It is most difficult to choose from among the many moving passages of Bernard's works an excerpt which would summarize his
concept of the highest degree of contemplation. Bernard often presents
St. Paul as the one who best exemplifies this experience:

> But the greatest of all is he who spurns the use of things
> which the senses can perceive (as far as human frailty can)
> and goes up not by steps but in great leaps beyond our
> imagining; he has learned to fly to the heights in contempla-
> tion at times. I think Paul's raptures were like that:
> raptures, not steps up, for he himself says that he was
> 'caught up' rather than that he 'ascended' (2 Cor 12:2). That
> is why he said, 'If we are beside ourselves, it is for God' (2
> Cor 5:13).

Further, these three (i.e., kinds of consideration)
come together when consideration, even in the place of its
exile, is brought higher by zeal for virtue and with the
assistance of grace, and either restrains sensuality so that it
does not get above itself or holds it so that it does not
wander, or flees it, so that it does not corrupt. . . . Indeed,
that flight is made on twin wings of purity and eagerness.

(De Consideratione II, 3)

In many other passages of the same work Bernard describes the
contemplative experience, likening it to the Seraphim's burning love for
God, to the Tabor event, and to the Bride's passionate love in the Song
of Songs. His descriptions of God as love are exceptionally rich in
biblical allusions and personal, experiential comments. He repeatedly
states that God's love has no boundaries, that He hates nothing that He
has made (cf. Ws 11:25), that He causes his sun to rise upon the good
and the wicked and rain to fall upon the just and the unjust (cf. Mt 5:45),
a biblical passage also quoted by Dante in his letter to Can Grande.
Bernard maintains that in contemplation the soul comprehends the very
heart of God, "Who takes care of those He has determined to save. He
carries them along, embraces them, and like a fire burns up the sins of
their youth and renders them pure and worthy of his love." Bernard also
insists that comprehension of these things is not the result of intellectual study and discussion, but rather of holiness:

Argument does not comprehend these things but holiness,
if that which is incomprehensible can be comprehended in
any way. But if it could not, the Apostle would not have said
that we should comprehend with all the saints (Rm 11:33).
So the saints comprehend it. Do you ask how? If you are
holy, you have comprehended it and you know. If not, be
holy and you will know from your own experience. Holy
love makes a man holy and it is twofold: holy fear of the Lord
and holy love. The soul moved entirely by them grasps as if
with its two arms, embraces, hugs, holds and says, 'I have
him and I will not let him go.' (Songs 3:4)

(De Consideratione XIV, 30)

Bernard's profound influence on Dante could be the topic of an entire book. A summary can be found in Edmund G. Gardner's classical study on the sources of Dante's mysticism, *Dante and the Mystics*. The topic of Dante's sources is a formidable one, and still occupies the scholars' attention and scrutiny. The astonishing aspect of all these studies is the discovery that Dante was able to integrate so many various biblical, patristic and medieval sources into his vision of Paradise. Dante in his letter to Can Grande merely mentions at random some of his sources.

One of those sources is St. Augustine's work *De Quantitate Animae,* usually translated as *The Magnitude of the Soul.* It is a small work in the form of a dialogue, written shortly after his conversion. In this book he examines the seven stages of the soul's progress from mere animation to the highest level of vision and contemplation of eternal truth: God Himself. Some scholars contend that Dante followed Augustine's pattern of seven stages as the framework for his journey through Hell, Purgatory and Paradise, the seventh stage being the soul's contemplation of God in the Empyrean. Arguments could also be given that Dante adheres more to Bonaventure's or Bernard's pattern of stages. It is difficult to identify which author Dante followed more closely.

It is equally difficult to single out any one passage as the most representative of a particular mystic's concept of such a complex and elusive experience as mystical contemplation, but the following seems somewhat representative of Augustine's thought on this topic. It may also be the one Dante had in mind in his letter:

At length, in the vision and contemplation of truth, we come to the seventh and last step, not really a step, but a dwelling place to which the previous steps have brought us. What shall I say are the delights, what the enjoyment, of the supreme and true God, what breath of undisturbed peace and eternity? These are the wonders that great souls have declared, so far as they brought themselves to speak of these realities, great souls of incomparable greatness, who, I believe, beheld and now behold these things.

> This I now dare to say to you in all simplicity, that if we hold with all perseverance to the course that God lays down for us and which we have undertaken to hold, we shall come by God's Power and Wisdom to that Highest Cause or Supreme Author or Supreme Principle of all things or whatever other name you would deem worthy of so great a Reality.   (*De Quantitate Animae* 33, 76)

We have noticed already that Dante also had a profound knowledge of Augustine's *Confessions.* No doubt Dante knew the outstanding passage in the ninth book of that work in which Augustine describes a foretaste of the Beatific Vision, experienced with his mother, St. Monica, as they gazed on the lovely garden at Ostia and were "caught up" into a vision of God. Augustine called it "this moment of understanding," when he and Monica "entered into the joy of the Lord." Augustine's influence on Dante can be found in almost all his works. We might even conclude that Augustine's conversion story, told in the *Confessions,* served as a model for Dante's own description of his "lost way" in the dark forest at the beginning of the *Inferno,* his purification of love on Mount Purgatory, and his joyful ecstasies in Paradise. Dante seems to have borrowed numerous images and expressions from many of Augustine's works. [18]

In the white rose of Paradise, Dante locates St. Augustine as the fourth in a direct line following St. John the Baptist, St. Francis of Assisi and St. Benedict. Augustine is placed opposite Sarah, often taken as a symbol of the official Church. Perhaps Dante is representing Augustine as a Doctor of the Church, an official exponent of her theology. [19] In any case, Dante expressed in numerous places his indebtedness to Augustine's theology, particularly his mystical theology. All the great mystics and theologians of the Middle Ages — Richard of St. Victor, Thomas Aquinas, Bernard, Bonaventure and so many others — reveal a deep indebtedness to St. Augustine.

The question of Dante's sources and the multiple influences on him — the Bible, the Fathers, the medieval Doctors and mystics — is a fascinating and interesting study which reveals Dante's genius for fusing into one vision such a multiplicity of sources. Perhaps Evelyn Underhill expresses best Dante's originality in this respect:

In Italy Dante is forcing human language to express one of the most sublime visions of the Absolute which has ever been crystallized into speech. He inherits and fuses into one that loving and artistic reading of reality which was the heart of Franciscan mysticism, and that other ordered vision of the transcendental world which the Dominicans through Aquinas poured into the stream of European thought. For the one the spiritual world was all love; for the other, law. For Dante it was both. In the *Paradiso* his stupendous genius apprehends and shows to us a Beatific Vision in which the symbolic systems of all great mystics, and many whom the world does not call mystics — of Dionysius, Richard, St. Bernard, Mechthild, Aquinas, and countless others — are included and explained. [20]

Evelyn Underhill's classic work, *Mysticism,* first published in 1911, is probably still the best one-volume study of mysticism in English. She was far ahead of her times in her scholarship and intuitions; and in spite of a veritable plethora of studies on mysticism in the twentieth century, her work still remains valid and a solid foundation for understanding Christian mysticism today. [21]

Her analysis of mysticism could serve as a "working definition" for our present study of Dante's mysticism. Her study, which embraces a broad spectrum of psychological, philosophical and theological approaches to the subject, seems particularly relevant to our study of Dante since she refers to Dante's mysticism more than thirty-three times in her book. One could possibly summarize Underhill's many descriptions of mysticism as "an authentic life process, involving transitory experiences, but transcending them with an ordered movement toward perfect consummation with the God of love." [22]

Underhill stresses throughout her work that authentic mysticism is the deep desire of the human person to surrender to the Mystery of total love. She insists that mysticism is not primarily concerned with what many people today consider its essence: spiritual highs and thrills, peak experiences or altered states of consciousness. She often emphasizes that the essence of mysticism is a complete way of life, not just occasional visions or extraordinary religious highs which, she affirms, can and do occur. In line with the best of Christian traditions — the testimony of the great saints and mystics themselves — she focuses on the God who initiates and directs the mystic's quest for absolute Truth and Love.

Underhill's understanding of genuine Christian mysticism has been confirmed by many outstanding theologians and spiritual writers of our century: Karl Rahner, Hans Urs von Balthasar, Bernard Lonergan, Thomas Merton, William Johnston, to name only a few.[23] Rahner, for example, insists that "mystical experience is not specifically different from the ordinary life of grace." He, of course, recognizes the unusual experiences of the saints — their visions, ecstasies, etc. — as mysticism in the strict sense; but he understands ordinary Christian experiences as mysticism in a wide sense. For Rahner the saints experienced in an extraordinary psychological way what all Christians experience in a more hidden way.

Von Balthasar also cautions us about placing too much emphasis on unusual experiences. He sees the modern quest for religious experience as an obsession for a scientific verification of our faith. Worldly science and psychology thus become a substitute for authentic religious faith. He views this as a contemporary heresy present in the Church today, and I think we have to face the painful truth of his observation. The mania today for religious experience, evidenced by the proliferation of "trendy," learnable techniques for inducing a religious experience of God has captivated, it seems, large numbers of Catholics to say nothing of other Christians, as well as the general public. This is not to say that the quest for a deeper experience of God is not good and valid in itself; but the subtle danger lies in the possibility that the quest may be a thinly disguised desire for "self-actualization" or self-fulfillment (or whatever may be the current term), which is ultimately a form of spiritual solipsism and narcissism. Many trends in the last three decades of American history are sufficient evidence of this search for transcendental experience — in many cases a quest for the traditional beliefs, values and practices of the authentic religions which have been scorned and abandoned. The void must be filled somehow.

Von Balthasar also insists in his writings on the mystics and saints that the most important thing is not their unusual visions and their personal accomplishments, but rather their unwavering obedience and commitment to their mission. Their utter humility and submission to the Lord who speaks to His servant is the true test of their mysticism and sanctity. Their selflessness and self-forgetfulness — their fidelity to the daily demands of faith, hope and love — are the authenticating signs of their Christian existence. Jesus' loving abandonment to His Father and to the world — his *kenosis* on the cross — is *the* model of Christian mysticism. The mystic's contemplation of the God who is Love will by His grace draw her into a radical immersion into that same kind of practical love. Thus the consummation of mystical experience overcomes the false dichotomy between contemplation and action. It becomes, as Underhill had insisted, a complete way of life. Selfless service to Christ, His Church and to the world, even when it results in apparent failure and seems foolish and futile, becomes then the most important criterion of real Christian mysticism.

Dante's life and writings seem to express that kind of authentic Christian mysticism. His life of service to the Church and the Empire (the world) was marked mainly by failure and disappointment, but he was sustained by his unwavering faith, hope and love and even experienced, it seems, at least one transitory moment of ecstatic joy. Many Dante scholars, however, are reluctant to describe him as a mystic in the strict sense. Some outstanding experts even flatly deny any such classification for Dante. [24] They cite his desire for fame and honor, his vocation as an artist and poet, and his deep involvement in politics, especially his concern for the welfare of the Empire. Some even cite his sensuality and erotic tendencies as obstacles to the attainment of authentic mystical experience.

There may also exist a lingering prejudice, even today, that a "mere layman" cannot be classified as a mystic. And there is his fascination with Beatrice, which seems for some readers an impediment to pure love of God. Dante thus would have had a divided heart, preferring the creature to the Creator. But Dante's sin, confessed on the summit of Purgatory, was not his love for Beatrice, but rather his neglect and betrayal of it! In the words of Hans Urs von Balthasar:

> The thoroughly earthly love of the *Vita Nuova* is carried as far as the heights of Heaven; indeed, it is extolled as the motive power for the whole journey through the hereafter.

The love, which began on earth between two human beings is not denied, is not bypassed in the journey to God; it is not, as was always, naturally enough, hitherto the case, sacrificed on the altar of the classical *via negativa;* no, it is carried right up to the throne of God, however transformed and purified. This is utterly unprecedented in the history of Christian theology.[25]

So Dante's worldly concerns, his love for Beatrice, his status as a layman, his vocation as poet and his human desire for earthly fame — all of these factors, or any one of them — have been cited as disqualifying him for classification as a mystic. Some critics even question his honesty in claiming an unusual mystical experience, as if God's grace could not operate in an extraordinary way in just an ordinary Christian layman. They refer to Dante's immense erudition and his genius for imitating classical writers, both pagans and Christians. As a supreme artist he therefore wrote a pure fiction, but really never had a mystical experience in the technical sense of the term. In other words, he never really "saw" anything; he had no real "vision" of Paradise, nor did he experience any "beatific vision."

Certainly it is plausible that as a gifted poet he was able to create such a vision and make it believable. He was indeed successful at this, if we read his *Comedy* as he intended it to be read. But was Dante "faking it"? Was he using his knowledge of the mystics' writings merely in the service of poetry? Such a suspicion, it seems, lurks in the minds of many Dante critics. With due respect for their serious studies of Dante's sources and his literary gifts, I think we should accept Dante's own claim that he truly "experienced" an extraordinary vision of God "as the Love that binds everything together." In Evelyn Underhill's words, "The mystic vision, then, is of a spiritual universe held within the bonds of love (cf. *Par.* XXXII, 85); and of the free and restless human soul, having within it the spark of divine desire, 'the tendency to the Absolute,' only finding satisfaction and true life when united with this Life of God. Then, in Patmore's lovely image, 'the babe is at its mother's breast, the lover has returned to the beloved.' "[26]

Dante throughout the *Comedy,* but especially in the closing cantos of *Paradiso* reveals a childlike naivete, a return to the mother's breast,

and a re-discovery of his true beloved one. Such images of infantile
confidence and amorous sighs abound in Paradise. It seems that Dante
really understood that one must become like a new-born babe again in
order to enter God's Kingdom, which is also an eternal wedding feast
with the beloved Lamb. So many experiential expressions, such as "I
saw" and "I tasted" are found in the final cantos of Paradise that I think
the open-minded reader should conclude that Dante was sincerely
narrating an extraordinary, personal experience which he also repeatedly attributed to a mysterious, undeserved grace from God. In his
monumental two-volume work on Dante's mysticism Giuseppe Parma
asks the crucial question: Did Dante truly see God in a real, mystical
rapture or ecstasy? His answer, with all the necessary qualifications, is
positive:

> Did Dante really see? The answer evidently can only be
> conjectural. The secrets of the soul escape all human
> history and are found in their truth only in the Father of
> Lights. Besides, these states of the soul (The scholars of
> experimental mysticism admit it and it is accepted and
> proven by Catholic writers) are not so rare, where Grace
> inspires and wills to give such a special gift. . . . Dante is the
> protagonist of the universal drama of Redemption, de-
> veloped in all its diverse and ascending moments. The
> sincerity of the poem and of the poet consists in the reality
> of the interpretation and in the real, intimate sentiment of
> the facts and the natural and supernatural meanings of its
> grand configuration. . . .
>
> Since the protagonist is the one 'who when Love in-
> spires, writes down and gives meaning in the way that Love
> dictates within him,' we should maintain his entire sincerity
> only when he has had the experience of what raises up his
> song. We are speaking of mystical experiences, properly
> so-called, of the wayfarer (*viator*) who was given a special
> gift of Grace; without experiences the profound mystical
> pages of the mystics would have enlightened his mind, but
> they would not have moved his heart to such an extent as to
> explode in a song which moves so many generations in the
> whole world. [27]

Besides this rather positive judgment on Dante's authentic mystical experience, we could quote many Dante scholars and theologians in our century who defend the *real* experience of Dante. One of the greatest Italian critics, Bruno Nardi, concedes that Dante's *Comedy* is certainly poetry and the highest kind of poetry, just as the prophetic books of the Bible are poetry, "but the central motive which animates such poetry is a moral and religious motive, to such an extent that the Dantesque vision and the rapture of the poet as 'literary fictions' distorts the meaning of what for Dante is primarily 'the *sacred* poem' which intends to narrate the wonderful revelation given to his poetic spirit by God."[28]

Nardi also maintains that Dante was a true prophet not because his plans for political and ecclesiastical reform were realized (they failed miserably!), but because he transcended the events of history and found the eternal ideal of justice which measures and judges the moral value of all human actions. But more than that: he projected his spirit into the Infinite and Absolute Spirit of God. Like Augustine, he joined his heart and soul to the Lord and found rest in Him. Nardi concludes that Dante experienced true rapture and ecstasy, just as the ancient saints and prophets such as Ezekiel, the author of the Book of Revelation and Paul had experienced it. Nardi expressed how absurd it is not to accept Dante's sincerity in these words: "No Christian of the Middle Ages, unless he were a fool or unbeliever, would have dared to parody the rapture of St. Paul in order to make of it, a poetic fiction, that is, a 'beautiful lie,' even if this hid a truth."[29]

Many other authorities could be cited to support the real mystical experience of Dante. A scholarly work of over seven-hundred pages by Egidio Guidubaldi was published in 1968, *Poema Sacro come Esperienza Mistica,* which analyzes from a Jungian perspective Dante's *Comedy* as a mystical experience. The tome is rich in its exploration of symbols, images and dreams as sources of Dante's artistic creation. Interpretations of the great theologian Romano Guardini, who also employed Jungian theories in his reading of Dante, are also included in this vast work which should be translated into English. But for those readers who cannot consult such a dense, scholarly tome on Dante as a mystic, the following conclusion of Edmund Gardner, I think, is true, to the point, and represents the fruit of rigorous scholarship:

The visionary experience upon which the whole sacred poem is based was simply a sudden realization of the hideousness of vice and the beauty of virtue, the universality and omnipotence of love, so intense and overwhelming that it came upon Dante with all the force of a special and personal revelation. But this passage in the letter (to Can Grande) clearly implies that, for the crowning vision or ecstasy of the *Paradiso,* he is claiming something more than such a mere realization, however intense; that he is claiming some ineffable spiritual experience of which he feels himself unworthy, and which he is utterly unable adequately to relate. These are manifestly the words of one who believed that he himself had experienced one of those contacts with the Divine that are attributed to the great saints and mystics of all creeds.

This experience of revelation, call it what you will, was undoubtedly the supreme event of Dante's inner life. . . . It would seemingly have been some absorbing subjective experience of the divine, completing and crowning what had gone before, some momentary flash of spiritual intuition, in which his mind 'was smitten by a flash, in which its will was fulfilled' (*Par.* XXXIII, 140); in which time and space were annihilated and the apprehension of the suprasensible, the divine and the eternal, was all in all. [30]

This extraordinary experience, which, I think, we can identify as a mystical experience in the strict sense, came to Dante not as a reward of his personal saintliness. He explicitly states in his letter that God at times sends this grace for the conversion of the sinner, implying that this revelation was needed for his own conversion. He even cites the outrageous example of Nebuchadnezzar, the very incarnation of the sinner in the biblical tradition, to demonstrate how God's grace is freely given to the most wicked.

I think there is the unmistakable ring of sincerity and truth in Dante's humble words, confirmed by his repeated profession in the cantos of *Paradiso* that the vision was pure gift from God. Dante, then, did not intend to place himself on a pedestal as a saint or mystic. His conversion came about through the most bitter sufferings: he had been publicly maligned, banished, maltreated and despised. He had endured endless physical hardships, not to mention the moral bewilderment over his own sinfulness and over the corrupt and chaotic state of the Church and Empire in his day. He had been pushed to the very limits of endurance, to the threshold of existential despair; but God's "amazing grace" had intervened to save him. His conversion occurred after extreme pressures from without and from within. Karl Vossler contrasts Dante in this respect with Augustine, Bernard and Francis of Assisi, noting that none of them had suffered so much in their conversion process:

> In comparison with Dante, Augustine, Bernard and Francis appear as natural, born, professional mystics, while from the stubborn material of the banished Florentine only unhappiness could rouse the holy flame.
>
> There was nothing habitual or professional in Dante's piety. I am inclined to call it occasional mysticism, using the word 'occasion' not in the sense of a chance occurrence, but of a concrete experience. What is true of occasional poetry applies also to occasional mysticism; they are both a direct, sincere, outpouring of the soul, arising not out of chronic exuberance, but from the momentary need of the heart.
>
> So there is nothing priestly or ministerial in Dante's piety, nothing of the virtuoso or of the monk. A pious man, but no saint. The lay spontaneity of Dante's piety fundamentally and favorably distinguishes his utterances from the sweetness, sanctity, and fanaticism of all apostles, prophets and men of God, of ancient and recent memory. It sets him apart, especially from the artificially aroused mediaeval mysticism. Herein Dante is modern, more modern than a modern preacher. [31]

This seems to be a very felicitous way to describe Dante: an occasional lay mystic. But the question often arises as to when and where this occasion or these occasions took place. Some scholars suggest the quiet monastic retreat of Santa Croce at Fonte Avellana high in the Apennines; others the delightful pine forest at Classe near Ravenna along the Adriatic coast; still others suggest the ancient Christian basilicas of Ravenna with their inspiring mosaics. Most scholars think that Dante wrote his *Paradiso* between the years 1318 and his death in 1321, but it is really impossible to determine when or where Dante's mystical experience occurred.

Another theory, which I think deserves serious consideration, is that Dante made a pilgrimage to Rome in the Jubilee year proclaimed by Boniface VIII in 1300 to commemorate the thirteen-hundredth anniversary of Christ's birth. [32] It is very likely that Dante was in Rome at that time, since in the *Comedy* he describes the crowds there and makes several allusions to that event, which was a call to spiritual conversion through confession, communion and the visitation of the basilicas where the remains of Saints Peter and Paul and other martyrs were venerated. The grand mosaics and icons depicting Christ, Mary and saints in glory in those basilicas must have impressed him deeply. Perhaps a "moment of understanding" occurred then; perhaps he had an extraordinary "vision" of sorts or a conversion experience then. In fact he deliberately chose Holy Week and Easter Week of the year 1300 as the ideal date of his journey through the realms of Hell, Purgatory and Paradise. Besides, the dominant themes of the *Comedy* are pilgrimage, conversion, confession and communion.

Could it be that like Paul on the road to Damascus, Dante experienced the glorious Christ through some sort of visionary medium during his pilgrimage in Rome and then later in life, after reflecting on it for a long time, entered more deeply into the meaning of that mysterious event? Dante often in Paradise compares his "visions" of Christ there to the flash of light that struck down and blinded Paul when the risen Christ appeared to him. We know from Paul's letters and the Acts of the Apostles how that divine revelation and that personal encounter with Christ was the single most significant event and turning point in his life, how he meditated on it for years before beginning his missionary journeys, and how it remained the very wellspring of his energy, zeal and love for Christ and His Church.

Paul's Christocentric spirituality so deeply impressed Dante that he consistently turned to it as the model for expressing his own spiritual experiences. As in all authentically Christian spiritualities the mystery of Christ stands at the very center. In writing of Newman's spirituality Louis Bouyer constantly reminds us of this:

> As the Fathers and the greatest of the schoolmen had recognized, the mystery of Christianity was simply the very mystery of Christ which itself opens out to us, through the Incarnation, the mystery of God in His Trinity. As a result we are introduced into this mystery's transcendent reality. And therefore the mystery appears as being eventually the mystery of the Church in her unity: the union of all her members with Christ the Head, through the Spirit, so that all become adopted by and recapitulated into the Father Himself, seen as the sole source of all. [33]

When discussing a book on Newman as a mystic, Bouyer gives some valuable insights on the essence of a Christian mystic:

> If Newman cannot be described as a "mystic" in the essentially psychological, modern sense of the term, his teaching *is* nonetheless mystical in the meaning attached to the word precisely by the followers of the Cappadocian Fathers. Let us understand that the whole of the Christian faith, for Newman as for them, is centered upon our apprehension by faith of the mystery of Christ, seen, according to the doctrine of St. Paul, as the mystery of His Cross, leading to His glorification and our own 'in Him.' That this mystery is fundamentally an object — *the* object — of faith implies that it will remain beyond the pale of our present experience. But that this object of faith — if our faith is alive — should consciously permeate the whole of our experience in varying degrees according to the individual is surely no less essential for Newman than for the Cappadocian Fathers as well as for St. Paul and St. John. [34]

Bouyer made these comments in the context of Newman's sermons on certain Pauline texts, particularly 2 Corinthians 3:18. Bouyer's comments about Newman's mysticism could be applied

equally to Dante's mysticism. In fact several Pauline texts which form
the basis of Newman's sermons are the very texts which are the basis of
Dante's Christocentric mysticism, expressed so exuberantly in his
three visions of Christ in Paradise.[35]

Many modern theologians, in the wake of Rahner and von Balthasar, are calling our attention to the value of the saints and mystics as
theological sources. According to these theologians, the mystics
through their lives and writings illuminate us on what is really taking
place in the lives of all persons of good faith. The mystics, according to
Rahner, illustrate what contemporary theology should be doing: initiat-
ing us into the experience of Mystery, Revelation and Love, which
haunts the roots of our being and has incarnated itself in the life, death
and resurrection of Christ.[36]

Mysticism then should not be isolated from other areas of theology
as many Catholic theologians in the past have done. Recently that call
for integrating mysticism once again into theology has been made by
William M. Thompson in a brilliant little work called *Fire and Light: The
Saints and Theology (On Consulting the Saints, Mystics and Martyrs in
Theology)*. In his Introduction, curiously enough, he explains his use of
the word "consult" in the sense of Newman's article "On Consulting the
Faithful in Matters of Doctrine." He recommends in that same Introduction that the great literary masters and artists, such as Dante, "who
have pondered and expressed the depths of the mystery of sanctity"
also be consulted because they gave us "an aesthetic expression of that
same powerful mixture of fire and light found in the saints."[37] Consulting Dante, then, a "lay mystic" whose poetic art gives an aesthetic
expression of that same fire and light found in the saints and mystics,
can and should be a source of enrichment for modern theology and a
source of inspiration for the faith of all Christians today. In the concluding chapters of this book we shall explore in more detail Dante's
mystical apprehension of the central Christian mystery: Christ and our
salvation through, with and in Him.

Chapter Seven

FIGURA CHRISTI

Dante throughout his writings never lets us forget that the central event of universal history for a Christian is the "Christ event." The mystery of Christ divides history into events and persons who preceded Him as types and figures and those who came after Him. These latter are also related to Him as "figures," whose complete meaning and destiny are understood only in reference to Him. In this respect Dante is following the first lesson which the Risen Christ gave to His disciples on the day of His resurrection (cf. Luke 24:27). He taught them to interpret universal history — "all the Scriptures" — as figures foreshadowing Himself.

This method of interpreting the Scriptures was sometimes called allegory by St. Paul (cf. Gal 4:22-26), and became the traditional key for interpreting Old Testament events and persons. It can be found in the writings of the "Apostolic Fathers," the apologists, Origen and all the Fathers and ecclesiastical writers throughout Christian history. Although this exegetical method has been called by different names — allegorical, mystical, figural, typological — it is still the same basic interpretation of history which understands Christ as the central person in whom the meaning of God's plan unfolds throughout universal history.

This method of interpretation, taught by Christ Himself, followed by New Testament writers and the Fathers, was also the fundamental technique employed by the great medieval Doctors. Dante, however, went beyond their use of the technique which was concerned with only the Bible. He freely and daringly adapted this biblical technique and extended it to all literature, including his own *Comedy*. In this respect Dante expressed a unique freedom and creativity which sets him in a class by himself.[1]

Dante, as we have seen, outlined the principles for interpreting his *Comedy* in his letter to Can Grande by explicitly placing "our salvation through Christ" as *the* allegorical or mystical center of the whole work. Thus the various characters in the *Comedy,* including himself the protagonist, are understood as so many "figures" which in some way or another find their full meaning only in relationship to Christ. They are "figures" or "shades" (*ombre*) of the one central reality: Christ. But they are not treated as "mere shadows" devoid of reality in a somewhat Platonic sense; rather, they are real, historical persons related somehow to the real, historical person of Jesus the Christ.

Many modern Dante scholars, such as Auerbach, Hollander and Singleton, have made this abundantly clear. Their understanding of Dante's "figural realism" and his "Christian Incarnational art" can help us see that Dante understood himself as writing history after the manner of "God's way of writing" found in the Bible. Thus Dante's allegorical method is biblical: it concerns facts, real events and real persons in history. For Dante even the events recorded in the literature of pagan antiquity have as much historical validity as the events recorded in the Bible. Thus the characters and events in Virgil's *Aeneid* and in other classical works have the significance of real persons and events in Dante's *Comedy*. In fact Virgil's works for Dante were the "pagan gospel" which he almost equated with the authority of the Scriptures. He treated the story in the *Aeneid* as history parallel to that recorded in Scripture and saw both as the two major components of universal history.[2]

In this respect Dante developed originally some earlier insights of the Fathers of the Church, such as Clement of Alexandria and Justin Martyr, whose positive appraisals of pagan literature, myths and philosophy discovered "seeds of the Logos" present in those pagan works. Augustine, who disowned Virgil in his *Confessions,* nonetheless in his *City of God* treated Virgil's *Aeneid* as historical record as far as the foundation of Rome was considered. Christian interpretation of Virgil and other classical writers is, however, a topic too vast to consider here. Let it suffice to say that Dante not only held classical literature, especially Virgil's *Aeneid,* in the highest regard as literature, but he also treated its heroes, heroines and even villains as historical persons who are somehow "figures" or "shades" of Christ. Some, of course, would be negative counterparts of Christ.

Dante's art as a poet is thus never separated from his theology as a Christian. In this sense he can aptly be described as the most original and the greatest of theological poets, or as a "poet-theologian," as some scholars would classify him.[3] His vast knowledge of the Bible and of theology is so creatively and artistically integrated with his knowledge of pagan literature and history that the *Comedy* can rightly be called one of the greatest — if not the greatest — masterpieces of a truly Christian humanism or, if you like, Christian theology as poetry.

Christ's entrance into human history — the event of the Incarnation — and the Redemption He accomplished for the human race are the two events which permeate all of Dante's writings, and in particular his *Comedy.* Dante makes us see and feel Christ's presence throughout the work, even in the *Inferno.* The very date he chooses for his descent into Hell is most significant: March 25, the feast of the Annunciation, which was the beginning of the Incarnation of Christ in Mary. According to some commentators this feast coincided with Good Friday in the year 1300, the anniversary of Christ's birth. Thus it was the ideal date which brought together the two central mysteries of the Incarnation and the Redemption. That is the date when Dante himself enters Hell to make the journey of descent once made by Christ for the salvation of the world.

Thus from the very beginning we see Dante imitating Christ's descent to the underworld so that he may rise with him and ascend to Paradise. Beatrice, too, we might recall, was a *figura Christi* when she descended into Hell in order to obtain Virgil's aid for the salvation of Dante. This same descent-ascent motif can be found in Aeneas' journey as well as in Paul's. But the most important descent-ascent event for our salvation is Christ's paschal mystery. Dante's journey — and every Christian's — is an imitation of Christ's death, resurrection and ascent to the Father's glory. Dante, then, as representative of every Christian *homo viator,* is truly a *figura Christi* — a follower and imitator of Christ in His descent and ascent.

The very location, structure and physical makeup of Hell will constantly remind us of Christ's death. Hell is located directly beneath the very center of the hemisphere of earth (i.e., directly beneath Jerusalem, the place of Christ's death). The pit of Hell is shaped like a funnel which reaches deep below the earth's surface to its most narrow place where Satan is located, the antithesis of Christ. Dante notices in his downward climb several enormous fissures and ruins in the rocks, caused by the earthquake at Christ's death on the cross.

Even though the name of Christ is never explicitly mentioned throughout the *Inferno,* there are several oblique allusions to His crucifixion as well as one clear description of His descent there to liberate those who had by faith looked forward to His coming for their salvation. This is, of course, a reference to that enigmatic article of the Apostles' Creed, "the Descent into Hell."[4]

The "Descent into Hell" remains for most Catholics and generally for most Christians today, an almost unknown aspect of the Christ event. It is rarely portrayed in religious art, except in traditional Eastern icons where it remains the usual way of depicting the Resurrection. That particular "moment" of the paschal mystery is often ignored or simply dismissed as too heavily laden with "mythological" elements. In Western liturgical art it seems to have been replaced in the Renaissance with the icon of the Risen Lord emerging from the tomb which had been guarded by soldiers. Or else His appearances to Mary Magdalen or to other disciples become the traditional portrayals of the Resurrection.

But in Dante's time the ancient Eastern Christian interpretation of the *Anastasis* (Resurrection) as Christ's Descent into Hell and His "Harrowing of Hell" was still a frequent theme in Western art. Splendid examples of this theme can still be seen in ancient mosaics and frescoes preserved in the churches of Rome, Venice, Siena and other cities throughout Italy.[5] It was also a much discussed topic with the medieval theologians, resulting in the solemn proclamation of the dogma of the Descent of Christ at the Fourth Lateran Council in 1215 and at the Council of Lyons in 1274.

Dante's understanding of Christ's Descent seems to follow substantially St. Thomas' interpretation of the dogma, although he adds some important and original details which are worth noting. In his

Summa Theologiae Thomas devoted an entire question, divided into eight articles, to this doctrine of the faith.[6] Thomas, through numerous quotations from the Old and New Testaments and the writings of Augustine, explains the dogma as a saving event which liberated only the "holy fathers," who were "joined to the Passion of Christ through faith formed by charity." By "holy fathers" he intends Abraham and other "just men" of the Old Testament who by faith and charity had a certain "conformity" with the charity of the suffering Christ. Thomas' concept of the Descent as a saving event was thus very restricted — unlike the cosmic interpretations of the Greek Fathers, such as Gregory of Nyssa. It excluded all unbaptized children and "infidels" in general. Thomas does not mention Adam or Eve, or any women at all.

Dante's interpretation of the event is uttered by Virgil, who as an "infidel" must remain in that section of Hell known as Limbo, where countless souls of men, women and infants are held for all eternity because "even though they had not sinned, they did not know Baptism, which is the gateway of faith. . . . they came before Christianity and did not worship God the way one should" (*Inf.* IV, 30-39). Dante is deeply troubled and saddened when he learns that Virgil and the other virtuous pagans will be "suspended in Limbo" forever. He asks Virgil if any souls had been freed in order to enjoy heaven's bliss. Virgil responds:

> I was a novice in this place
> when I saw a mighty Lord descend to us
> who wore the sign of victory as his crown.
> He took from us the shade of our first parent,
> of Abel, his good son, of Noah, too,
> and of obedient Moses, who made the laws;
> Abram, the Patriarch, David the King,
> Israel with his father and his children,
> with Rachel, whom he worked so hard to win;
> and many more he chose for blessedness;
> and you should know, before these souls were taken,
> no human soul had ever reached salvation.
> (*Inf.* IV, 52-63)

Although Dante generally follows Thomas' theology on this dogma, he explicitly states who some of these "holy fathers" were and even names Rachel, one of the "holy mothers." Besides, he notes that the number of those saved was great. Later in the *Comedy*, on the planet of Venus, he will see that the brightest light there is a woman, Rahab, the whore of Jericho, "the first to rise among the souls redeemed by Christ's great triumph." This allusion in Paradise to the Descent of Christ is worthy of our attention. Its context is an answer to Dante's question about the identity of an extraordinary splendor there:

> Know, then, that there within Rahab has peace,
> and once joined with our order, she impressed
> her seal upon it at the highest rank.
> To this sphere where the shadow of your earth
> comes to an end, she was the first to rise
> among the souls redeemed in Christ's great triumph.
> It was most fitting that she be received
> and left in one of our spheres as a palm
> of that great victory won by those two palms,
> for it was Rahab who made possible
> Joshua's first glory in the Holy Land —
> which seems to matter little to the Pope.
> Your city — which was planted by the one,
> the first to turn against his Maker's power,
> and whose fierce envy brought the world such woe —
> creates and circulates the wicked flower
> that turns the shepherds into ravening wolves
> and breaks the fold and lets the lambs run wild.
>   * * *
> But Vatican and every sacred place
> in Rome which marked the burial-ground of saints
> who fought in Peter's army to the death,
> shall soon be free of this adultery.
>   (*Par.* IX, 115-142)

Dante's choice of Rahab, a prostitute, as the "first fruits" of Christ's redemptive death on the cross and His triumphant harrowing of Hell is extremely significant. It is an example of Dante's keen insight into the meaning of "pure gospel": "The tax collectors and the harlots enter the Kingdom of Heaven before you." Rahab is compared to the "palm" of Christ's victory, won by his outstretched "palms" on the cross. Dante may be excused, or perhaps praised, for this somewhat precious, but felicitous, pun on the word *palm,* since it evokes here so much theological depth and imaginative associations.

Palm trees flourished, and still do, in the city of Jericho where Joshua's victory took place — his first significant triumph in the conquest of the Holy Land, an event understood as a figure of Jesus' victory on the cross. Joshua as a figure of Jesus (their names in Hebrew were the same, meaning "God saves") was familiar in the Christian exegesis of the Old Testament. Joshua's outstretched palms in prayer called down God's powerful victory, just as Jesus' outstretched palms on the cross called down His Father's act of vindicating victory in the resurrection.

Rahab, a pagan and a harlot, became in Christian exegesis not only an example of faith and good works (cf. James 2:25; Hebrews 11:31) but also a prophetess who foretold Christ's shedding of blood on the cross. The detail of her giving Joshua a signal with a scarlet cord (cf. Joshua 2:17) was interpreted in early Christian literature as a figure pointing to Christ's blood. In Matthew's genealogy she was listed as an ancestor of Christ and later in patristic and medieval theology she was often cited as a figure of the Church, composed of Gentiles and sinners, but saved by Christ through her faith and works of charity.

Rahab, who is described as the brightest light in that sphere, is significantly contrasted with Pope Boniface VIII. She cooperated in Joshua's victory in the Holy Land, while the leader of the Church in Dante's time was so consumed by greed — love for the wicked flower of Florence, the gold florin — that he had no concern for the recovery of the Holy Land as a place for Christians' pilgrimage. In this passage Dante alludes to Boniface's infidelity to Christ and His Church as the sexual sin of adultery. The Pope's infidelity is thus bluntly contrasted with the fidelity of the prostitute Rahab, a humble outsider to God's people who became the courageous, faithful one who was "assumed" by Christ as the first trophy in his victorious harrowing of Hell.

Dante's reference in Paradise to Christ's triumphant descent into Hell should not surprise us, since many Fathers of the Church and medieval writers, influenced by the "kenotic" Christology of St. Paul, understood Christ's descent to the lowest regions — the underworld — as an essential phase in the redemptive process. Many Pauline texts (Ep 4:10; Col 1:18; 1 Cor 15:20) stress Christ's descent and destruction of the Kingdom of death as a necessary "moment" in his ascent to glory and universal supremacy. Paul emphasized this descent-ascent pattern of salvation throughout his letters to proclaim that the whole cosmos was affected by Christ's all-embracing salvific power. This interpretation of the descent was not lost in Christian tradition, as patristic literature, ancient iconography and the liturgy abundantly testify.

This theme of *Christus Victor* in His descent and harrowing of Hell was familiar in medieval sermons, hymns and poetry. As Helen Gardner noticed, "Many students of medieval literature have commented on the remarkable persistence and popularity of the theme of the Harrowing of Hell in English poetry and the survival in England of the older doctrine of the Atonement . . . as the rescue of humanity from the power of the devil. The figure of Christ as humanity's champion, rather than as sacrificial victim, not making satisfaction to God for man's sins, but outwitting and defeating his and mankind's enemies, survives into the later Middle Ages because of the continuing strength of the old heroic tradition."[7] Gardner cites such masterpieces of Anglo-Saxon religious poetry as the early *Dream of the Rood* and the later *Piers Plowman* as examples of medieval literature where the themes of the Harrowing of Hell and Christ as Hero dominate. She comments that the *Dream of the Rood* is a parallel in the vernacular of the magnificent Latin hymn by Venantius Fortunatus, the *Vexilla regis prodeunt,* which Dante quotes at the very bottom of Hell. [8]

Besides the many Latin hymns and popular vernacular poems which celebrated the Harrowing of Hell, there were sermons, too, which kept this mystery before the eyes of the faithful. One such sermon by St. Bernard describes Christ's first coming — His Incarnation — as culminating in His descent into Hell: "He came from the heart of God the Father into the womb of the Virgin Mother; He came from the highest heaven into the lower regions of the earth. . . . But now, as I see, he descended not only to the earth, but also to Hell itself: not as one bound but as the free man among the dead."[9]

Mark Musa cites this passage from St. Bernard as the background for Dante's reenactment of the Harrowing of Hell in another passage of the *Inferno*: Canto IX. The event is preceded by Dante's admonition to the reader: "All of you whose intellects are sound, look now and see the meaning that is hidden beneath the veil that covers my strange verses." This is one of only two addresses to the reader which explicitly invites him to see a figurative meaning in the literal sense of the narrative about to unfold. The scene that follows the admonition is an important passage which, in highly dramatic and even theatrical terms, recreates the Harrowing of Hell. The context is the delay and terror of Virgil and Dante at the gates of Dis, the city in the lower Hell. The hideous devils have slammed the gates shut in Virgil's face — the only time in the *Comedy* when Virgil is dismayed and frustrated in his mission of guiding Dante through Hell. The inability of reason and human nature, represented by Virgil, to overcome the power of evil forces is expressed here. Power has to come from a higher source, and it arrives in the sudden and astonishing advent of a heavenly messenger:

> and then, above the filthy swell, approaching,
> a blast of sound, shot through with fear, exploded,
> making both shores of Hell begin to tremble;
> it sounded like one of those violent winds,
> born from the clash of counter-temperatures,
> that tear through forests; raging on unchecked,
> it splits and rips and carries off the branches
> and proudly whips the dust up in its path
> and makes the beasts and shepherds flee its course!
> He freed my eyes and said, "Now turn around
> and set your sight along the ancient scum,
> there where the marsh's mist is hovering thickest."
> As frogs before their enemy, the snake,
> all scatter through the pond and then dive down
> until each one is squatting on the bottom,
> so I saw more than a thousand fear-shocked souls
> in flight clearing the path of one who came

walking the Styx, his feet dry on the water.
From time to time with his left hand he fanned
his face to push the putrid air away,
and this was all that seemed to weary him.
I was certain now that he was sent from heaven.
I turned to my guide, but he made me a sign
to keep my silence and bow low to this one.
Ah, the scorn that filled his holy presence!
He reached the gate and touched it with a wand;
it opened without resistance from inside.
(*Inf.* IX, 64-90)

This scene is a true masterpiece of dramatic art, but the theological content is what interests us here. Most commentators have interpreted the "one sent from heaven" as an angel; Musa is one of the
few scholars to discover the full Christological dimension of this passage
as a reenactment of Christ's descent and harrowing of Hell. [10] Certain
details, such as the walking on the water and the wand or scepter, are
unmistakable and traditional references to Christ's universal power.
Christian iconography normally depicted the *Christus Victor* in Hell
carrying either the cross or a banner bearing the sign of the cross. Often
in the art known to Dante the scepter in Christ's hand is in the shape of a
cross. A familiar image of Christ, certainly seen by Dante in the mosaics
of Ravenna and elsewhere, showed Christ as a young warrior with the
cross in his right hand, his feet trampling a serpent or lion.

This ancient image of Christ as victor, warrior and hero for humanity in its struggle with Satan and his devils had deep roots in the New
Testament as well as in the Old Testament figures of Christ, such as
Moses, Joshua, David and Daniel. It had received imaginative and
mythological embellishments in some of the apocryphal gospels popular
in the Middle Ages, such as the Gospel of Nicodemus which described
in great detail the devils' resistance to Christ's entry into Hell and His
dramatic victory there.

The memory of Christ's triumph through his cross and descent
into Hell accompanied Dante all through his own descent into Hell in
imitation of Christ. At the very bottom of Hell (cf. Canto XXXIV) Virgil
points out to Dante Satan and introduces him with the words of the Latin

liturgical hymn *Vexilla regis prodeunt* (The banners of the King go forth). The word *inferni* is added to these words to express that Satan is the very antithesis of Christ. Satan as the King of Hell is thus the hideous parody of Christ. Satan's banners (his *vexilla*) are his ugly, bat-like wings which generate the freezing cold wind which punishes the sinners and keeps them frozen in the icy lake. The wings are the counterpart of Christ's cross which expressed God's warm love for the world.

The *Vexilla Regis,* one of the Church's greatest hymns, was written in the late sixth century to celebrate a relic of the True Cross brought in solemn procession to Poitiers. It has remained in liturgical use for Holy Week, especially on Good Friday, and for the feast of the Exaltation of the Cross on September 14. The opening verses sound the triumphant note:

> The banner of the King goes forth;
> Now shines the mystery of the Cross,
> by which Life bore death,
> And by death brought forth life.

The hymn contains many memorable phrases, such as: "God reigned from the tree"; "The beam which held His Body raised up Hell's prey"; and "Hail, O Cross, our only hope." For Dante the mystery of evil, Hell and Satan could be understood only as a perversion of Christ's goodness and love revealed through His cross. All the descriptions of Satan are thus counterparts of divine qualities; his three faces and their colors ape the Trinity. The three souls chewed by Satan are Judas, Brutus and Cassius, figures which also suggest the three crosses on Calvary, besides being the men who betrayed Christ and the Roman Emperor, Julius Caesar.

The suicidal death of Judas on a tree also served as a perverted Christological figure in the *Inferno* (cf. Canto XIII), where the suicides have been transformed into trees. Their infernal existence as trees apes Christ, often symbolized by the tree of the cross in Christian art. In fact Dante followed the tradition that after Christ's final coming as judge, the bodies of the suicides would hang upon trees, as once Christ's body hung on the cross.[11] Throughout the *Inferno* there are many passages — too numerous to mention here — in which the souls of the damned are presented as those who disfigured the image of their Creator and thus reflect a perverted Christological figure.

The entire *Inferno* can be understood, then, as modeled on Christ's descent, foreshadowed in such Old Testament figures as Joseph, betrayęd by his brothers and cast into a cistern, Israel's descent into the waters of the Red Sea and later in the Jordan — all figures of Christ's baptism, which in the New Testament is the basic figure of His death and resurrection. The frozen lake of perdition at the bottom of Hell is a perversion of the waters of baptism, energized with divine, saving powers through Christ's triumphant descent into Hell. The paschal mystery of Christ simply permeates the entire *Inferno,* although, as Dante warns us, we must pierce the veil of poetry to see the allegorical and mystical meaning.

At the beginning of the *Inferno* Virgil had announced to Dante, who was terrified by the three evil beasts, that a Savior would come to drive back into Hell the bestial evil. The beasts who block Dante's way are usually interpreted as the radical sins of pride, avarice and lust. The Savior figure, symbolized as a greyhound, has been the object of endless interpretations; but I think we should keep in mind that many of the first commentators on Dante in the early fourteenth century interpreted the mysterious Savior as Christ in His final coming. Many also identified this figure with the DUX predicted by Beatrice on the summit of Mt. Purgatory. Certainly the divine attributes of the greyhound — wisdom, love and power (cf. *Inf.* I, 104) — suggest a more than human person. We should note that these are the same three divine qualities written over Hell's entrance to describe the creator of Hell: Divine Justice (cf. *Inf.* III, 4-6). The same three attributes are perverted at the bottom of Hell into the black, yellow and red colors of Satan's three faces: Divine Wisdom became the black of ignorance; Power became the yellow of impotence; Love was perverted into the red of hatred (cf. *Inf.* XXXIV, 43-45).

Much more could be written on the Christological pattern of the *Inferno,* but before we leave the topic we might take an overview of Hell's basic structure and Dante's journey there. At the beginning Dante was told that his descent into Hell was arranged by Beatrice who had descended there for his salvation. She was the "one sent" by Mary and St. Lucy, two figures who together with Beatrice represent the Trinity of Divine Persons. Beatrice, as we have seen extensively, is the Christ figure sent by the Father (Mary) and the Holy Spirit (St. Lucy) to save Dante, who represents humanity lost in a forest of sin. The three heavenly ladies are moved by God, Who is Love (cf. *Inf.* III, 70-138). Thus the genesis of Dante's journey through Hell had its initiative in God's descending love, incarnate in Christ, who "left his footprints in Hell" for mankind's salvation. Christ is the victor and "the way" of victory over death and evil once and for all.

All the regions of Hell with its nine circles, ever diminishing in circumference, were visited by Dante in his spiral descent. This downward, spiral movement will be reversed into a upward, circular movement when Dante, in imitation of Christ's resurrection, will ascend the mountain of Purgatory to reach the earthly Paradise. A similar circular pattern of ascent will continue through the nine spheres of Paradise, culminating in the Empyrean, where God's love will be fully revealed. The theme of following in the footsteps of Christ, the Victor and Lover of humanity, will thus always be in Dante's mind and heart as he journeys through all these realms.

After the arduous journey through the eternal, starless night of Hell, Dante emerges with Virgil at the base of the mountain-island of Purgatory, which rises out of the watery southern hemisphere of the earth. The contrast between the gloomy darkness of Hell and the enchanting colors and light of this new atmosphere is most striking, and Dante describes it exquisitely in the opening Cantos of *Purgatory*. The time is Easter morning and Dante gives us numerous allusions to Christ's resurrection as he depicts the dawn and rising sun, typical symbols for the rising, triumphant Christ, who has vanquished darkness.

References to Christ's resurrection are too numerous to describe here, but we should notice the first person who meets Dante and Virgil, since in many ways he is a figure of Christ. It is Cato of Utica, a Roman Stoic philosopher and statesman who, in opposition to Julius Caesar, committed suicide for the sake of political freedom. This is quite a surprise to us, especially after Dante had just witnessed the eternal punishment of two men who betrayed Caesar: Brutus and Cassius, both symbols of opposition to Divine Justice which ordained human peace and happiness through the Roman Empire. And here in the place of salvation and grace we encounter Cato, a pagan suicide who had opposed Caesar. And besides, Cato is the very guardian of Purgatory and the first guide for the two pilgrims, Dante and Virgil. Dante keeps reminding us of the surprises of God's grace.

Cato was probably chosen by Dante for many reasons; we may see in him a typical example of Dante's figural art by which he blends into one person various figures — the virtuous pagan who is saved, Moses, Christ, and Dante himself as Everyman or Every Christian. These multiple levels of meaning and this figural density usually escape the reader's first encounter with Cato, but careful study and reflection reveal that Dante had several meanings in mind.

Although Cato as a figure of Christ interests us most, the other levels also serve to illuminate Cato's meaning in the *Comedy*. At first Cato would seem a most unlikely candidate to serve as a figure of Christ, but we should investigate Dante's high esteem for this pre-Christian philosopher and statesman. Dante, in accord with classical Roman authors such as Cicero and Lucan, regarded Cato as an outstanding martyr of freedom since he opposed the tyranny of Julius Caesar. Praise of Cato abounds in Dante's works: in his *De Monarchia* he interprets Cato's suicide as an "unspeakable sacrifice" and refers to Cato as "the severest champion of true liberty, who, in order to kindle in the world the passionate love of liberty, chose to pass out of life a free man rather than without liberty to abide in life."

In his *Convivio* Dante exclaims: "O most sacred heart of Cato . . . what earthly man was more worthy to symbolize God than Cato? Certainly none. Surely it is better to be silent about him, in imitation of Jerome, who on the subject of St. Paul thought it better to be silent than to say too little." In the same passage Dante adds that in remembering the lives of such "divine citizens" as Cato we can see "some light of the Divine Goodness added to their good nature in order to produce such wonderful actions."[12]

Here at the base of Mount Purgatory Virgil introduces Dante to Cato with these words:

> May it please you to welcome him — he goes
> in search of freedom, and how dear that is,

> the man who gives up life for it well knows.
> You know, you found death sweet in Utica
> for freedom's sake; there you put off that robe
> which will be radiant on the Great Day.
> (*Purg.* I, 70-75)

Cato, "who for liberty gives up life," is a figure which foreshadowed Christ's self-sacrifice. His act of suicide was a sort of pre-imitation of Christ's death; and Virgil, so often the prophet, predicts that Cato will re-clothe himself in a glorious body on that "Great Day," a clear allusion to the Resurrection of the Body and Final Coming of Christ. This prophecy comes so soon after our contemplation of Judas the suicide, awaiting in Satan's mouth the last day when his body would hang eternally from a tree. But Cato's suicide was understood as a martyr's death, prefiguring Christ's sacrificial death on the cross for "the glorious liberty of the children of God."

That Cato was a pagan, i.e., an unbaptized infidel, raises a question which haunted Dante: the salvation of the virtuous heathens. It is a question which Dante addresses more fully in *Paradise* (cf. Cantos XIX and XX), but it strikes our curiosity here. Dante knew the Church's teaching, based on the Scriptures, on the necessity of faith in Christ for salvation as well as the need of baptism and charity. His primary master in theology, St. Thomas, strongly defended these necessities, but also admitted the possibility of implicit faith in Christ which came through extraordinary revelations given to "many Gentiles." Thomas cites the example of Job, the Sibyl and examples from Roman history of individual pagans who were enlightened by God's Holy Spirit and thus came to have implicit faith in Christ. Thomas contended that these pagans came to believe in Christ and in God "by ways pleasing to Him": the Spirit revealed these truths to them. [13]

Thomas also admitted different kinds of baptism besides sacramental baptism by water. They were baptism of blood and baptism of desire, "which proceeds from faith working through charity, by which God sanctifies the interior person; God's power is not bound to the visible sacraments." [14] Thomas even justified the popular belief in the eternal salvation of the pagan Roman Emperor Trajan, a curious tradition which Dante also accepted (cf. *Par.* XX) in order to demonstrate the mysterious Justice of God which baffles human reason. In fact, on the thorny question of the salvation of the pagans Dante always humbly bowed to God's mysterious judgments, expressed in the Scriptures and Church teaching. In the *Convivio* he confessed: "For human reason cannot of itself see this (i.e., the relegation to eternal Limbo of morally good persons who had no explicit faith in Christ) to be just, yet by faith it can." Dante's compassionate heart struggled with this "hard saying" found in the Church teaching of his time. So often in the *Comedy* he expresses sadness and pathos over Virgil's being "suspended" eternally in Limbo, not because of sin but only through lack of faith in Christ. Virgil normally represents the limitations of human nature and the pagan world deprived of the supernatural gift of faith.

We might wonder why Cato, also a pagan like Virgil, should be the guardian of Purgatory destined to be saved on the Last Day. Many commentators admonish us to interpret individual characters as Dante intended them to be interpreted. A character should not be considered in all his various historical aspects, but only in one or two aspects which served Dante's representational purposes for that character. Here Cato, although a real, historical person, represents mainly freedom and sacrificial heroism. Cato is not considered in all the possible interpretations of his life: his opposition to Caesar as Roman Emperor, for example, is not considered. That would be a reason for consigning him to Hell together with Brutus and Cassius. Nor are all aspects of Virgil considered by Dante. His love and esteem for Virgil would have prompted him to place him among the saved, but Virgil's symbolic role is mainly as the representative of the limits and inability of human nature and wisdom to reach full salvation on its own.

Dante does not explain to us here how Cato meets the requirements for salvation taught by Thomas, that is, implicit faith or baptism of desire. Perhaps Cato's death was a kind of baptism of blood in Dante's mind. But Dante also refers here (*Purg.* II, 81) to Cato's love for his wife Marcia, which in his *Convivio* he cites as a symbol of God's love. Marcia had left Cato to marry his friend Hortensius, but later wanted to return to Cato, who forgave her and took her back. In that context Dante repeats his former praise: "What earthly man was more worthy to signify God than Cato? Certainly none."[15] So Cato, besides representing moral freedom, the basic purpose of the purgatorial process, also represents divine love for the repentant sinner, who, like Marcia, turns to the Lord for forgiveness. Freedom, repentance and divine mercy are the dominant themes in *Purgatory* and Cato represents them all as the champion of freedom and the lover who forgives. He therefore was a most appropriate figure for the Risen Christ, victorious over the tyranny of sin and death through His love-sacrifice which forgave and liberated humanity.

Cato as a figure of Moses, who was a figure of Christ, is also prominent here. The details of his physical appearance recall biblical descriptions of Moses. His face, so radiant "as if the sun were shining on it," recalls Moses' vision of God on Mt. Sinai, a figure of Mt. Purgatory. Moses, the liberator of his people through the Exodus event, also foreshadows Christ's liberating action through His death and resurrection — His Exodus. Such a rich typology (and we have mentioned only a few aspects) abounds in this passage that a more detailed analysis would be impossible here.[16] Let us conclude our discussion of Cato's figural functions by mentioning that Cato is also a figure of Dante himself, a pilgrim making his Exodus journey to the summit of the mountain where he will behold Beatrice, the figure of Christ in His glorious Final Coming as Judge and Savior.

Toward the end of the first canto of *Purgatory* Dante must go to the very bottom, the shore of the island, in order to wash himself from the filth of Hell and to gird himself with one of the reeds growing there. The descent, bathing, and the reed have many figurative meanings: humility, the Passion of Christ (His beating with a reed), baptism and rebirth. Dante ends the canto by describing a miracle: "Upon pulling out the reed a second humble plant sprang up!" The real miracle is Dante's putting on the death of Christ and his rising and rebirth with Him.

At the base of the mountain the role of Cato, the guardian of Purgatory, comes abruptly to an end, but the role of guardian angels is most prominent throughout the upward journey on Mount Purgatory. They also serve as figures of Christ and keep before our minds the mystery of Christ and His redemptive work. Most commentators overlook this Christological aspect of the angels. Without delving into a theology of angels, we might merely recall that a primitive Christology understood Christ in terms of an angel. Jean Danielou has explored this fascinating subject.[17] There are deep Old Testament roots to this tradition, which can be found in the New Testament and the extant writings of the Apostolic Fathers which preserve many aspects of a lost Jewish-Christian theology which flourished briefly before Christian theology became so influenced by Greek philosophical concepts. The basic Old Testament concept of an angel as a messenger of God — one sent with good news or a minister of God's will on earth — certainly contributed to one of the earliest understandings of Christ. A clear distinction, however, was maintained between angels and Christ Himself. This is evident throughout the New Testament (cf. Heb 1:6-14). The angels are His servants, since He is the only Son of God and universal Lord. But we should also notice that their ministry as intermediaries between God and humanity parallels Christ's ministry in many ways.

The first appearance of an angel in Purgatory serves as a typical example of the role of angels as mediators analogous to the unique mediator, Christ. It is the angel who pilots the souls across the sea to Purgatory. The scene is described brilliantly by Dante who tantalizes our curiosity about the identity of the strange, unearthly light that moves swiftly and effortlessly across the water (cf. *Purg.* II, 13-27). Virgil commands Dante to kneel and fold his hands, just as he had ordered him to do so at the arrival of the angel at the gates of Dis, the scene which reenacted Christ's triumphal descent into Hell. Dante certainly knew the Scriptural injunctions against the adoration of angels (cf. Rv 12:10; Col 2:18), but this "bird of God" so closely resembles Christ in His redemptive action that the angel's creaturely status is absorbed into his ministry as a "divine" messenger. The angel's outstretched wings and unbearable brightness are further details which suggest Christ on the cross. In fact he signs the souls whom he has transported with the "holy cross" as they sing the famous Passover song, *In Exitu Israel de Aegypto* (Psalm 113). This psalm announces the main theme of *Purgatory*: Exodus, the pilgrimage of freedom and salvation, the fundamental figure or allegory which foreshadows salvation through Christ, as Dante explicitly stated in his letter to Can Grande. Obviously the angel as the liberator and bearer of souls to the shores of salvation is a figure of Christ the Liberator and Savior, whose death and resurrection effected the new Passover and Exodus.

Another important scene in which angels function as figures of Christ is found at the base of Purgatory before the two pilgrims enter the gate of Purgatory itself. It takes place in the Valley of the Princes (*Purg.* VIII), and corresponds in significant ways to the scene described in *Inferno* IX. The ninth canto of *Inferno* is really the eighth, since *Inferno* I is an introduction to the entire *Comedy.* So *Purg.* VIII and *Inf.* IX have much in common. In fact, both cantos describe, as Mark Musa has so admirably demonstrated,[18] two comings of Christ. The passage in *Inf.* IX described His first coming, the Incarnation, which culminated in His descent and victory in Hell; the passage in *Purg.* VIII describes His daily coming into the Christian soul. This "second" coming was included in the traditional theme of medieval spirituality: the three advents of Christ. The second coming was understood as Christ's daily presence and all-powerful grace in every Christian's soul as she struggles with temptation and evil forces in her earthly pilgrimage. The "third coming" was understood as Christ's final advent as universal judge.

The souls in the Valley of the Princes are singing the *Salve Regina,* a compline hymn which calls on Mary, the new Eve, to help "the exiled children of Eve in this valley of tears." She is asked to show them "after this exile the blessed fruit of your womb, Jesus." After the second hymn Dante gives his second admonition to the reader, very similar to his first, given at the scene of the angel's arrival at the gates of Dis. The admonition and the scene that follows should be quoted to show the similarity with the episode in Hell:

> Sharpen your sight, Reader: the truth, this time,
> is covered by a thinner veil, and so,
> the meaning should be easy to perceive.
> I saw that noble host of souls, who now
> in silence kept their eyes raised to the heavens,
> as if expectant, faces pale and meek,
> and then I saw descending from on high
> two angels with two flaming swords, and these
> were broken short and blunted at the end.
> Their garments, green as tender new-born leaves
> unfurling, billowed out behind each one,

> fanned by the greenness of their streaming wings.
> One took his stand above us on our side,
> and one alighted on the other bank;
> thus, all the souls were held between the two.
> My eyes could see with ease their golden hair,
> but could not bear the radiance of their faces:
> light that makes visible can also blind.
> "From Mary's bosom both of them descend
> to guard us from the serpent in the vale."
>   (*Purg.* VIII, 19-38)

Soon after the arrival of the angels the ancient serpent "that offered Eve the bitter fruit to eat" slithers into the valley, but is swiftly put to flight by the "two holy falcons." This little victory scene is intended for all Christian pilgrims who are still in the valley of tears, subject to various temptations. The action described is a miniature mystery play in which the serpent, the traditional figure of Satan, is put to flight by the divine messengers. The detail of the color of the angels' wings is significant since green is the symbol of hope, a dominant theme throughout *Purgatory*. Also significant is their origin: "from Mary's bosom," which continues the theme of the *Salve Regina* in which the coming of "the blessed fruit of Mary's womb" — Her Son, Jesus — is the hope of the souls.

This little "mystery play" is a theologically meaningful dramatization of the daily presence of Christ through His powerful grace in the life of every Christian. The angels as figures of Christ reenact the intervention of Christ's power, which should reassure every Christian that the fear-inspiring enemy — whatever form it should take — can be overcome by Christ's presence. "My grace is all you need: for my power is strongest when you are weak" were Christ's words to Paul when he suffered an affliction from Satan (cf. 2 Cor 12:9). Dante, who was "frozen by fear," was strengthened and given hope by the arrival of the angels. Christ's daily presence should give every Christian exile in this valley the same kind of hope and strength.

Throughout Purgatory angels will function as figures of Christ who aid Dante in his ascent. Although Christ is not mentioned by name in Purgatory (just as His name was not mentioned in Hell), He is present through the guardian angel on each of the seven terraces of the mountain. Christ never speaks as a character in the *Comedy,* but His words are spoken by the angels on each storey who erase the marks or vestiges of the seven capital sins from the penitent's forehead. The angels pronounce Christ's words from the Sermon on the Mount: the beatitudes. On each level the soul not only cleanses itself from one of the capital sins, but in a positive way learns the opposite evangelical virtue taught by Christ in His Sermon on the Mount. Thus Purgatory is, in Dante's phrase, "the discipline of the mountain." The original Latin meaning of *disciplina* is "learning process." The soul learns to be refashioned into the image of Christ.

So, on each storey of the seven-storey mountain the soul acquires one of the beatitudes taught by Christ on that unnamed mountain in Galilee. It is important to notice that Mary, the perfect "disciple" is always presented first as the outstanding exemplar of each beatitude. She is the model for every Christian disciple. Her face is the "face that most resembles Christ," as St. Bernard will describe her in Paradise.

We should notice also that Dante describes the angels' actions and words on each terrace as very tender and moving. Rather than inspire fear, the angels comfort Dante and often fan him and caress him with their wings. They radiate joy and confidence as they give directions to Dante and Virgil, who do not know the way. On the last terrace, where lust is purified by fire (the only time fire is an instrument of the purgatorial process), the guardian angel of that terrace, the angel of chastity, also called "the angel of joy," sings to Dante from the other side of the wall of fire with the words: "Blessed are the pure of heart." Then the ninth and final angel says to Dante, also with the words of Christ: "Come, blessed of My Father." The process is now over; and Dante, free and upright, enters the Earthly Paradise.

Dante's *Purgatory* is a masterpiece, not only of poetry but also of theology. His original contributions as "a theologian of Purgatory" are simply too many to enumerate here. The very structure of the mountain, his classification of sins and their gravity, the general atmosphere and mood of the mountain were striking innovations to the popular concept of Purgatory in his time. To mention just a few of his original insights: he considered sins of the spirit committed against one's neighbor, such as pride, envy and wrath, to be far more serious than sins of the flesh, usually committed against oneself, such as avarice, gluttony and lust. He also considered Purgatory to be a place primarily of repentance, i.e., *metanoia,* the radical change of one's heart, rather than a place of punishment and torment. In the words of Jacques Le Goff, "He rescued Purgatory from the infernalization to which the Church subjected it in the thirteenth century. Dante was in a sense more orthodox than the Church, more faithful to Purgatory's underlying logic."[19]

Dante's Purgatory is a "place" where hope reigns supreme. The souls there pray and sing with the words of the liturgy. "Dante had the secret of integrating into his poem the liturgy that the Scholastics usually kept out of their writings."[20] The Scholastics wondered whether demons or angels attended to the souls in Purgatory; but Dante's answer leaves no doubt: it is the angels, who at every turn comfort, reassure and give assistance to the souls. Dante's angels perform the role of Christ who caresses the penitent soul, heals it, and erases all stain of sin. This is indeed a far cry from the popular idea of Purgatory which dominated in the preaching, writings and art of Dante's time: a place of fiery torment like Hell, different only in so far as it is temporal and not eternal like Hell. Such a popular misconception of the Church's authentic (and extremely minimal) teaching on Purgatory still persists today. Dante's poetic and theological originality in giving us relevant images that express true *metanoia* and hope can, and should, be the corrective to any persistent misrepresentation of Purgatory. His Purgatory not only offers us a lesson on how to die with hope, but also gives us a much-needed lesson on how to live today with hope. Dante's Purgatory offers an honest and salutary confrontation with the evil within the human heart as well as the firm conviction that the human soul, energized by divine grace, can change and become little by little the very image of God.

Dante conceives Purgatory not merely as an after-life experience, but one that is lived now by the Christian pilgrim whose weakness is transformed by the abiding presence of Christ whose grace constantly forgives, heals and divinizes us. The Purgatorial process is actually our baptism being "lived out" on a daily basis — a putting to death of the selfish ego and a putting on of Christ: an ongoing death and resurrection with and in Him.

Dante's arrival at the summit of Mount Purgatory has already been discussed in great detail in the preceding chapters. The culmination of the ascent focused on the arrival of Beatrice who came as a figure of Christ in His third and final advent as universal judge. We have considered her stern indictments and Dante's confession of sin. We have also seen the reenactment of Christ's redemption in the mystical pageant there. But we did not focus sufficiently on the moment when Beatrice unveiled the beauty of her eyes to Dante. At that moment Beatrice's handmaids said to Dante: "Look deeply for now you stand before those emeralds from which Love once shot loving darts at you." Dante sees reflected in her eyes the image of Christ, represented by the griffin, a mythological animal that was part-eagle and part-lion. These two "natures" symbolize the heavenly, divine nature (high Christology) and the earthly, human nature (low Christology) of Jesus. The eagle parts were gold (divinity), and the lion parts were white and red, suggesting His flesh and blood in the Eucharist:

> A thousand yearning flames of my desire
> held my eyes fixed upon those brilliant eyes
> that held the griffin fixed within their range.
> Like sunlight in a mirror, shining back,
> I saw the twofold creature in her eyes,
> reflecting its two natures, separately.
> Imagine, reader, how amazed I was
> to see the creature standing there unchanged,
> yet, in its image, changing constantly,
> And while my soul, delighted and amazed,
> was tasting of that food which satisfies
> and, at the same time, makes one hungrier,
> the other three, revealing in their mien
> their more exalted rank, came dancing forth
> accompanied by angelic melody.
> "Turn, Beatrice, turn your sacred eyes,"
> they sang, "and look upon your faithful one
> who came so very far to look at you!
> Of your own grace grant us this grace: unveil
> your mouth for him, allow him to behold

> that second beauty which you hide from him."
> O splendor of the eternal living light!
> Who, having drunk at the Parnassian well,
> or become pale within that mountain's shade,
> ·   could find with all of his poetic gifts
> those words that might describe the way you looked,
> with that harmonious heaven your only veil,
> when you unveiled yourself to me at last?
> (*Purg.* XXXI, 118-148)

In this moving scene Dante sees and tastes the beauty and goodness of the Lord in the eyes and smile of Beatrice. His experience of
knowing Christ is complemented by tasting Him as delightful food. One
thinks of the Eucharist here.[21] Beatrice, as Divine Wisdom present in
the Church's Word and Sacrament, reveals not just intellectual
knowledge about Christ but also experiential knowledge of Christ.
When she unveils her second beauty to Dante — her smile — she
communicates a further revelation which might be described as the
emotion of joy which accompanies the revelation of truth. Dante,
overwhelmed by this second grace, admits that no poetic gifts, no
inspiration from the Muses, are adequate to express this extraordinary
joy. One is reminded of St. Peter's words, "So you rejoice with a great
and glorious joy which words cannot express, because you are receiving the salvation of your souls, which is the purpose of your faith in
Him." (1 Peter 1:9)

And yet these experiences, marvelous and joyous as they are, pale
before the "transhumanizing" experiences of the heavenly Paradise. In
the earthly Paradise we are still seeing, to paraphrase St. Paul, only dim
images in a cloudy mirror. The joyful experience of faith is still only a
kind of darkness when compared with the "face-to-face" vision in
Paradise (cf. 1 Cor 13:12). There we shall read of Dante's three
rapturous visions of Christ in glory.

Chapter Eight

PILGRIM *IN PATRIA*

Dante's journey through the nine spheres of the heavenly Paradise is a marvelous description of the stages of the soul's ascent and pilgrimage to the "face-to-face" vision of God in the Empyrean. The blessed souls whom he encounters on each planet reflect the influence in their earthly lives of the particular planet on which Dante meets them. They also reflect a stage in Dante's own gradual ascent. They all, however, radiate a common joy and love because God's love and peace fills them all according to their capacities. Thus in the third sphere, the planet of Venus, the souls there such as Rahab, who had been moved once by erotic love, are now transformed by the perfect love, *agape*. Venus, according to Dante, was the last planet which was touched by the shadow of the earth.

When Dante with his guide Beatrice ascend to the next planet, the sun, a quite different phase in their journey begins. The sphere of the sun is populated with the great theologians of the Church whose gifts of divine wisdom and contemplation had illuminated Christ's spouse on earth. Dante will tell us that they all now sing and dance, forming two circles or garlands which encompass him and Beatrice. They sing praises to the Trinity and to the Incarnate Son. Dante's poetry now simply soars with ecstatic revelry in praise and adoration of God — His love, beauty, wisdom and power.

Dante's arrival in the sun begins with these magnificent tercets:

> Looking upon His Son with all that love
> which each of them breathes forth eternally,

> that uncreated, ineffable first One,
> has fashioned all that moves in mind and space
> in such sublime proportions that no one
> can see it and not feel His Presence there.
> Look up now, Reader, with me to the spheres;
> look straight to that point of the lofty wheels
> where the one motion and the other cross,
> and there begin to revel in the work
> of that great Artist who so loves His art,
> His gaze is fixed on it perpetually.
> (*Par.* X, 1-12)

After this terse but inspiring contemplation of the Trinity as Persons whose essence is Love and whose Love generates the universe, their work of art, Dante proceeds to a contemplation of the universe, beginning with "the most sublime of Nature's ministers," the sun. The sun in Dante's poetic imagination is the most appropriate symbol of God. Often in his works he dwells on this analogy. In his *Convivio* he had written:

> There is nothing perceptible by the senses in the whole world which is more worthy to serve as an example of God than the sun. . . . Just as the sun illuminates all the heavenly bodies . . . so God illuminates with intellectual light the heavenly and other intelligent creatures. . . . Just as the sun gives life by its warmth, so God vivifies all things by His goodness.
> (*Conv.* III, XII, 7-8)

It was thus fitting that the souls in the sphere of the sun should be the great wise men who, illuminated by divine wisdom, enjoy with such intensity the beatific vision of God "as He is" in the Trinitarian mystery. The sun, as symbol of God and of Divine Wisdom, will become more frequently the specific symbol of Christ, the Incarnate Wisdom of God. It is at this stage of the journey that Beatrice is finally "eclipsed," as she gently turns Dante away from his infatuation with herself to the contemplation and praise of God:

> Then Beatrice said: "And now give thanks,
> thanks to the Sun of Angels by whose grace
> you have ascended to this sun of sense."
> No mortal heart was ever more disposed
> to do devotion and to yield itself
> to God so fully and so readily
> than mine was at her words. So totally
> did I direct all of my love to Him,
> that Beatrice, eclipsed, had left my mind.
> But this did not displease her, and she smiled
> so that the splendor of her laughing eyes
> broke my mind's spell. Again I was aware
> of many things: flashes of living light
> made us a center and themselves a crown —
> their voices sweeter than their aspect bright:
> (*Par.* X, 52-63)

This is a definite step in Dante's journey to God. Beatrice's role as guide to the contemplation and love of God has been successful. She smiles with her lips and laughs with her eyes, as she sees Dante directing all the love of his heart to God. We see in this passage that Dante's love for Beatrice reached its perfection and fruition in total love for God. Beatrice, the woman and symbol of Revelation, is happy and overjoyed, not jealous because her lover has forgotten her. Dante has found God, perfect joy and love, through and with Beatrice, who rejoices in his find. Verse 64 is significant here. It literally states: "my mind united in many things divided." Dante's mind was united, even though he was contemplating many things: God, Beatrice and the things around him. His mind is "united and divided" at the same time. From now on he will gaze on God, Beatrice and the universe around him with one, undivided love.

Dante and Beatrice find themselves surrounded by a circle of souls, described as jewels, stars, flames of light, dancing ladies, and flowers forming a crown or garland. As the dance comes to a halt, one of the souls introduces himself. It is Thomas Aquinas, who discourses on God's wisdom and providence:

The Providence that governs all the world
with wisdom so profound none of His creatures
can ever hope to see into Its depths,
in order that the Bride of that sweet Groom,
who crying loud espoused her with His blood,
might go to her Beloved made more secure
within herself, more faithful to her Spouse,
ordained two noble princes to assist her
on either side, each serving as a guide.
One of the two shone with seraphic love,
the other through his wisdom was on earth
a splendor of cherubic radiance.
Now I shall speak of only one, for praise
of one, no matter which, is praise of both,
for both their labors served a single end.
(*Par.* XI, 28-42)

Thomas then gives his famous encomium of St. Francis of Assisi. He describes Francis as "a sun which rose to the world as radiantly as this sun here does." He notes that the ancient name of Assisi — *Ascesi* — means "I have ascended," and then gives a more precise word: *Oriente,* a term familiar from Luke's Gospel where Christ is called the *Oriens ex alto,* the rising sun which visited us from on high. Dante was not the first to compare Francis to the rising sun: the analogy can be found often in St. Bonaventure's *Life of St. Francis* and in the writings of the Spiritual Franciscans. In those sources Francis is also identified with the Angel "ascending from the rising of the sun, having the seal of the living God (Rv 7:2)." In a prayer to Francis Bonaventure had exclaimed:

Now, finally toward the end of your life you were shown at the same time the sublime vision of the Seraph and the humble figure of the Crucified, inwardly inflaming you and outwardly marking you as the 'second Angel, ascending from the rising of the sun and bearing upon you the sign of the living God.'
(*Life of St. Francis,* 13)

Bonaventure throughout his works described Francis in terms of Christ. Another typical example would be: "Now fixed with Christ to the cross, in both body and spirit, Francis not only burned with a Seraphic love of God but also thirsted with Christ crucified for the salvation of men."[1]

Of all the human beings in history after the coming of Christ, Francis was the one, according to Dante, who most resembled Christ. Mary and John the Baptist rank above Francis in the Rose of Paradise for obvious reasons, but immediately below John the Baptist is Francis, followed by Benedict and Augustine. Edmund Gardner's remarks on this order are worth noting: "Dante's idea, then, in the relative order of these three saints may well be that while theology (represented by Augustine) is a sacred thing, contemplation (represented by Benedict) is higher, and the perfect imitation of Christ, represented by St. Francis, is higher still."[2]

Dante perceived Francis as a second Christ and as a sun "whose invigorating powers penetrated the earth with a new strength." He described Francis on the bare rock (Mount La Verna) where "he took upon himself Christ's holy wounds and for two years wore this final seal." He also described him as a guide and reformer of Christ's spouse, the Church, and as a prince who shone "with seraphic love." But for Dante the way in which Francis most resembled Christ was in his marriage to Lady Poverty, the Spouse of Christ who "widowed, despised and ignored, waited eleven hundred years and more, living without a lover until he (Francis) came." For Dante Francis was the passionate lover of Christ's Spouse, Lady Poverty, "to whom all bar their door, as if to death itself" (*Par.* XI, 60).

We might call this "the moment most full of Dante's Franciscanism."[3] For Dante the movement of evangelical poverty begun by Francis was superior to any other in the entire history of the Church and of the world. In this canto the two greatest heroes of history, Christ and Caesar, both affirm the superior worth of Lady Poverty. Poverty — Christ's and Francis' beloved lady — was the only spiritual force, according to Dante, which could purify the Church and the world of the root of all its evils and injustices: greed.

Francis, then, in Dante's eyes, was the perfect imitator of Christ because he embraced with passionate ardor Christ's abandoned

Spouse, Poverty. By his marriage and sacred bond with Poverty Francis was freed from the various chains and vanities, mentioned at the beginning of Canto XI — law, medicine, priesthood, politics, sexual pleasure — which made men's wings beat in downward flight. Poverty liberated Francis to love God and all His creatures with the same seraphic love which inflamed Jesus. For this reason — that Francis by his poverty was able to imitate Christ perfectly — Dante considered him the greatest of all saints, whose "wonderful life were better sung by Heaven's highest angels," than merely recited by a wise, holy human (even the great Thomas Aquinas!) on a lower sphere. Dante admired in Francis above all the fearless champion of Christ's poverty, but he also saw in him the reformer of the Church who remained a loyal son of the Church. Dante also saw in Francis the martyr who accompanied the Fifth Crusade to Egypt, where "urged by a burning thirst for martyrdom, he preached Christ."

Even though Dante himself did not embrace poverty willingly, most of his mature years were spent in poverty; and he too, like Francis, was a prophet and apostle for Church reform and a return to the pure gospel of Christ. It would not seem an exaggeration to claim that Dante saw in Francis not only a kindred spirit, but more importantly a perfect model for imitation. We might recall that Dante's youth paralleled Francis' in many ways: military service, frivolous living, and flirtation with the ideals of the troubadour tradition. Both men underwent radical conversion experiences and gave bold witness to a "lay spirituality" centered on the mystery of Christ.

It would be beyond our scope to dwell on the other providential champion of Church reform, St. Dominic, whom Thomas mentioned along with St. Francis. St. Bonaventure, the great Franciscan mystic and scholar, gives a magnificent encomium of Dominic in the following canto (*Par.* XII). Let us simply note that Francis is described as "seraphic," i.e., like the Seraphim, the highest angels whose love for God is the most intense. Dominic, however, is compared to the Cherubim, the angels who enjoyed the highest knowledge of God. The medieval debate over which approach to God was superior — knowledge or love — is too complex to discuss here. Let us merely mention that the two circles of theologians which encompass Dante and Beatrice represent two theological "schools": the Dominicans, led by

Thomas, are the inner circle, knowledge; the outer circle, led by Bonaventure, represents love. Dante is probably following Thomas' doctrine that knowledge precedes love.[4] But we shall see at the very end of *Paradiso* that Dante's final word about God and our relationship to Him is "love."

The two circles which Dante describes go in opposite directions, as if they were two cog-wheels, whose teeth fit into and drive one another. By this imagery Dante expresses a reconciliation of the much-disputed question concerning the primacy of love or knowledge. The contrary movements of the head and heart, represented by the Dominican and Franciscan schools of theology, really fit into and produce one another. Knowledge and love belong together and complement one another. Both Thomas and Bonaventure were intellectual lights *and* mystics whose love of God enriched the Church.

As a conclusion to this exploration of Dante as a mystic we will consider the three visions of Christ which Dante the pilgrim enjoyed in Paradise, his true homeland, or *patria*. The first one follows the cantos which described the sphere of the sun (X-XIII), where the two concentric circles joyously sang and danced. Dante remarked that their song was "not a Bacchic hymn; they sang of Three Persons in one God and of One Person, human and divine" (*Par.* XIII, 27). Thus the mysteries of the Trinity and of the Incarnation are the themes of their jubilation. The "One who was pierced by the lance, and gave the satisfaction for future and past, such that it outweighed all of mankind's guilt" (*Par.* XIII, 40-42) is always, however, *the* mystery that is celebrated. We shall see that the final vision in Paradise will be focused more on the mystery of the Incarnation, the union of the divine and the human in Christ.

In the first vision (Canto XIV) Christ will flash forth from the cross in the company of all those who shared in His sufferings. Then in the second vision (Canto XXIII), Christ will appear in His triumphant glory as the central Sun of the starry throngs of His saints in their victory with Him over death and hell. Then in the final vision (Canto XXXIII) the mystery of the Incarnation will come as a flash of lightning, in which Dante will see the union of humanity and divinity in Christ.

We will notice certain common features and patterns in all three visions. The upwardly spiral movement of Dante toward the Empyrean where he will enjoy the ultimate experience of God is the fundamental pattern and thrust of the entire *Comedy*. The images of circles and light dominate, and in each vision Christ is described as the sun or the central circle of light. Dante thus discovered the real center of the universe in Christ, the sun. As a scholar he naturally followed the medieval cosmology of the earth as the center of the material universe, but in these mystical visions the sun symbolism takes over and expresses a heliocentric structure of the universe. Even though he had clearly stated in his *Convivio* that "It is quite enough for people on the authority of Aristotle to know that the earth with the sea is the center of the heavens" (*Conv.* III, 5), here in Paradise he seems to be unconsciously contradicting that theory and preparing the world for the acceptance of the heliocentric theory. Several modern scholars have noticed how the medieval mystics' symbolism actually leads to scientific truth. Even though medieval astronomy strongly maintained the earth as center, the mystics saw the centrality of the Divine Sun. [5]

We have already considered some aspects of the first vision of Christ in previous chapters, but let us here focus on the figure of Christ which illuminates this scene. Dante and Beatrice have left the sun and are now in the planet Mars, whose red glow fills Dante with a further grace and a "more exalted bliss." The experience causes him to exclaim:

> Then in the language common to all men,
> with all my heart, I made an offering
> unto the Lord befitting His fresh grace.
> Nor had the sacrifice within my breast
> ceased burning when I knew my prayer of thanks
> had been accepted, and propitiously,
> for with such mighty sheen, such ruby glow,
> within twin rays, such splendor came to me,
> I cried: "O Helios, who adorns them so!"
> (*Par.* XIV, 86-96)

Dante sees the souls in Mars as so many rays of light which form the figure of a cross within a circle. He cries out again:

> but here my memory defeats my art:
> I see that cross as it flames forth with Christ,
> yet cannot find the words that will describe it.
> But who takes up his cross and follows Christ
> will pardon me for what I leave unsaid
> beholding Heaven's whiteness glow with Christ.
> (*Par.* XIV, 103-108)

The vision holds Dante in a trance while he hears a hymn sung. "Arise" and "Conquer" are the only words he hears. The music raises his heart to "heights of love." Dante confesses that "until that moment nothing had existed that ever bound my soul in such sweet chains." And yet the chains, he declares, produce "a sacred joy" which grows in perfection as he rises. This extraordinary passage expresses clearly, I believe, a real mystical experience of Dante. He surrenders himself, by divine grace, to Christ's sacrificial love shining forth in His cross, formed by the glowing lights of the martyrs. The language of sacrifice and love permeate this ecstatic vision.

Could Dante be expressing in verbal form the meaning of the stupendous mosaic in the apse of St. Apollinare in Classe: the glorious golden circle filled with the cross of Christ whose face appears at its center? I think so. As we have seen, the mosaic depicts the Transfiguration and the Exaltation of the Cross as one mystery. Below the circle-cross gaze the three apostles as sheep and below them stands with outstretched arms in the shape of a cross the figure of the martyr St. Apollinaris. The martyr in Christian tradition was the person who perfectly imitated Christ in His complete sacrificial love. Dante in his final years stood below this mosaic and perhaps saw himself in Apollinaris, the martyr captivated by Christ's sacrificial love.

Dante's cry of "O Helios" is most significant here. *Helios* is the Greek word for the sun and for the sun god. In medieval etymology it was associated with the Hebrew word *Eli,* "my God." It suggests Christ's words from the cross: *"Eli, Eli, lama sabachtani,"* the Hebrew for "My God, my God, why have you forsaken me?"[6] Here in Paradise Christ as Helios, the Sun, shines upon the cross and kindles in Dante the same sacrificial abandon — suffering, love and joy. We might remember that Dante in Purgatory (cf. *Purg.* XXIII, 70-75) quoted these words of Christ from the cross to express the profound joy which the souls there experienced as they offered their sufferings and themselves as a sacrifice to God.

Dante no doubt found in this vision — whether in reality it was a visual, audible or purely spiritual grace — the incentive and strength to rise and continue his life and work as a conquering martyr — a witness to Christ's truth and love. By this experience he became willing to be a "holocaust," a sacrificial victim entirely consumed by the fire of divine love. He remarks that only the one who takes up his cross and follows Christ can understand what he was unable to put into words. The crushing defeats of his life — his exile, his distress at the dual tragedies of Church and Empire, all his sufferings and failures — are finally clarified and given ultimate meaning in the glorious victory of Christ on the cross. Dante sees not only the final, underlying meaning of his own life in the cross of Christ, but also the ultimate significance of universal history.

Dante's Christocentric mysticism, expressed so eloquently here, has the ring of authentic Christian experience, proclaimed in St. Paul's epistles of the New Testament, such as Ephesians and Colossians. The mystery of Christ's cross as the central revelation of God's "secret plan" for universal salvation shines out in those letters. They express the primitive mysticism of St. Paul and St. John: a theology of the cross which is at the same time a theology of glory. In the last analysis — paradoxical though it may seem — there is no dichotomy between cross and glory. Christ's visceral cry of *Eli* is a real plea from the depths of darkness and the emptiness of "God-forsaken" suffering. In that moment His anguished soul must have felt the absence and silence of God, but He trusted and waited for His Father's response. God answered by raising Him and exalting Him to the glory of the heavens — to the *Helios*. A Christian following Him knows through the gift of faith that his life is a re-living of the total mystery of Christ — in both His sufferings and finally in His glorification.

After the vision of Christ's cross we now come to the second vision of Christ: His glorious triumph with the throngs of the redeemed, the Church Triumphant. Beatrice, whom Dante compares to a mother bird awaiting with anxious desire the dawn in order to feed her young, sees the sky growing ever brighter and exclaims to Dante: "Behold the hosts of Christ in triumph; see all the fruit harvested from the circling of these spheres!" (*Par.* XXII, 19-21). Up until this point — we are now in the eighth heaven, the fixed stars — all that Dante has seen, even the flash of light from Christ's cross, has been but darkness in comparison with the light and glory which will be revealed to him as Christ the Sun rises with His trophies, the hosts of the redeemed souls. Dante perhaps based his images on the triumphant processions of Roman conquerors carrying back their trophies in chariots along the *Via Sacra* of Rome. Christ is depicted here in similar images: the conquering hero who brings with Himself the "spoils" of His victory: the saints from Limbo and the Christian saints — all the souls of "the Old and New Covenants," as the concluding words of the canto state.

In this canto of exceptional poetic beauty and exuberance Dante expresses how his vision grew stronger and brighter as he ascends with Beatrice. The higher he climbs the more his vision expands because he is receiving further graces. He is being transformed, as St. Paul wrote, "from glory to glory" (2 Cor 8-18). Christ is revealing Himself more and more to Dante whose mind is seeing in ever greater degrees the glory of the Lord which enlightens and transforms him. One is reminded of St. Gregory of Nyssa's concept of Paradise (and of a Christian's life on earth) as a progressive, unending activity of enlightenment and transforming love, not a dull state of eternal repose and sleep. Dante, too, experiences this dynamic progress in glory. He now attempts to describe what he saw:

> I saw, above a myriad of lights,
>   one Sun that lit them all, even as our sun
>   illuminates the stars of his domain;
> and through its living light there poured the glow
>   of its translucent substance, bright, so bright
>   that my poor eyes could not endure the sight.
> O Beatrice, loving guide, sweet one!
> She answered: "That which overcomes you now
>   is strength against which nothing has defense.
> Within it dwell the wisdom and the power
>   that opened between Heaven and earth the road
>   mankind for ages longed for ardently."
>   (*Par.* XXIII, 28-39)

We recognize here St. Paul's designation of Christ as "the Power and Wisdom of God" (1 Cor 1:24). The "translucent substance" would be His humanity or His body, once veiled in the humiliation of the flesh and the Passion, but now shining with the glory of the Resurrection, a glory which He communicates to all the redeemed, His "mystical" Body.

Dante's mind at this moment "swells until it broke its bounds." He compares his experience to lightning which explodes from a cloud. In medieval terms lightning was fire which, contrary to its true nature of rising, sometimes crashes to earth when it cannot be contained. Dante also employs several other metaphors to express this moment of ecstasy, such as a dream which he cannot remember or a small boat in a vast sea, images which will reappear in the final vision. He confesses that his mind is staggering here and is totally incapable of putting into words such an extraordinary rapture.

Beatrice then commands him to look straight into her face, since now he has the power to endure her smile, but next she reprimands him for not turning to the vision again:

> Why are you so enamored of my face
> that you do not turn to the lovely garden
> flowering in the radiance of Christ?
> There is the Rose in which the Word of God
> took on the flesh, and there the lilies are
> whose fragrance led mankind down the good path.
> (*Par.* XXIII , 70-75)

Dante obeys, and surrenders his "frail eyes to the battle of the light." This blinding light, Christ the Sun, has now ascended, but he continues to send His "rays of love" on the garden of the blessed souls:

> Sometimes on cloudy days my eyes have seen
> a ray of pure sunlight come streaming through
> the broken clouds and light a field of flowers,
> just so I saw there hosts of countless splendors
> struck from above by ardent rays of love,
> but could not see the source of such a blaze.

O Mighty Force that seals them with such light,
You raised yourself on high so that my eyes,
powerless in your presence, might perceive.
(*Par.* XXIII, 79-87)

This last tercet is Dante's prayer of thanksgiving to Christ, the *Kind* Power who ascended in order to give him this vision of His glory. Musa's translation, "O Mighty Force," does not follow literally Dante's *O Benigna* (kind) *Vertu.* Dante seems to be echoing St. Paul again: "The kindness (*benignitas*) and love of God our Savior has appeared to us" (Titus 3:4).

Dante then directs his attention, following Beatrice's command, to Mary, the Rose of the mystical garden of the Church. The rest of the canto is an extravagant praise of Mary, overflowing with filial devotion and childlike love. Dante describes here a coronation scene of Mary as the Queen of Heaven. The angel Gabriel, the flaming crown which encircles Mary, sings:

I am angelic love encompassing
the joy supreme who breathed from out the womb
which was the place where our Desire dwelt,
and I shall circle you, Heavenly Lady,
while you follow your Son, to highest heaven
and with your presence make it more divine.
(*Par.* XXIII, 103-108)

This coronation scene is actually a reenactment of the Annunciation, which evokes the moment of the Incarnation when "supreme joy" came to the world because "our Desire" made His dwelling place in Mary's womb. Christ, "the desire of the everlasting hills," (Gn 49:26) was also the one "whom the angels desire to see" (1 Peter 1:12). Jesus, "the joy of man's desiring," is the climax of salvation history both for angels and for humans.

As Mary rises and follows Her Son, Dante contemplates the angels whose love for Mary is compared to an infant raising its arms for its mother after it has suckled. The angels express Dante's own filial love for Mary as they sing the *Regina Coeli,* the Church's Easter hymn to the Queen of Heaven who rejoices because "He whom you deserved to bear has risen, as He said." Christ's victory with Mary and all the saints is the triumph which Dante sees on this glorious day in the Easter Week of 1300, a day when he is given a glimpse of "the joyous treasure which is reserved for those who rejected gold in their tearful exile in Babylon." Dante, in the spirit of Augustine's *City of God,* once again reflects on self-love, expressed in greed, as the root of all sins. In Dante's mind Christian souls are delivered from this self-love (symbolized by the city of Babylon) by their love of God, which is a foretaste of the joy in store for them in the Heavenly City.

Some commentators have noted that Mary's triumph is given more attention in this canto than the triumph of Christ.[7] Others claim that Dante's Christ here is an impersonal, intellectual concept based on the medieval Summas and Councils of the Church.[8] Dante's high Christology, according to some scholars, obscures the Jesus of the gospels: the tender, human Savior who is present also in the pages of St. Bernard or in the mystical spirit of St. Francis and the Franciscan poets, such as Jacopone da Todi. Dante's Christ, it is argued, is so remote and transcendent that He is enclosed in His own divinity and inspires only awe and reverence in Dante. As a result, these scholars assert, Dante's affections are moved only by his love for Beatrice and Mary. According to these interpreters, Christ's humanity evoked only admiration in Dante: wonder at how God could become man. The human Jesus, then, does not stir Dante's heart, but only his mind, formed by the intellectual theologians of medieval Scholasticism, who based their Christology mainly on the precise, but dull and dry, dogmatic definitions of Nicea and Chalcedon. Thus Dante saw only the divinity of Christ as a Light which illuminates and causes stupor and holy awe.[9]

There is some truth in these observations, and perhaps the Byzantine art in the majestic mosaics of Florence, Rome and Ravenna reinforced this image of the transcendent Christ of the dogmas in Dante's mind. Nonetheless, Dante expresses in this passage and elsewhere deep feelings of affection and love for Christ, whose tender humanity touched his heart. In his prayer here, for example, Christ is addressed as a kind (*benigna*) power. Dante alludes to Christ's love repeatedly throughout this canto, describing Him as the source of the highest "joy" and as the "desire" of all creatures, words charged with emotions. Besides, the Sun is not just a symbol of divine power and light, but also a metaphor for Christ's warmth, which continuously gives life and nourishes the garden.

Dante's tender love for Mary, the Rose of the garden, is also expressed in very affectionate terms, even though she is always the Queen who is approached with the greatest reverence. His attention to Mary and to Beatrice in this canto echoes the typical medieval piety which instinctively gravitated toward Mary and women saints because they mirrored the warm, maternal aspect of God's love.

Before we arrive at the final vision we should notice that, as Dante ascends, he increases his references to Christ as the Spouse who consummated His marriage to His Bride, the Church, by shedding His blood on the cross. The image of Christ the Victor, although not abandoned, yields more and more to Christ the Lover, whose nuptial feast with the Church is the supreme joy of Paradise. Allusions to His maternal love which nourishes the Church with His own blood will also appear. We will notice too how Dante's affections are increasingly inflamed as he enters more deeply into a contemplative consciousness of Christ's love for His Church and for Dante himself.

Dante's desire to see Christ grows more intense. In fact, the face of Christ becomes the image that dominates the higher he ascends. Expressions such as "seeing" and "tasting" become more frequent as Dante's desires and longings — his hunger and thirst for divine love — are intensified and gradually satisfied. Although the desire for intellectual knowledge always persists in Dante's mind, the affections of his heart are increasingly stirred and in the end it will be those desires that will be satisfied, not his intellectual thirst.

After the stirring vision of the triumph of Christ and His Church Beatrice addresses all the blessed souls of that triumph:

> O fellowship of those chosen to feast
> at the great supper of the Lamb of God
> Who feeds you, satisfying all your needs,
> if by the grace of God this man foretaste
> of what falls from the table of the Blest
> before the hour death prescribes for him,
> consider his immeasurable thirst;

> bedew him with a few drops, for you drink
> forever from the Source of this man's thoughts.
> *(Par.* XXIV, 1-9)

But before Dante will be able to taste that heavenly food he must pass an "entrance exam" on the three fundamental virtues necessary for any Christian: faith, hope and love. The three apostles closest to Jesus, the ones with Him on Mt. Tabor at the Transfiguration, are the examiners. Peter, James and John conduct this examination in the manner of medieval Scholastic doctors who question a candidate for a degree in theology. We have quoted portions of this passage in previous chapters: Peter's examination on Dante's faith and James' examination on his hope. Some commentators consider these examinations to be dull and arid, but the third one reveals some outstanding aspects of Dante's spirituality. St. John, the examiner on love, is introduced by Beatrice with these words:

> This is the one who lay upon the breast
> of our own Pelican; he is the one
> who from the Cross assumed the great bequest.
> *(Par.* XXV, 112-114)

Jesus as the pelican was a familiar symbol of Christ in medieval art and liturgical hymns. In a famous Eucharistic hymn attributed to St. Thomas Aquinas, the *Adoro Te Devote,* Jesus is addressed in these tender terms:

> O Loving Pelican, Lord Jesus,
> Cleanse me, a sinner, with your blood,
> Of which one drop can save
> The whole world from all sin.

In medieval times it was believed that when food failed, the pelican fed her young with her own blood. Another legend held that the pelican revived her dead young with her blood. One can easily see how the pelican became a symbol of Christ. Jesus as mother bird can also be found in the gospels (cf. Luke 13:34). St. John, who rested on the

breast of Jesus at the Last Supper and received Mary as his mother at
the cross — "the great bequest," in Dante's words — became for the
early Christians the apostle of divine love. Origen, who wrote the first
commentary on John's Gospel, observed that "No one can apprehend
the meaning of it (i.e., John's Gospel) unless he has lain on Jesus' breast
and received from Jesus Mary to be his mother also."[10]

When John questions Dante on the nature of love he is not satisfied
with Dante's intellectual responses, but requires an answer that expresses Dante's existential and emotional experience of love. One is
reminded here of Newman's famous distinction between "real" and
"notional" assent to religious truth, or of Pascal's "reasons of the
heart." John insists on a real assent and a reason from Dante's heart,
even though Dante had quoted from philosophy and from Scripture to
demonstrate his love for God:

> "But tell me, are there other ties you feel
> that draw you to Him? Let your words explain
> the many teeth with which your love can bite."
> The sacred purpose in the questioning
> of Christ's own eagle here was clear to me —
> I knew which way my answer had to go.
> (*Par.* XXVI, 48-53)

Dante, realizing what kind of response John demanded, gives an
answer straight from his heart:

> I spoke again: "All of those teeth with strength
> to move the heart of any man to God
> have bitten my heart into loving Him.
> The being of the world and my own being,
> the death He died so that my soul might live,
> the hope of all the faithful, and mine too,
> joined with the living truth mentioned before,
> from that deep sea of false love rescued me
> and set me on the right shore of true Love.

> I love each leaf with which enleaved is all
> the garden of the Eternal Gardener
> in measure of the light he sheds on each."
> (*Par.* XXVI, 57-66)

Dante has passed the final test with flying colors! All the hosts of heaven applaud with a resounding "Holy, Holy, Holy!", the eternal song of the Seraphim around God's throne (Is 6:2-3), echoed in John's visions (Rv 4:8), and still sung in the Church's liturgy on earth. Dante has clearly acknowledged that "the heart has its reasons, which reason cannot understand." His heart knows that God is love, as John stated in his first epistle, and that He showed that love principally in Christ's death on the cross for us.

Throughout the remaining cantos of *Paradise* Dante will witness the blessed souls singing joyfully "Glory to the Father and to the Son and to the Holy Spirit." Their song inebriates Dante, as he exclaims:

> I seemed to see all of the universe
> turn to a smile; thus, through my eyes and ears
> I drank into divine inebriation.
> O joy! O ecstasy ineffable!
> O life complete, perfect in love and peace!
> O wealth unfailing, that can never want!
> (*Par.* XXVI, 4-9)

Dante describes his experience more and more in terms of the heart and the emotions: his mind now is "in love," burning more than ever with divine delight. God's own joy and happiness is reflected in Beatrice's smile and face, drawing Dante into the ultimate experience. His attitude toward Beatrice becomes more childlike as he seeks his mother's milk (cf. Canto XXX, 84) and the peace which will be his in beholding God soon. He now invokes God's grace — not the inspiration of the Muses or Apollo, as he had previously done — for the power to find words adequate for expressing what he saw (cf. Canto XXX, 97-99).

What now appears to him is the entire company of heaven "in the form of a white rose . . . all those whom with His own blood Christ made

His bride" (XXXI, 1-3). This vision of unearthly beauty fills him with unspeakable delight as he sees all the saints of the Old and New Covenants focus their "look and love upon one goal . . . the Triune Light and Fulfiller of full joy!" (XXXI, 29). He compares his experience to a pilgrim's awe and joy when he arrives in Rome and beholds the splendor of the Lateran, the mother church of Christendom in Dante's time. The present structure still bears the inscription "mother and head (*mater et caput*) of all the churches of the city and of the world."

The Lateran basilica, originally dedicated to Christ our Savior, was magnificently decorated with mosaics in Dante's time. One of the principal ones, still preserved in the apse today, shows the face of Christ, which, according to tradition, appeared miraculously in the sky on the day of the basilica's dedication by Pope Silvester in the time of Constantine. In Dante's time the Lateran basilica, the cathedral of Rome, was one of the principal "station churches" in the circuit of churches visited by pilgrims. The papal residence, which was connected with the basilica, housed a chapel called "the holy of holies" (*sancta sanctorum*) in which an icon of Christ was venerated, believed to be made by "other than human hands."[11] Dante's reference here to the Lateran, which "outsoared all mortal art" (XXXI, 35), could be understood in the sense of the pilgrims' joy in seeing this icon of Christ or the mosaic of Christ's face in the apse of the basilica. Dante's own joyous vision seems to echo theirs. He in fact refers to himself now as a pilgrim "refreshed with joy," wondering how he will describe it when he returns home (XXXI, 43-45).

And now Dante turns to ask Beatrice more questions about the new splendors he beholds. She is no longer at his side. He finds instead an old man whose face is filled with divine joy. He is like a loving, tender father. It is St. Bernard of Clairvaux, who now replaces Beatrice as Dante's guide. This "holy elder," symbol of mystical love, had been sent by God's love and the prayers of Mary and Beatrice to prepare Dante for the ultimate vision of God. On seeing him Dante exclaims:

> As one who comes from some place like Croatia —
> to gaze on our Veronica, so long
> craved for, he now cannot look long enough,
> and while it is displayed, he says in thought:

> "O Jesus Christ, my Lord, the One true God,
> is this what your face truly looked like then?" —
> just so did I while gazing at the living
> love of the one who living in the world,
> through contemplation, tasted of that peace.
> (*Par.* XXXI, 103-111)

Dante once again evokes the typical pilgrim's experience at Rome. This time he refers to the famous "Veil of Veronica," venerated at St. Peter's basilica. It was considered to be the true image (*Veronica* comes from *vera,* true, and *icon,* image) of Christ's face, imprinted on a cloth which had wiped blood and sweat from His face on the way to the cross. [12] It is possible that Dante saw this icon during his pilgrimage to Rome in the Jubilee year of 1300. In any case, he sees on the face of Bernard a reflection of that love and joy felt by pilgrims upon beholding Christ's face on the "true icon."

Bernard, the "contemplative soul rapt in love's bliss," now assumes the role as Dante's guide. He is the one who will describe the beauty and order of the celestial rose to Dante. He does so by first revealing the divisions of the rose, described here as a great rose window in a medieval cathedral. The vast circular arena is divided vertically into those who believed in Christ to come and those who believed after His coming on earth. We see the Incarnation again as the supreme event which divides universal history into two parts. Bernard first points out Eve, who had opened the wound "which Mary was to close and heal" (XXXII, 1-3). This is a reference to the familiar *EVA-AVE* symbolism of Mary as the second Eve, who reversed Eve's sin by obeying the message of the angel who addressed her with *Ave,* the Latin word for "hail." Bernard now tells Dante to look at Mary:

> "Now look at that face which resembles Christ
> the most, for only in its radiance
> will you be made ready to look at Christ."
> I saw such bliss rain down upon her face,
> bestowed on it by all those sacred minds
> created to fly through those holy heights,
> that of all things I witnessed to this point

nothing had held me more spellbound than this,
nor shown a greater likeness unto God;
and that love which had once before descended
now sang, *Ave, Maria, gratia plena,*
before her presence there with wings spread wide.
(*Par.* XXXII, 85-93)

Bernard then prepares Dante for the pilgrim's ultimate vision: to look at Christ. Before they can turn their eyes upon "the Primal Love," that is, God, they must pray for the grace to do so, since human power cannot attain to that. Bernard then addresses his famous prayer to Mary, which is the beginning of the final canto of *Paradise*:

O Virgin Mother, daughter of your son,
most humble, most exalted of all creatures
chosen of God in His eternal plan,
you are the one who ennobled human nature
to the extent that He did not disdain,
Who was its Maker, to make Himself man.
Within your womb rekindled was the love
that gave the warmth that did allow this flower
to come to bloom within this timeless peace.
For all up here you are the noonday torch
of charity, and down on earth, for men,
the living spring of their eternal hope.
(*Par.* XXXIII, 1-12)

The remaining words of the prayer and the rest of the canto are of such incomparable beauty and spiritual depth that they must be contemplated and prayed rather than merely read and studied. Dante realizes that he is now approaching the very "end of all man's yearning." He will now see the vision with new eyes — through the eyes of Mary, most lowly and most exalted. Dante, so keenly aware of his own lowliness and also of his grace-given exaltation, is now writing the climax of his sacred poem, which is a comedy, a "lowly" form of poetry, as he stated in his letter to Can Grande. But it is at the same time a most exalted work because it is inspired by God's grace. Mary is thus the image of Dante's own soul and of his greatest achievement, the *Comedy*.

Mary seems to be raised to such an exalted position by Dante and other medieval writers, that some commentators, especially those outside the Catholic tradition, are scandalized that she is practically considered a fourth divine person. According to these interpreters, the Trinity has been transformed into a quaternity. Among others, Carl Jung has observed this by commenting that Mary "became involved in the Trinitarian drama as a human being. The Mother of God can therefore be regarded as a symbol of mankind's essential participation in the doctrine of the Trinity." His comments, however, were not intended to be derogatory or in any way disparaging toward Catholic tradition. He wrote that Mary is a "fourth" in the Trinity through the mystery of God's Incarnation in her and the mystery of her Assumption and Coronation as Queen of Heaven. [13] Jung's analysis of the human psychological need for a feminine, maternal God would find this need filled in the person of Mary; and Jung was delighted when Pope Pius XII defined the dogma of Mary's Assumption in 1950. He considered the definition as most important for Catholics and for all other Christians as well.

But a closer examination of Dante's Mary reveals that he does not raise her to divine status as a fourth person in a quaternity. Mary, even as Queen Mother in Heaven, is always a creature, saved and "divinized" as are all Christians, who are partakers of Jesus' humanity and sharers also in His divinity. As Robert Faricy explains so well, "The feminine principle of God is Jesus Christ risen in so far as He is the whole Christ that includes especially His body, the Church, and also the whole world and all in it as it enters, in Christ, into the Triune God." [14] Mary as the image of the Church, the Body of Christ, was extensively developed by the Vatican II document on the Church, *Lumen Gentium*.

As Dante enters into his vision of the Triune God, empowered by the divine grace given through the prayers of Mary, Beatrice, and Bernard — the Communion of Saints — he becomes overwhelmed by the "Light Supreme" of God's glory. He prays to God that his mind will be able to put into verses what he sees so that "more of Your might will be revealed to men." He thus understands his vision as a divine gift which will be a revelation for the salvation of the world. Like St. Paul, he

perceives a revelation from God as a charismatic message for the good
of all (cf. 1 Cor 14:16-33).

But what did Dante see? What was this "beatific vision"? We can
only turn to his own words, the final tercets of the *Comedy*:

> Within Its depthless clarity of substance
> I saw the Great Light shine into three circles
> in three clear colors bound in one same space;
> the first seemed to reflect the next like rainbow
> on rainbow, and the third was like a flame
> equally breathed forth by the other two.
> How my weak words fall short of my conception,
> which is itself so far from what I saw
> that "weak" is much too weak a word to use!
> O Light Eternal fixed in Self alone,
> known only to Yourself, and knowing Self,
> You love and glow, knowing and being known!
> That circling which, as I conceived it, shone
> in You as Your own first reflected light
> when I had looked deep into It a while,
> seemed in Itself and in Its own Self-color
> to be depicted with man's very image.
> My eyes were totally absorbed in It.
> As the geometer who tries so hard
> to square the circle, but cannot discover,
> think as he may, the principle involved,
> so did I strive with this new mystery:
> I yearned to know how could our image fit
> into that circle, how could it conform;
> but my own wings could not take me so high —
> then a great flash of understanding struck
> my mind, and suddenly its wish was granted.
> At this point power failed high fantasy
> but, like a wheel in perfect balance turning,
> I felt my will and my desire impelled
> by the Love that moves the sun and the other stars.
> (*Par.* XXXIII, 118-145)

So much commentary has been written over the centuries on these final tercets of Dante's *Comedy* that one is simply overwhelmed by its sheer volume. Perhaps the best commentary is silence — the silence of contemplative prayer. Dante himself tells us that he has no words to describe it. Word becomes silence, as the mystics so often confess.

The vision of the Trinity described here as three united circles was a traditional image. Perhaps Dante based his version of this image on Joachim of Fiore's "figures." The three circles representing the three Divine Persons and their intimate relations would thus be the symbol and metaphor chosen by Dante from Joachim's famous *Liber Figurarum*. In that book Joachim represented the Trinity as three equal circles, side by side and inter-linked. They are of three distinct colors: the third circle is fiery red and the other two are green and blue — the three colors of the rainbow in most medieval art. A modern Joachim scholar, Marjorie Reeves, believes that Dante was "struck by the clarity of Joachim's concept and the beauty of its expression."[15] According to Reeves, the simple and "awe-ful" *circumincessio* of the Trinity would be expressed by "this flashing, quasi-electric contact of each circle with the other two."

But is the mystery of the Trinity and the inner relationships of the Three Persons really the essence of the final vision that beatifies Dante? Many scholars think that the vision is not so much an intuition of the Trinitarian mystery as an insight into the mystery of the Incarnation.[16] We should always keep in mind that the two mysteries cannot be separated. Christian faith always understood the Incarnation and the Trinity in terms of each other. The Christian experience of the Incarnation — mystery revealed — is at the same time the Trinitarian mystery — ultimately unknowable. It is through the Incarnate Son that we enter the mystery of the Trinity.

Dante's vision actually focuses on the central circle which holds the image of Christ, God and man. Dante sees the perfect image of God in the human figure of Christ. At this final stage of his pilgrimage he too has become what Beatrice is: an image of Christ, "rooted in the Trinity," as he stated in his *Vita Nuova*. He has become also what Mary is: an image of Christ. Bernard, we recall, had described her as having "the greatest likeness unto God." Both Beatrice and Mary — and all the saints of the

Church — form the one image of Christ, who is the only perfect image of God.

Even in this final vision Dante does not penetrate with his mind into the mystery of the Trinity. It remains unknowable — a supreme light, but one that blinds and leaves only darkness in his mind. We are reminded of the ancient "apophatic" experiences of the Eastern Fathers of the Church, such as St. Gregory of Nyssa, Dionysius and many others, who expressed this paradox of "bright darkness." Many of the Western medieval mystics expressed this same experience.

The "new mystery" which amazes Dante is how "our image," that is, humanity, fits into the middle circle, which represents Christ. This is the mystery of the Incarnation, the union of humanity with divinity. Throughout the *Comedy* Dante had expressed awe that God became man in Christ; now he is astounded at how our humanity is in God. He states that "a great flash of understanding struck my mind," but it is an understanding that does not enlighten his intellect on the mystery of the Incarnation or on the mystery of the Trinity. (If it did, he doesn't tell us what it was.) Instead, he describes it as a feeling — an experiential knowledge — that his "will and desire" are now in complete harmony with "the Love that moves the sun and other stars."

Dante's intellectual thirst has apparently not been satisfied, nor is ours, if we expected to gain here a greater intellectual penetration into the divine mysteries. Instead, a deeper desire — the pilgrim's deepest desire to love and to be loved — has been satisfied by entering into the inner life and movement of God who is Love. This unique experience which Dante claims to have received as a divine grace is, I believe, the same grace which St. Paul sang of in his hymn of Trinitarian praise:

> In our union with Christ Jesus, God has raised us up with Him to rule with Him in the heavenly world. He did this to demonstrate for all time to come the extraordinary greatness of His grace in the love he showed us in Christ Jesus. (Ep 2:6)

This divine grace is given to all of us pilgrims when we seek and probe with faith and hope into the depth of our Christian experience. We discover, as Dante did, that God is the tremendous Lover who is seeking us, calling us even now into a unique experience — call it mystical — by which we know, feel and sing His all-embracing, never-ending love for us. This unique experience — inexpressible as it is — is none other than the "union" and "divinization" that the great mystics of the Eastern and Western traditions of the Church have transmitted to us in their writings. This mystical union with God has two sides, which seem to coincide in Dante's final vision. The one side is the brightness of God's ecstatic love for us — His movement outwards — manifested in creation, His presence and glory in the material universe which culminates in His self-revelation in the Incarnation of Christ. This is often called the affirmative or "cataphatic" aspect of the experience. The other side — the "apophatic" aspect — is the soul's apprehension of His hidden presence within us. This is the dark, imageless, unknowable mystery of His loving presence which satisfies the soul's movement of ascent into Him and effects the soul's ecstatic union of love with Him. [17] Both ecstasies — God's and ours — reach a union which surpasses concepts and words. It is a pure grace from God, who is love. To Him be praise and glory. Amen.

NOTES

Chapter One

1. Cf. *Jacopone da Todi - The Lauds,* translated by Serge and Elizabeth Hughes (New York: Paulist Press, 1982), p. 55.
2. Denzinger, Henricus (editor), *Enchiridion Symbolorum* (Freiburg: Herder, 1963) 875 (p. 281).
3. Cf. Anderson, William, *Dante the Maker* (New York: Crossroad, 1982), p. 84.
4. Cf. Fallani, Giovanni, *Dante e la Cultura Figurativa Medievale* (Bergamo: Minerva Italica, 1976), p. 44.
5. Cf. Cosmo, Umberto, *L'Ultima Ascesa* (Florence: "La Nuova Italia," 1968), p. 189.
6. *Ibid.,* pp. 171-172.
7. Dinsmore, Charles Allen, *Aids to the Study of Dante* (Boston: Houghton, Mifflin and Co., 1903), p. 117.
8. Cf. *Fonti Francescane,* Editio Minor (Assisi: Casa Editrice Francescana, 1986), pp. 204-205; 330.
9. Chesterton, G.K., *St. Francis of Assisi* (New York: Doubleday and Co., 1957), pp. 45-46.
10. *Ibid.,* p. 48.
11. Leclercq, Vandenbroucke, Bouyer, *The Spirituality of the Middle Ages : A History of Christian Spirituality, Vol. II* (New York: The Seabury Press, 1968), p. 296.
12. Cf. Anderson, *op. cit.,* p. 413.
13. Cf. Tardiolo, Franco, *Dante Alighieri Francescano* (Roma: Editrice Nuovi Autori, 1983), pp. 36-38. See also Gilson, Etienne, *Dante and Philosophy,* Translated by David Moore (New York: Harper and Row, 1963), p. 34.
14. Cf. Leclercq, *et al. op. cit.,* pp. 112-113.
15. Cf. Fox, Ruth, *Dante Lights the Way* (Milwaukee: Bruce, 1958) pp. 303-343.
16. *Ibid.,* p. 303.
17. Panichas, George, editor, *The Simone Weil Reader* (New York: David McKay Co., 1977), p. 15.
18. *Conv.* IX, 28, 9.
19. Cf. Leclercq, *et. al., op. cit.,* p. 352.

Chapter Two

1. Cf. Coulton, G.G., *From St. Francis to Dante: Translations from the Chronicle of the Franciscan Salimbene* (Philadelphia: University of Pennsylvania Press, 1972), p. 14.
2. Cf. Anderson, *op. cit.,* p. 86.

3. *Ibid.*, p. 137.
4. Musa, Mark, *Dante's Vita Nuova: A Translation and an Essay* (Bloomington: Indiana University Press, 1973), p. 174.
5. Singleton, Charles S., *An Essay on the Vita Nuova* (Cambridge: Harvard University Press, 1949), p. 114.
6. Musa, *op. cit.*, p. 129.
7. Singleton, *op. cit.*, p. 4.
8. *Ibid.*, p. 116.
9. Cf. Fallani, Giovanni, *Dante e la Cultura Figurativa Medievale,* pp. 32-35.
10. Cf. *Vita Nuova,* XXIX.
11. Singleton, *op. cit.*, p. 124.
12. *Ibid.*, p. 123.
13. *Vita Nuova,* XXVIII.
14. *Bonaventure - The Soul's Journey into God,* translation and introduction by Ewert Cousin, (New York: Paulist Press, 1978), p. 2
15. *Ibid.*, p. 77.
16. Milward, Peter, *A Commentary on The Sonnets of G.M. Hopkins* (Chicago: Loyola University Press, 1969), p. 128.
17. *Ibid.*, p. 114.
18. *Ibid.*, p. 118.
19. Cf. Deschene, James, "The Divine Comedy: Dante's Mystical and Sacramental World-View," *Studia Mystica* 4 (1981), pp. 36-46.
20. Musa, *op. cit.*, p. 164.
21. Eliot, T.S., *Dante* (New York: Haskell House, 1974), p. 68.
22. Cf. DVE, II, IV.
23. Cf. Anderson, *op. cit.*, p. 305.
24. Cf. Gilson, Etienne, *Dante et Beatrice: Etudes Dantesques* (Paris: Librairie Philosophique J. Vrin, 1974), p. 85.
25. Weaterby, Harold L., *The Keen Delight* (Athens, GA: University of Georgia Press, 1975), p. 15.
26. Maritain, Jacques, *Creative Intuition in Art and Poetry* (Princeton University Press, 1977), p. 393.
27. *Ibid.*, p. 370.
28. *Ibid.*, pp. 373-374.
29. Ferguson, Francis, *Dante* (London: Weidenfeld and Nicolson, 1966), p. 66.
30. Davis, Charles T., *Dante's Italy and Other Essays* (Philadelphia: University of Pennsylvania Press, 1984), p. 11.
31. Cf. Gilson, Etienne, *Dante and Philosophy,* pp. 79-80.

Chapter Three

1. Dinsmore, Charles Allen. *Aids to the Study of Dante* (Boston: Houghton, Mifflin and Co., 1903), pp. 102-103.
2. *Ibid.*, p.118.
3. Fergusson, Francis, *Dante* (London: Weidenfeld and Nicolson, 1966), p. 43.
4. *Ibid.*, pp. 42-43.
5. *Ibid.*, p. 45.
6. *Ibid.*, p. 44.

7. Delmay, Bernard, *I Personaggi della Divina Commedia* (Florence: Leo S. Olschki, 1986), p. 150.

8. Cf. Gilson, Etienne, *Dante and Philosophy* (New York: Harper and Row, 1963), p. 63.

9. *Enciclopedia Dantesca* (Roma: Istituto della Enciclopedia Italiana, 1984), Vol. I, p. 609.

10. Cf. Gilson, Etienne, *Dante and Philosophy*, p. 63.

11. *Ibid.*, p. 69.

12. Cf. *Inf.* XV, 106-108.

13. Chubb, Thomas C., *Dante and his World* (Boston: Little, Brown and Co., 1966), p. 73.

14. Cf. Rowse, A. L., *Homosexuals in History* (Dorset Press, 1983), pp. 6-23.

15. Cf. Anderson, *op. cit.*, p. 145.

16. *Ibid.*, p. 154.

17. *Ibid.*, p. 159.

18. Cf. Weatherby, Harold, L., *Cardinal Newman in His Age* (Nashville, Vanderbilt University Press, 1973), pp. 128-131.

19. Cf. Gilson, *Dante and Philosophy*, p. 93.

20. Cf. von Balthasar, Hans Urs, *The Glory of the Lord: A Theological Aesthetics* (San Francisco: Ignatius Press, 1986) Vol. III, p. 43.

21. Cf. *Conv.*, II, II, 3.

22. Cf. von Balthasar, *op. cit.*, pp. 45-46.

23. Cf. *Conv.*, II, I, 2-4.

24. Pelikan, Jaroslav, *The Christian Tradition*, Vol. III: *The Growth of Medieval Theology (600-1300)* (Chicago: University of Chicago Press, 1978), p. 291.

25. Cf. Gilson, *Dante and Philosophy*, pp. 114-116.

26. *Ibid.*, p. 119.

27. *Ibid.*, pp. 138-139.

Chapter Four

1. Cf. Chubb, *op. cit.*, p. 58.

2. Cf. *Enciclopedia Dantesca*, Vol. I, p. 627. The article on *La Bibbia* by Angelo Penna is an excellent summary of Dante's knowledge and use of the Bible.

3. Hollander, Robert, *Allegory in Dante's Commedia* (Princeton University Press, 1969), p. 20.

4. *Ibid.*, p. 28.

5. *Ibid.*, p. 28.

6. Cf. Singleton, Charles S., *Dante Studies I: Commedia: Elements of Structure* (Cambridge: Harvard University Press, 1954), p. 15.

7. Cf. Singleton, Charles S., *The Divine Comedy: Paradiso 2: Commentary* (Princeton University Press, 1975), p. 81.

8. Cf. Smalley, Beryl. *The Study of the Bible in the Middle Ages* (University of Notre Dame Press, 1964), pp. 363-364.

9. *Ibid.*, p. 371.

10. Cf. Singleton, *Dante Studies I*, p. 98.

11. Cf. Hollander, *op. cit.*, p. 52.

12. Cf. Trevor, Meriol, *Newman: The Pillar of the Cloud* (New York: Doubleday and Company, 1962), pp. 75-76.
13. Cf. Chesterton, G.K., *Chaucer* (New York: Sheed and Ward, 1956), p. 40.
14. Huntington, George, *Comments of John Ruskin on the Divina Commedia* (Boston: Houghton, Mifflin and Co., 1903), pp. 168-169.
15. McDonnell, Thomas (editor), *Blaze of Recognition* (New York: Doubleday and Co., 1983), p. 15
16. Adler, Mortimer J., "God and the Professors" (unpublished lecture). See his *How to Think About God* (New York: McMillan, 1980), pp. 8-17.
17. Cf. Fallani, Giovanni, *Dante e la Cultura Figurativa Medievale,* pp. 99-100
18. Cf. Sayers, Dorothy L., *Further Papers on Dante* (London: Methuen and Co., 1957) p. 192.
19. Bloom, Allan, *The Closing of the American Mind* (New York: Simon and Schuster, 1987), p. 374.
20. Newman, John Henry Cardinal, *The Idea of a University* (Westminster: Christian Classics, Inc., 1973) Discourse IX, pp. 217-218.
21. Cf. Paolini, Shirley J., *Confessions of Sin and Love in the Middle Ages: Dante's Commedia and St. Augustine's Confessions* (Washington, D.C.: University Press of America, 1982), pp. 72-80.

Chapter Five

1. Fallani, Giovanni, *L'Esperienza Teologica di Dante* (Lecce: Edizioni Milella, 1976), pp. 41-43.
2. Cf. Brezzi, Paolo, *Enciclopedia Dantesca,* Vol. I, pp. 960-968. Brezzi's article on *Chiesa* is an excellent summary of Dante's ecclesiology.
3. *De Monarchia* III, XIII, 4.
4. Newman, John Henry, *Apologia pro Vita Sua*, pp. 270-275.
5. Cf. Femiano, Samuel, *Infallibility of the Laity: The Legacy of Newman* (New York: Herder and Herder, 1967), pp. 30-31.
6. Cf. Patterson, Webster, *Newman Pioneer for the Layman* (Washington: Corpus Publications, 1968), pp. 49-84; see also Dessain, C.S., *The Spirituality of John Henry Newman* (Minneapolis: Winston Press, 1977), p. 30.
7. Cf. Patterson, *op. cit.*, p. 139.
8. Cf. Denzinger, *op. cit.*, Bulla *"Ne Super His,"* 990 (p. 295).
9. Cf. Jedin, Hubert (editor), *History of the Church* (New York: Crossroad, 1982), Vol. IV, pp. 371-373.
10. Cf. Patterson, *op. cit.*, p. 137.
11. *Apologia pro Vita Sua,* Part IV, p. 157.
12. Cf. Dessain, *op. cit.*, p. 26.
13. *Ibid.*, p. 26.
14. *The Idea of a University,* p. 316.
15. Cf. Bouyer, Louis, *Newman's Vision of Faith* (San Francisco: Ignatius Press, 1986), p. 44.
16. Cf. Jedin, *op. cit.*, Vol. IV, p. 356.
17. Cf. Gilson, Etienne, *Dante and Philosophy,* pp. 162-224.
18. *Ibid.*, pp. 184-185.
19. Cf. *De Monarchia* I, XVI, 1-2.

20. Cf. Anderson, *op. cit.*, p. 452, note 48.
21. Cf. Gilson, *op. cit.*, p. 278.
22. *Ibid.*, pp. 270-275.
23. Von Balthasar, *The Glory of the Lord* Vol. III, p. 24.
24. *Conv.* IV, IV.

Chapter Six

1. Cf. McBrien, Richard, *Catholicism* (San Francisco: Harper and Row, 1981) Study Edition, pp. 506-511; for a summary of Dante's Christology see Kenelm Foster's article on *Cristo* in *Enciclopedia Dantesca,* Vol. II, pp. 262-269.
2. Cf. O'Connell, Timothy, *Vatican II and Its Documents: An American Reappraisal* (Wilmington: Michael Glazier, Inc., 1986), p. 127.
3. Cf. McBrien, *op. cit.*, pp. 464-465.
4. Cf. Sloyan, Gerard, *The Jesus Tradition* (Mystic, Conn.: Twenty-Third Publications, 1986). This small, readable volume is an excellent summary of these mystical approaches to Christology.
5. Cf. Leclercq, *et al.*, *The Spirituality of the Middle Ages,* pp. 344-356.
6. Cf. Gershom, Scholem, *Kabbalah* (New York: New American Library, 1978), pp. 373-376.
7. Cf. Anderson, *op. cit.*, p. 293.
8. *Bonaventure, The Soul's Journey into God, op. cit.,* 1978), 7:6 (p. 115).
9. Cf. von Simson, Otto, *Sacred Fortress: Byzantine Art and Statecraft in Ravenna* (Princeton University Press, 1987), pp. 41-46.
10. Cf. Kaske, Carol, ' "Mount Sinai" and Dante's "Mount Purgatory," ' *Dante Studies* LXXXIX, 1971, pp. 1-18.
11. Demaray, John, *The Invention of Dante's Commedia* (New Haven: Yale University Press, 1974), pp. 114-115.
12. Cf. *Summa Theologiae* II-II, 172, 4.
13. *Ibid.*, 175, 3.
14. Von Balthasar, Hans Urs, *First Glance at Adrienne von Speyr* (San Francisco: Ignatius Press, 1981), p. 89.
15. *Ibid.*, pp. 57-58.
16. Von Balthasar, *The Glory of the Lord*, Vol. III, p. 13.
17. *Ibid.*, p. 21.
18. Cf. Gardner, Edmund G., *Dante and the Mystics* (New York: E.P. Dutton and Co., 1913), pp. 44-76.
19. *Ibid.*, p. 76.
20. Underhill, Evelyn, *Mysticism* (New York: E.P. Dutton and Co., 1961), p. 462.
21. Cf. Egan Harvey, *What are They Saying About Mysticism?* (New York: Paulist Press, 1982).
22. *Ibid.*, p. 40.
23. *Ibid.*, pp. 98-108.
24. Cf. Anderson, *op. cit.*, pp. 401-407.
25. Cf. von Balthasar, *The Glory of the Lord*, Vol. III, p. 32.

26. Underhill, *op. cit.*, p. 135.
27. Parma, G.B., *Ascesi e Mistica Cattolica nella Divina Commedia* (Subiaco, 1927), Vol. II, p. 476.
28. Nardi, Bruno, *Dante e la Cultura Medievale* (Bari: Laterza, 1985), p. 308.
29. *Ibid.*, p. 287.
30. Gardner, Edmund, *op. cit.*, pp. 34-36.
31. Vossler, Karl, *Medieval Culture: An Introduction to Dante and His Times*(New York: Frederick Ungar Publ., 1929), Vol. I, p. 82.
32. Cf. Anderson, *op. cit.*, pp. 152-153.
33. Bouyer, Louis, *Newman's Vision of Faith*, p. 13.
34. *Ibid.*, p. 157.
35. Cf. Guidubaldi, Egidio, *Dante Europeo III: Poema Sacro come Esperienza Mistica* (Florence: Leo S. Olschki, 1968), pp. 599-608.
36. Cf. Egan, *op. cit.*, p. 98.
37. Cf. Thompson, William M., *Fire and Light: The Saints and Theology* (New York: Paulist Press, 1987), p. 7.

Chapter Seven

1. Cf. Hollander, Robert, *Allegory in Dante's Commedia*, p. 133.
2. *Ibid.*, p. 75; p. 103.
3. Cf. Costa, Dennis John, "Dante as a Poet-Theologian," *Dante Studies* LXXXIX, 1971, pp. 61-77; see also Fallani, Giovanni, *Dante Poeta e Teologo* (Milan: Marzorati, 1965), pp. 9-22.
4. Cf. Marthaler, Berard L., *The Creed* (Mystic, Conn.: Twenty-Third Publ., 1987), pp. 164-174. These pages give an excellent summary of traditional and recent interpretations of this article of faith.
5. Cf. Kartsonis, Anna, *Anastasis, The Making of an Image* (Princeton University Press, 1986), pp. 82-93.
6. *Summa Theologiae* III (Tertia Pars) 52, 1-8.
7. Gardner, Helen, *Religion and Literature* (Oxford University Press, 1983), p. 150.
8. *Ibid.*, p. 149.
9. Bernard of Clairvaux, *First Sermon on the Advents* (PL CL XXXIII, 38). Translation is by Mark Musa, *Advent at the Gates*, p. 147.
10. Cf. Musa, Mark, *Advent at the Gates* (Bloomington: Indiana University Press, 1974), pp. 65-84.
11. Cf. Cassell, Anthony, *Dante's Fearful Art of Justice* (University of Toronto Press, 1984), p. 33.
12. *Conv.* IV, 5, 16.
13. *Summa Theologiae* II-II, 2, 7.
14. *Summa Theologiae* III, 68, 2.
15. *Conv.* 28, 15.
16. Cf. Hollander, op. cit, p. 128.
17. Cf. Danielou, Jean, *The Theology of Jewish Christianity* (London, 1964), pp. 117-147. See also Grillmeier, Aloys, *Christ in Christian Tradition* (Atlanta: John Knox Press, 1975), Vol. I, pp. 47-53.
18. Cf. Musa, Mark, *Advent at the Gates*, pp. 85-109.

19. Le Goff, Jacques, *The Birth of Purgatory* (University of Chicago Press, 1986), p. 346.
20. *Ibid.*, p. 349.
21. Cf. Sayers, Dorothy L., *Further Papers on Dante* (London: Methuen and Co., 1957), p. 192. See also Demaray, *op. cit., p. 123.*

Chapter Eight

1. Bonaventure, *The Life of St. Francis* in *Bonaventure - The Soul's Journey into God, op. cit.*, p. 315.
2. Gardner, Edmund, *Dante and the Mystics*, p. 76.
3. Cosmo, Umberto, *L'Ultima Ascesa*, p. 132.
4. Cf. Carroll, John S., *In Patria: An Exposition of Dante's Paradiso* (Port Washington, N.Y.: Kennikat Press, 1911), p. 181.
5. Cf. Anderson, *op. cit.*, p. 403.
6. Cf. Carroll, *op. cit.*, p. 241.
7. Cf. Musa, Mark, *The Divine Comedy,* Vol. III: *Paradise* (New York: Penguin Books, 1985), p. 275.
8. Cf. Cosmo, *op. cit.*, p. 250.
9. *Ibid.*, p. 251.
10. Origen, *Commentary on the Gospel of John,* I, 6 (*The Ante-Nicene Fathers,* Vol. X, p. 300: Wm. B. Eerdmans Publ. Co., Grand Rapids, Michigan).
11. Cf. Demaray, John, *The Invention of Dante's Commedia,* p. 42; p. 90.
12. *Ibid.*, p. 91; p. 183.
13. Faricy, Robert, "Jung and Teilhard: The Feminine in God and the Church," *Raising the Torch of Good News,* edited by Bernard Prusak (College Theology Society, Vol. 32, 1986), p. 243.
14. *Ibid.*, p. 246.
15. Reeves, Marjorie, *Joachim of Fiore and the Prophetic Future* (New York: Harper and Row, 1977), pp. 65-66; see also McGinn, Bernard, *The Calabrian Abbot: Joachim of Fiore in the History of Western Thought* (New York: Macmillan, 1985), pp. 175-181.
16. Cf. Costa, Dennis John, *op. cit.*, p. 67.
17. Cf. Louth, Andrew, *The Origins of the Christian Mystical Tradition* (Oxford: Clarendon Press, 1983), pp. 175-177.

SELECT BIBLIOGRAPHY

Anderson, William, *Dante the Maker*, New York (1982)

Auerbach, Erich, *Mimesis: the Representation of Reality in Western Literature*, Princeton (1953)

_____, *Dante, Poet of the Secular World*, Chicago (1961)

Balthasar, Hans Urs von, *The Glory of the Lord: A Theological Aesthetics*, 3rd Vol., San Francisco (1986)

Barbi, Michele, *Problemi di Critica Dantesca*, Florence (1975)

Bergin, Thomas, *An Approach to Dante*, London (1965)

Brown, Raphael, *True Joy from Assisi*, Chicago (1978)

Bucke, Richard, *Cosmic Consciousness*, Philadelphia (1972)

Buonaiuto, Ernesto, *La Prima Rinascita*, Milan (1977)

Carroll, John, *Exiles of Eternity*, Glasgow (1906), reprint London (1971)

_____, *Prisoners of Hope*, Glasgow (1906), reprint London (1971)

_____, *In Patria*, Glasgow (1906), reprint London (1971)

Cassell, Anthony, *Dante's Fearful Art of Justice*, Toronto (1984)

Cervigni, Dino, *Dante's Poetry of Dreams*, Florence (1986)

Cosmo, Umberto, *L'Ultima Ascesa*, Florence (1968)

Davis, Charles Till, *Dante's Italy and Other Essays*, Philadelphia (1984)

De Sanctis, Francesco, *Storia della Letteratura italiana*, Milan (1945)

Eco, Umberto, *Art and Beauty in the Middle Ages*, New Haven/London (1986)

Enciclopedia Dantesca, ed. Umberto Bosco, 5 Vols., Rome (1976)

Fallani, Giovanni, *Dante, Poeta Teologo*, Milan (1965)

_____, *Dante Autobiografico*, Naples (1975)

Fergusson, Francis, *Dante's Drama of the Mind*, Princeton (1953)

_____, *Dante*, London (1966)

_____, *Trope and Allegory*, Athens, GA (1977)

Foster. Kenelm, O.P., *The Mind in Love*, London (1956)

Freccero, John, ed., *Dante: A Collection of Critical Essays*, Princeton (1965)

Frye, Northrop, *The Great Code*, New York (1982)

Gardner, Edmund, *Dante and the Mystics*, London (1913)

————, *Dante's Ten Heavens*, New York (1900)

Gilson, Etienne, *Dante and Philosophy*, New York (1963)

Guardini, Romano, *Landschaft der Ewigkeit*, Munich (1958)

Guenon, Rene, *L'Esoterisme de Dante*, Paris (1925)

Guidubaldi, Egidio, *Poema Sacro Come Esperienza Mistica*, Florence (1968)

Hollander, Robert, *Allegory in Dante's Commedia*, Princeton (1969)

Kirkpatrick, Robin, *Dante: The Divine Comedy*, Cambridge (1978)

Leclercq, Jean; Vandenbroucke, Francois; Bouyer, Louis, *The Spirituality of the Middle Ages*, New York (1961)

Maritain, Jacques, *Creative Intuition in Art and Poetry*, London (1954)

Mazzotta, Giuseppe, *Dante, Poet of the Desert*, Princeton (1979)

Moore, Edward, *Studies in Dante*, 3 Vols., Oxford (1903), reprint New York (1968)

Morghen, Raffaello, *Dante Profeta*, Milan (1983)

Musa, Mark, *Dante's Vita Nuova*, Bloomington and London (1973)

————, *Advent at the Gates*, Bloomington and London (1974)

————, *The Divine Comedy*, 3 Vols., Bloomington (1984, 1985, 1986)

Nardi, Bruno, *Dal Convivio alla Commedia*, Rome (1960)

Papini, Giovanni, *Dante Vivo*, New York (1935)

Ralphs, Stella, *Dante's Journey to the Centre*, Manchester (1972)

Reeves, Marjorie, *Joachim of Fiore and the Prophetic Future*, London (1976)

Sayers, Dorothy, *Introductory Papers on Dante*, London (1954)

————, *Further Papers on Dante*, London (1957)

Singleton, Charles, *An Essay on the Vita Nuova*, Cambridge (1949)

————, *Dante Studies I*, Cambridge (1954)

————, *Dante Studies II*, Cambridge (1958)

————, *The Divine Comedy*, Translation and Commentary, 6 Vols., Princeton (1973)

Toynbee, Paget, *A Dictionary of Proper Names and Notable Matters in the Works of Dante*, revised by Charles Singleton, Oxford (1968)

Underhill, Evelyn, *Mysticism*, New York (1961)

Vossler, Karl, *Medieval Culture: An Introduction to Dante and His Times*, 2 Vols., London (1929)

Wilkins, Ernest, *Dante: Poet and Apostle*, Chicago (1921)

INDEX

W